Money as a Social Institution

T0331346

Money is usually understood as a valuable object, the value of which is attributed to it by its users and which other users recognize. It serves to link disparate institutions, providing a disguised whole and prime tool for the "invisible hand" of the market.

This book offers an interpretation of money as a social institution. Money provides the link between the household and the firm, the worker and his product, making that very division seem natural and money as imminently practical. *Money as a Social Institution* begins in the medieval period and traces the evolution of money alongside consequent implications for the changing models of the corporation and the state. This is then followed with double-entry accounting as a tool of long-distance merchants and bankers, then the monitoring of the process of production by professional corporate managers. Davis provides a framework of analysis for examining money historically, beyond the operation of those particular institutions, which includes the possibility of conceptualizing and organizing the world differently.

This volume is of great importance to academics and students who are interested in economic history and history of economic thought, as well as international political economics and critique of political economy.

Ann E. Davis is Associate Professor of Economics at Marist College, USA. She serves as the Chair of the Department of Economics, Accounting, and Finance, and was the founding director of the Marist College Bureau of Economic Research, 1990–2005. She was the Director of the National Endowment for Humanities Summer Institute on the "Meanings of Property," June 2014, and is the author of *The Evolution of the Property Relation*, 2015.

Routledge Frontiers of Political Economy

For a full list of titles in this series please visit www.routledge.com/books/series/SE0345

Money as a Social Institution

The Institutional Development of Capitalism

Ann E. Davis

Routledge
Taylor & Francis Group

LONDON AND NEW YORK

First edition published 2017
by Routledge

2 Park Square, Milton Park, Abingdon, Oxfordshire OX14 4RN

52 Vanderbilt Avenue, New York, NY 10017

Routledge is an imprint of the Taylor & Francis Group, an informa business

First issued in paperback 2018

British Library Cataloguing-in-Publication Data
A catalogue record for this book is available from the British Library

Library of Congress Cataloging-in-Publication Data
Names: Davis, Ann E., 1947- author.
Title: Money as a social institution : the institutional development of capitalism / Ann E. Davis.
Description: Abingdon, Oxon ; New York, NY : Routledge, 2017. |
Includes index.
Identifiers: LCCN 2017000587| ISBN 9781138945869 (hardback) |
ISBN 9781315671154 (ebook)
Subjects: LCSH: Money—Social aspects. | Social institutions. | Capitalism.
Classification: LCC HG220.A2 D39 2017 | DDC 332.4—dc23
LC record available at https://lccn.loc.gov/2017000587

ISBN: 978-1-138-94586-9 (hbk)
ISBN: 978-0-367-19414-7 (pbk)

Typeset in Times New Roman
by DiacriTech

To Bob, as always

Contents

Figures

Tables

Preface

Money is usually understood as a valuable object. On the contrary, the contention defended here is that money is a symbol utilized by a sovereign nation to enforce discipline for the achievement of national priorities. The value of money is attributed to it by its users, which other users recognize.

In other words, this book offers an interpretation of money as a social institution. The method is "historical institutionalism," which makes use of linguistic statements, related institutions, and the associated expertise. This institutional complex evolves historically, with changing meanings over time.

This particular application to the concept of money makes use of recent contributions to the "linguistic turn" by such philosophers as John Searle. That is, money is a form of symbolic communication, with explicit documentation and implicit meanings. Second, money relates to the discipline of modern institutions, an analysis drawing upon Foucault's critique of modernity and Marx's critique of political economy. Third, money relates to the history of the state, drawing upon historians of the fiscal/military state such as Brewer, Tilly, and Schumpeter. Legitimacy and expertise also relate to the strength of the state, drawing upon the work of Habermas and Poovey. Finally, the persistence of core institutions like the corporation draws upon the analysis of John Padgett and John Powell, as well as Brian Arthur and Harold Berman.

The first chapter begins with a discussion of these three distinctive characteristics of money: its symbolic nature, disciplinary aspects, and relation to sovereignty. The key theorists of money—Marx, Keynes, and Simmel—are discussed and their major insights compared. The role of the individual is explored in the context of such a complex social institution, which improbably seems to empower solitary agents.

The second chapter considers the social theorists John Searle and Michel Foucault and provides a dialogue between them regarding the contradictory aspects of money. This dialogue helps to further develop the method of historical institutionalism in relation to money, drawing insights from both.

The third chapter explores the analysis of capitalism as a model of labor exchange via money. Again the contributions of Marx and Keynes are further considered in this context. The prominent social divisions, such as the public/private divide, are examined to better understand how the role of labor is rendered relatively invisible.

The fourth chapter provides a long-term history of money in the context of related institutional changes. This chapter begins with coin, the prototype of money, but emphasizes the social and institutional nature of the use and interpretation of coin. The widening use of money in long-distance trade provides a context for examining the development of the monetary genres and the changing structure of the corporation as a vehicle for various types of monetary exchanges.

The fifth chapter examines money and the changing form of the state in relation to changing monetary genres and corporate forms. The evolution of the "tax/credit state" is analyzed, along with changing theories of money and methodologies.

The sixth chapter considers fetishism and financialization in the context of the financial crisis of 2008. Revisiting Marx and Keynes, the reification of money and efforts to stabilize its value become even more important after the end of the Bretton Woods financial system in the 1970s. The potential conflict between the institutional priorities of stabilization of money values and the expansion of money may lead to slower growth and financial crisis.

The seventh chapter examines the role of the corporation in the liberal state. With the complex and interdependent flows of money, labor, and materials, the corporation is the integrating institution and a key agent in the modern economy.

The eighth chapter concludes with a summary and consideration of future prospects, revisiting the three aspects of money as symbol, discipline, and sovereignty, in contrast to the mainstream economic theory of money and finance. The increasingly frequent financial crises threaten the discipline of money and portend the rise of political reaction. The novel forms of money and the impact of information technology are considered in historic and institutional contexts.

Money provides the link between the household and the firm, the worker and his product, making that very division seem natural and money as imminently practical. Financial accounting, first developed in medieval long-distance trade, provides the common template for discipline of the household, the firm, and the nation, as well as international commerce. The ultimate aim of this analysis is to provide a framework for examining money historically, beyond the operation of those particular conventions and institutions, which includes the possibility of conceptualizing and organizing the world differently.

Acknowledgements

I would like to thank Marist College for supporting my study in Florence on three separate occasions: fall 2010, summer 2011, and summer 2015. The Vassar College library has been extraordinarily generous with access to its extensive holdings and interlibrary loan functions. A special thanks is due to the National Endowment for the Humanities (NEH) for the privilege of serving as director for the Summer Institute on the Meanings of Property, June 2014.

Conversations with Sven Beckert, Amy Bloch, Melinda Cooper, Frank Decker, Duncan Foley, Todd Gitlin, Richard Goldthwaite, Edith Kuiper, Michael Hannagan, Hendrik Hartog, Paddy Ireland, Jeff McAulay, Robert McAulay, John Najemy, John Padgett, Moishe Postone, Mary Poovey, Paddy Quick, and John Searle have been very extremely helpful. Discussants and participants at the Allied Social Science Association meetings in Boston in 2016 and the World Interdisciplinary Network on Institutional Research in Bristol, UK, in April 2016 were also very useful, along with participants in the NEH Summer Institute in June 2014.

My family has been supportive and encouraging throughout. I thank my parents for inspiring my lifelong search for knowledge and insight, as well as social betterment.

1 Introduction and Selected Review of the Literature

I. Methodologies in Flux

A. Current Period

In the current period, methodologies are in flux. There is a wide range of different approaches, including, for example, economics as a science (Mirowski 1989), as well as historical institutionalism (Mahoney and Thelen 2010), evolutionary institutionalism (Hodgson 2015), literary studies (Poovey 1998), behavioral economics (Kahneman 2011), new institutional economics (Greif 2006), philosophy (Searle 2010); technology (Arthur 2015), historical materialism (Wickham 2007, 2016), game theory (Quint and Shubik 2014), world systems theory (Arrighi 1994), network theory (Blockmans 2010; Latour 2005; McLean 2007; Powell 1990; Tilly 2010; Castells 1996; Padgett and Ansell 1993), and cognitive science (Fauconnier 2003; Hutchins 1996). There are disciplines that have risen and fallen, only to reemerge, such as the history of ideas (McMahon and Moyn 2014).

According to Davis (2015), this is a sign of institutions in flux, with key categories in question, such as "property" and "money," and the associated expertise undergoing reassessment and critique. Yet few methodologies examine money as an institution rather than a self-evident object of convenience. This work will proceed to consider money as an integral aspect of social institutions, subject to the same methodological approaches.

B. Money as a Social Institution

Building on Davis (2015), the organizing concept for this book is that money is a social institution (Desan 2014; Seigel 2012, 271–272, 280; Wray 2004), usefully studied with the method of historical institutionalism. By applying this methodology, one would focus on the category of money, along with the financial institutions and the expert knowledge associated with them. Although the associated literature is voluminous, this approach will focus on the language, the specific terminology, and the shifting meanings over time. Exploring these definitions in a historical context will provide a method for tracing shifting institutions over time and their complex interconnections.

There are several aspects to this proposition, specifically in the case of money. First, money is a symbol, part of a coded system of communication (Habermas 1989; Hutter 1994; Luhmann 2012; Simmel 1978). Second, money is a disciplinary device (Poovey 1998, 2008). Third, money is a form of sovereignty, integrally related to the state (Barkan 2013; Ingham 2004, 49; Kelly and Kaplan 2001, 2009; Santner 2016).

After discussing each of these aspects, the chapter will proceed by a review of the literature, highlighting Marx, Simmel, and Keynes. The three aspects of money emphasized here will be contrasted with other treatments in the literature.

Finally, this discussion will be used to consolidate the proposed framework for the analysis of money for the remainder of the book and key questions and issues to be resolved.

II. Symbol

First, money is a symbol. Money takes a physical, material form that is visible, recognizable, and quickly interpreted, like Kahneman's "thinking fast" (2011). In this sense, an instantaneous message is communicated subliminally, without the participants' awareness. As such, money becomes "naturalized," and its use becomes habitual, not the subject of scrutiny or inspection under normal circumstances. Money is often taken as valuable in itself, which may enhance its functionality (Searle 2010, 107, 140; Poovey 2008, 26).

As a symbol, the message is interpreted by users of a distinct community, who recognize each other as participants, who know the "language" (Hutchins and Johnson 2009; Padgett 2014e, 98). This group becomes a closed community, with its limits delineated by social signs (such as age and gender), as well with the possession and effective utilization of the symbol. The message must be repeated to maintain its meaning, but in this process its message can become distorted and ambiguous. Under these circumstances, the form and content of the message can vary over time, leading to a form of "evolutionary" development (Hutter 1994, 123–128; Luhmann 2012, 38, 114–115; Padgett 2012d, 55–60).

For the sign to maintain its meaning, there must be an operation of "observing repetitions" (Hutter 1994, 114).

> Every sign needs another sign to validate its existence: only the next sign proves that the prior sign had meaning, i.e. *was* a sign. (Hutter 1994, 114; italics in original)

In this process of repetition, communication is differentiated from its environment (Hutter 1994, 116). The boundary of understanding of these signs is called "society" (Hutter 1994, 118) in certain contexts. Money is a type of self-referential system of code, related to property and transactions (Hutter 1994, 119–122). In this sense, money is "fictional," referring to a meaning that is only understood by the mutually recognized participants, whether clan, group, or organization (Hutter 1994, 127, 136).

Money is a type of, and the subject of, specialized writing, or "expertise," which reproduces its meanings by professional standards and protocols. One example is double-entry bookkeeping, which has precise rules for representation and for "balancing" the flows of money and commodities (Poovey 1998, 29–65). Money is subject to the "problematic of representation," nonetheless, whereby the concordance of word and thing becomes questionable (Poovey 2008, 4–7, 14–19). This instability of reference between money and value in general becomes particularly acute in periods of financial crises. At such times, even professional economists can resort to types of "fiction" writing and storytelling to help explain its breakdown. According to Poovey, the development of modern academic disciplines like economics and literary studies, and the distinction between "fact" and "fiction," can help stabilize the meanings of money even in such times of crisis (Poovey 2008, 77–85).

III. Disciplinary Device

Money has most often been linked to the political authority and served as a disciplinary device, albeit in different ways. In the history of money there have been several stages: money as tribute, taxes, and the capacity to exchange "property" as designated by the official hierarchy; the capacity to hire living labor; and the capacity to make use of money itself by means of a regulated financial market (Ferguson 2008; Goetzmann 2016). Money may be an instrument of "liberal governmentality" in the liberal state (Davis 2015, 214–215).

The meaning of money is stabilized by the *qualitative* relationship of the power to command commodities, resources, and labor; the *quantitative* ratios of relative prices; and the substitution among various types of financial assets to create "liquidity" (Davis 2015, 149–150). In order to rationalize and analyze the quantitative relationship between money and commodities, a distinction was made by Smith and Marx between "productive" and "unproductive" labor (Smith 1994; Marx 1967; Christophers 2013, 40–51). Only productive labor creates "value," and competition among producers systematizes the exact quantitative relationships reflected in market prices. Productive labor is distinguished by types of products as well as locations of production. For Smith and Marx, services were not "productive," and even for contemporary economists, the household does not produce value. Money as a symbol includes the qualitative relationship, the potential of money to command labor power, and the quantitative equivalence of money and commodities in exchange. Yet these relationships are in flux over time (Postone 1993), influenced by relative bargaining power and improvements in methods of production, from skill, science, and mechanization. Yet there is a "normal" or "equilibrium" value that represents the social average, expressed in measures of labor productivity for each sector and in each time period.

In economies characterized by the separation of factory from households, another discipline on the worker is to locate and qualify for employment. Wages from employment typically become the primary means of acquiring necessities as well as luxuries. This search for employment requires the development of skills to produce products that are valued on the market (Meister 1991).

IV. Form of Sovereignty

As an abstract concept, the state has been made analogous to concrete "bodies," for individual persons, monarchs, and nation-states (Howland and White 2009, 1–2; Padgett 2012a, 122–123; Poovey 1995, 2002). Coin has further represented the political power of the state (Hutter 1994, 132; Spufford 2002; Polanyi 1944), and the issue of money is often the monopoly of the state (Rogoff 2016, 17-30). Hobbes imagined the state as a creature, the Leviathan, larger than life (Barkan 2013, 21–25), a single entity composed of the collective of individuals. For a mercantilist state, corporations were instruments of trade and colonization (Kelly 2006, 160–167), with power beyond the territory of the state (Barkan 2013, 89–109). On the other hand, private business corporations became separate entities, "the legal embodiment of capital separate from the state," and capable of challenging that state (Barkan 2013, 57).

With the rise in the use of money to mediate trade and production, there also emerged a new composition of the elite and a new form of the state, a type of "co-constitution" (McLean and Padgett 2004, 193–195).

As public debt became a means of raising funds to wage war, the power of the state increased. This new capacity to extend the scale and territory of the state then facilitated increases in fundraising capacity (Arrighi 1994). At the same time, this increasing importance of money in supporting the military and the extension of state power caused the form of the state to change to a state founded on financial flows (Weber 1978, 166–174, 199–201). This concept is further developed in a discussion of the tax/credit form of the state discussed in Chapter 5.

In particular, the modern money school emphasizes money as the creation of the state. Rather than viewing money as always the "creature of the state" (Tcherneva 2016, 6), nonetheless, this analysis stresses the interaction of the state and money. On the one hand, a sovereign currency can enhance the power of the state (Ferguson 2001). On the other hand, hegemonic currencies used to dominate world trade can be an instrument of subordination for peripheral states. The currency hierarchy reflects the competitive status among nation-states. A long-term history of money would highlight the changing role of money along with the changing form of the state, as suggested in Table 1.1.

Another clue to the salience of money as a coordination/control device is the emergence and the flux among competing theories of money in different eras, as illustrated in Table 1.2.

In other words, the term "money" and what counts as money, the related institutions, and the expertise are all important components of a related complex that evolves historically.

Table 1.1 Forms of State and Money

Type of State	Form of Money
Empire	Precious metal or standard commodity
Commercial revolution among competing states (Lopez 1971; Spruyt 1994)	Precious metal; private bankers
Hereditary monarchical states (Polanyi 1944)	Precious metal (*haute finance*)
British Empire	Gold standard (1880–1914)
Liberal trade empire (U.S. dominated)	Dollar/gold standard under Bretton Woods; hegemonic fiat currency post Bretton Woods

Table 1.2 Theories of Money and Time Period

School/Theorist of Money	Time Period
Aristotle	Ancient Greece
Church	Medieval Period
Mercantilist	Early Modern
Classical (Locke 1988; Smith 1994)	Early Industrial
Neoclassical (Marshall 1923); Austrian (Hayek 1933)	Industrial
Keynes	Modern Global Trade Regime
Modern Theory (Wray 2016)	Post-Neoliberal

V.   Review of the Literature

It is important to review, compare, and build on major contributions to the analysis of money, including Marx, Simmel, Keynes, and others.

A.   Marx

For Marx, labor is the central relationship between humankind and the material world and provides an insight into a method for comparing different historical epochs, such as historical materialism. Marx's labor theory of value is shared by Locke, Smith, and Ricardo, although in a particular form related to the specifics of the institutions of capitalism. In this specific historical form of capitalism, money expresses the value represented by abstract labor time (Postone 1993).

For Marx, money is "ideological" in the sense of hiding a deeper reality compared with the surface appearance (Poovey 2002, 132), which can only be adequately understood by means of a "critique of political economy." Money can be understood as a symbol (Marx *Capital,* Vol. I 1967, 90–93, 126–127, 129), capable of becoming "the private property of any individual" (Marx 1967, 132). Money is the abstract form of human labor generally, the "universal equivalent" (Marx 1967, 67). Money is "the individual incarnation of social labour, as the independent form of existence of exchange-value, as the universal commodity" (Marx 1967, 138). With the emergence of money, "value" takes an active independent form and appears to expand automatically (Marx 1967, 92–93, 152–155).

Marx draws upon Aristotle to understand the distinction between use value and exchange value (Marx 1967, 152–155, 164). "The secret of the expression of value, namely, that all kinds of labour are equal and equivalent, because, and so far as they are human labour in general, cannot be deciphered, until the notion of human equality has already acquired the fixity of a popular prejudice ... [when] the dominant relation between man and man is that of owners of commodities" (Marx 1967, 60). This symbolic expression of exchange value in the money form is contradictory, particularly in a crisis.

> On the eve of the crisis, the bourgeois, with the self-sufficiency that springs from intoxicating prosperity, declares money to be a vain imagination. Commodities alone are money. But now the cry is everywhere: money alone is a commodity! As the hart pants after fresh water, so pants his soul after money, the only wealth. In a crisis, the antithesis between commodities and their value-form money, becomes heightened into an absolute contradiction (Marx, 1967, Vol. I, 138)

The coded nature of money does not reveal its foundation in labor time and its role in facilitating the exchange of labor and commodity by that common standard. That is, the worker in the factory is paid a wage per hour, which presumably compensates him for the entire length of his working day. The wage goods that he can *purchase* with that wage payment, nonetheless, represent less than the value *produced* during his entire working day. That is, the labor time necessary to produce the wage goods he can purchase is less than the total number of hours during which he was productively employed. This is the origin of surplus value (Marx 1967, Vol. I). The appearance of equal rights and equivalence, and the payment of the worker for each hour, masks the reality of exploitation. Both the worker and the owner have "equal rights" of ownership (Marx 1967, 167–176; Wolff 1988). The owner of the factory has the rights of property, which include ownership of the product produced, and the right to mark up the price of that product to include profit, a standard rate of return on the amount of money that he advanced to purchase the commodity labor power and raw materials. The worker has the right to sell his own commodity, labor power, for the time necessary for the production of his necessities, even though his working day is longer. Money appears to expand on its own, but the origin of this ostensible return to money, or profit, is the labor embodied in the commodity produced.

> Money itself is a commodity, an external object, capable of becoming the private property of any individual. Thus social power becomes the private power of private persons ... The desire after hoarding is in its very nature unsatiable [sic]. In its qualitative aspect, or formally considered, money has no bounds to its efficacy, i.e., it is the universal representative of material wealth, because it is directly convertible into any other commodity. But, at the same time, every actual sum of money is limited in amount, and, therefore, as a means of purchasing, has only a limited efficacy. This antagonism between the quantitative limits of money and its qualitative boundlessness, continually acts as a spur to the hoarder in his Sisyphus-like labour of accumulating. (Marx 1967, Vol. I, Ch 3, Section 3.a, 132–133)

Balance for the economy as a whole is achieved when total labor employed is equal to total aggregate value, or gross domestic product (GDP), and the aggregate price markup over costs of production is equal to the sum of unpaid labor time, or surplus value (Moseley 2016). When these equivalents are not met, there is a change in the value of money, which is not "accounted" for by mainstream economics, except perhaps by attribution to improper policies of the central bank. In spite of having achieved the modern status as a "science," changes in the money form have been manifested in party politics (Poovey 2002; Pincus 2007; Wennerlind 2011).

Another example in which common terms can have different meanings is the corporation. For modern usage, the business corporation is an example of individual private property. For Marx, it is an example of social collaboration (Marx 1967, Vol. I, Ch. 31, 755; Vol. III, Ch. 20, Ch. 27, 436–441).

B.   *Simmel*

Simmel begins his *Philosophy of Money* by assuming two categories: being and value (Simmel 1978, 59–62), drawing on Plato and Kant. The basis for valuation is subjectivity, which develops along with the differentiation of subject and object (Simmel 1978, 62–65). For Simmel, the central relationship between humankind and the material world is subjective valuation, and most social relationships take the form of exchange, including work (Simmel 1978, 79–85).

> The projection of mere relations into particular objects is one of the great accomplishments of the mind ... The ability to construct such symbolic objects attains its greatest triumph in money ... Thus money is the adequate expression of the relationship of man to the world. (Simmel 1978, 129)

Simmel views money as the means to develop independence and freedom (Simmel 1978, 306–314, 321–331) and to support individualism (Simmel 1978, 347–354).

> Money, as the most mobile of all goods, represents the pinnacle of this tendency. Money is really that form of property that most effectively liberates the individual from the unifying bonds that extend from other objects of possession. (Simmel 1978, 354)

Simmel is critical of Marx's labor theory of value, but misconstrues it as representing labor expended in production, rather than socially necessary labor based on competition in commodity production (Simmel 1978, 426–428).

C. *Keynes*

In Chapter 17 of *The General Theory*, money is defined in relative terms, as the asset with the highest liquidity premium relative to its carrying costs (Keynes 1964). Keynes draws upon classical economics, adapted to a monetary economy. For Keynes, money is an asset with its "own rate of return," like all other assets (Keynes 1964, 222–244). The unique "liquidity" of money can also be due to its use in payment of wages, taxes, and debt (Keynes 1964, 167, 232–234, 236–239), which is by convention instead of inherent physical characteristics of its production. Keynes uses a form of supply and demand to explain market prices. For example, scarcity of supply can partly explain the value of money and capital (Keynes 1964, 213–215, Mann 2015). Further, his analysis of demand focuses on "psychological" factors, such as the marginal propensity to consume (MPC), the marginal efficiency of capital (MEC), and liquidity preference (pp. 28, 30, 91, 96, 141–145, 170–173, 194–199, 202–203, 234–242, 246–247, 251–253, 315–316). In summarizing his "general theory" in Ch. 18, Keynes writes

> We can sometimes regard our ultimate independent variables as consisting of (1) the three fundamental psychological factors, namely, the psychological propensity to consume, the psychological attitude to liquidity and the psychological expectation of future yield from capital assets. (Keynes 1964, 246–247)

This is along with (2) the wage unit and (3) the quantity of money.
  The interest rate is determined by liquidity preference, or

> The rate of interest at any time, being the reward for parting with liquidity … It is the "price" which equilibrates the desire to hold wealth in the form of cash with the available quantity of cash. (Keynes 1964, 167)

There are contradictions of liquidity nonetheless. There is no such thing as liquidity for the economy as a whole (pp. 151, 153, 155, 160–161), even though each individual investor can experience the liquidity of any particular asset by his ability to trade that asset for others in a given time period. In turn, liquidity preference is a key determinant of the rate of interest, which is a threshold for the rate of investment (MEC) (pp. 165–167, 194–209, 212–213, 222, 234–235, 308–309). In period of crisis, there is a possibility of infinite demand for liquidity (pp. 174, 207–208, 316), which could contribute to further declines in investment.

Money facilitates control of the system, on the one hand. On the other, if there is infinite desire for cash, real investment will suffer (p. 212–213). The interest rate on money is a standard threshold for investment (p. 222), but also affects the choice of *form* of investment (money vs. debt) (pp. 166–167, 212–213).

The separation of ownership and control facilitates the rise of the stock market (pp. 150–151), which may aid financing of investment. On the other hand, the stock market has a tendency to operate like a casino, subject to waves of speculation (pp. 156–161). The cure for this instability may be the "euthanasia of rentier" and an increased role of the state (pp. 164, 220–221, 320, 325, 376–381), even though that may conflict with norms of "capitalist individualism" (pp. 160–161, 380–381).

Important dimensions of Keynes' analysis of money include the follow key points:

1 There is a micro/macro split, as revealed in the critique of the neoclassical theory of wages (Keynes Ch. 19), sometimes called the "fallacy of composition." For example, reducing wages may improve the profitability of a single employer, but may reduce effective demand for the system as a whole. This macro effect of lower wages would decrease employment instead of increasing it. Second, liquidity is possible for the individual investor, but not for the system as a whole.

> With the separation between ownership and management which prevails to-day and with the development of organized investment markets, a new factor of great importance has entered in, which sometimes facilitates investment but sometimes adds greatly to the instability of the system ... The Stock Exchange revalues many investments every day and the revaluations give a frequent opportunity to the individual (though not to the community as a whole) to revise his commitments. It is as though a farmer, having tapped his barometer after breakfast, could decide to remove his capital from the farming business between 10 and 11 in the morning and reconsider whether he should return to it later in the week. (Keynes 1964, 150–151)

2 Keynes notes the link between money and time (pp. 68–71, 135–137, 145–146, 293–294), as evidenced by his observation that money and durable equipment are the links between the present and the future and the effect of expectations of the future on the present market price of

durable equipment. He expresses sympathy for the classical school of economics, which regards labor as the sole factor of production. Labor is the "sole physical unit" in Keynes' analysis as well, along with "units of money and of time" (pp. 213–214).

Keynes repudiates his earlier contention that there is a single "natural rate of interest" (pp. 242–244). The interest rate is influenced by psychology as well as central bank policy. The MEC is influenced by the quantity of capital, but also by expectations (pp. 135–137), and may be influenced by speculation in the financial markets.

The role of the interest rate in setting the standard for the MEC (p. 235) provides the central bank a tool for the management of the system, but there are limits to its effectiveness (pp. 204, 207–208, 215, 308–309), such as the zero lower bound in the context of a sudden collapse of the MEC. His resort to "animal spirits" serves to rescue the system, but at the cost of an additional psychological variable (pp. 161–163).

3   Money as the symbolic marker of the social system, a point made by Luhmann but not sufficiently appreciated by Keynes.

Keynes discusses the unique characteristics of money as an asset with its "own rate of return" (pp. 225–229), but does not conceptualize the conditions of production of money as a symbol.

The money-rate of interest, by setting the pace for all the other commodity-rates of interest, holds back investment in the production of these other commodities without being capable of stimulating investment for the production of money, which by hypothesis cannot be produced (Keynes 1964, 235).

4   Keynes sees money as an object, with conditions of production (pp. 229–232), rather than a relationship, in contrast to Marx. He does nonetheless focus on the "psychological factors" in the development of the general theory.

Keynes has succeeded in shifting the grounds for economic theory from marginal productivity and marginal utility to money units and cash flows. For example, the marginal efficiency of capital is based on expected future cash flows (pp. 135–149). He provides a critique of Marshall's theory of interest as circular (pp. 137, 140, 184), founding his own on liquidity preference based on psychology. The unique role of money is due to its liquidity, which occurs because money is the unit for the payment of wages, debt, and taxes. "Sticky" money wages are a condition of the stability of the system (pp. 236–239, 250–251).

A further examination of the concept of liquidity in Keynes' work helps us understand how money becomes the primary variable for him in the economic system. First it seems that liquidity is an attribute of money. Then it seems that the definition of money is based on its liquidity. Further there is no absolute standard of liquidity (Keynes 1964, 240), and in fact liquidity is a function of the business cycle. Liquidity preference is a way of expressing the wishes of wealth holders and their willingness to part with cash, reflected in the interest rate. The "feelings" of wealth holders are expressed in a financial indicator in terms of the trade of assets with other wealth holders. That is, "liquidity" is a human attribute, expressed in financial markets by a quantitative measure of the relative substitution of financial assets at various stages of the business cycle. In this way, the financial markets are no longer perceived as human, but as price signals that communicate among themselves, a form of reification.

D. Game Theory

A very different approach can build on game theory. Rather than a settled technical matter of "price determination," recent theories allow for a diversity of strategic agents and varieties of objective functions. For example, Quint and Shubik begin with a fully developed money economy and apply the techniques of game theory. To simplify the model, it is assumed that government provides the rules and is one of the agents in the financial system. There is no production in this model, but only exchange (pp. 5–6) in order to focus on the strategic role of money "in the financial control of the economy" (Quint and Shubik 2014, 2).

> This book is about a fundamental phenomenon in economic life. This is the use of money and credit in transactions, and their role as substitutes for trust. Money is the catalyst that enables the flow of goods and services to the body economic. The financial system is the neural network and control system, directing the money and credit flows of the economy. A good model of the financial system should take into account the physical aspects of money, the role of government within a society, and dynamics … We suggest here that much of the financial system can be viewed as a formal dynamic game, where government supplies the rules and the pressures of politics and society help modify many of these rules in the fullness of time. (Quint and Shubik 2014, 1)

This analysis is grounded in long-term history, but formalized by equations that express key relationships in abstract terminology.

"History and anthropology teach us that there have been thousands of variations in money and financial institutions over the past 4,000 years. Coinage has existed for only about 2,500 years, central banks for 300 years" (Quint and Shubik 2014, ix).

"To erect a sound basis for a theory of money and financial institutions, we believe, it is worth starting simply, with primitive concepts aimed at understanding an already monetized economy with markets" (Quint and Shubik 2014, x).

The models of money as a medium of exchange can be studied while omitting production, according to this analysis, due to the additional complexity involved (Quint and Shubik 2014, 5–6).

"Conceptually our models start hardly earlier than 1650 A.D., although Rome and Babylon appear to have had some aspects of a market economy" (Quint and Shubik 2014, 17).

E. Sociology of Money

In contrast with Zelizer (1997), who discusses the embeddedness of money in social networks with various meanings, the approach here is to consider money itself as social. Other sociologists stressed the "performativity" of money (Callon, Millo and Muniesa 2007; Christophers 2013, 9–12; MacKenzie 2006). That is, economic concepts such as money and property exist in human understanding as well as human action, the latter of which makes the concepts "real."

VI. Money as a Representation of Time

In modern capitalist economies, money is a symbolic representation of time—work time, life time—linking money to "perpetuity," or infinite time. Time is the basic unit of analysis of all economic categories (Postone 1993), even if only implicitly. This is true of the income categories wages, rent, interest, and profit, as well as productivity. There is the imperative to increase the "throughput" of factories (Chandler 1990) as well as to increase the rate of turnover of inventory or money, or to increase capacity utilization, the portion of a year at which an existing factory is operational. There are various denominations of time, such as the carefully measured work time in factories, compared with the leisure time "to be filled" of the household, or the life expectancies of the overlapping generations in perpetuity.

As expressed in the typical circular flow diagram in introductory economics courses, the basic units of the economy are the firm and the household. The exchange of labor and product is mediated by money on the respective factor and product markets. The "realization" of profit would not take place without the mobile labor force producing the commodity during the working day for a wage. Then that wage becomes the payment for the product produced in the factory and acquired by the household for leisure time consumption. Without the productivity differential between firm and household, there would be no motivation for this exchange of labor and product by means of money. Yet this implicit comparison occurs even though the time of household production is not measured or disciplined and is not recognized as producing economic "value."

Financial circuits differentiate household from factory—specific places as well as discrete times. Each site "produces" a commodity that circulates via money, labor, and product, respectively. That is, money delineates a financial circuit *between* firm and household. Yet the money relationships *within* firm and household are distinctive. The relationships within the firm are mediated by contract by unit of time; during the performance of the contract, there is no exchange of money. The relationships within the household are mediated by a marriage contract (Pateman 1988) and legal custody of minors. While money is shared within the household, there is no payment for household "services." Such a money payment would be considered taboo, a violation of the personal, sharing relationships that are the norm for household behavior.

The ironies of the labor relationships abound. Labor is the source of the "value" of the product but is also a cost of production. Labor is also the origin of the "realization" of the value of the product in final sales to the household in the role as consumer, in the process of the reproduction of the worker and the next generation. Distinct "spheres" or "domains" (Poovey 2002) reduce the potential contradictions among the various components of value production and realization process, all of which are denominated in labor time. There is no standard measure of time across the boundaries of factory and household, other than human lifetimes.

Profit is the result of the distinct rules for mediation between household and firm. Profit is the residual between the sales price of the product and the costs of production, primarily labor costs. Profit can result if the productive labor time embodied in the product is greater than the time costs of wage goods paid to the workers who produced that product. This differential is the bonus paid for the productivity of the firm relative to the household in the production of consumer goods and the reward for continuing gains in productivity at the firm. This notion of the labor value of production is common to Locke, Smith, and Marx, but remains contested in modern economic theory (Moseley 2016; Postone 1993; Shaikh 2016). The "shut down price" in modern microeconomics nonetheless reflects the minimum unit labor costs: wage divided by labor productivity.

By contrast in modern economics, the sales price of the product is attributed to the subjective "utility" of the consumer, rather than the value of the labor time embodied in production. Although there remain issues in the precise measurement of labor time as the foundation of "value," there is no independent measure of "utility" other than the sales price itself. This tautological notion of "utility" could be considered an example of a reifying abstraction common to the "modern fact," by which a conjectural feature of "human nature" is measured and "verified" by abstract mathematical representation (Poovey 2002). With the separation of the household from factory, the sphere of domesticity becomes identified with "privacy" and "leisure" (McKeon 2005; Veblen 1934), and the pleasure of the autonomous "individual" becomes the purpose of the system. Such an abstraction as "utility" is part of the modern theory of "governmentality," by which human nature can be explained by consistent "natural laws" originating inside the individual, which can be objectively observed by experts (Poovey 2002, 126, 131, 138–140).

Even though the household is not considered "productive," there is a cultural objective of relative status and upward mobility, which are nonetheless measures of household "industriousness" (Veblen 1934; de Vries 2008).

A Puritan mentality would regard the accomplishments of a lifetime from the perspective of the final Judgment Day (Brown 2015; Christensen 2012; Weber 1958), a metaphor not unrelated to the balancing of the accounting books (Soll 2014).

VII.   Money and the Representation of Space

Although money is issued by the sovereign nation, it is also a vehicle for trade among nations. Money was used in long-distance trade, in the form of gold coin, after the collapse of the Roman Empire (Fox, Velde, and Ernst 2016). Abstract money as a unit of account was most common in local exchange. The ability to protect territory was associated with gold coin as the means of hiring mercenaries. As trade developed and city-states acquired more surplus, these gold reserves were useful in military expenditures to expand territory. This formed a type of virtuous circle, by which trade helped to finance military, which extended territory to expand more trade. Arrighi (1994) expressed this relationship between money and territory by as a type of circuit, $T - M - T'$, instead of Marx's typical circuit of $M - C - M'$. As further discussed later, this importance of money in turn altered the form of the state to a "tax/credit state."

VIII.   Money and Capitalism

The role of money is important in the institutions of capitalism, yet money existed for centuries before the emergence of capitalism. There is a large literature regarding the origins and definition, as well as the transition to capitalism (Emigh 2009).

Specifically there is ongoing discussion regarding the characterization of the economy in the Renaissance. For example, rather than see early "capitalism" in Florence, the view here is that the use of money was in the process of extension for trade and production, but commodity production was primarily textiles and luxury goods, rather than all necessities. Wage labor was not yet the dominant type of employment, but rather sharecroppers and apprentices were common. Markets had not yet penetrated land, which could be acquired by inheritance, through families, or through conquest, by the city-states. Confidence in credit instruments was not yet widely established, and company stock, bills of exchange, and banks were not yet established "in perpetuity," including public debt. Early merchants and bankers still tended to invest surplus in land for the enjoyment of the countryside, extra income, collateral, inheritance, and the possibility of noble title. With the usury prohibition still affecting some institutions, the use of money to make more money was not yet firmly established and normative. Profits were calculated at the end of the contract and distributed to shareholders, but companies were not yet perpetual corporations. Merchants, although increasingly respected, tended to have lower status than nobility. Modern political theory was in development, with "civic humanism" and Machiavelli's writings, but not yet political economy. Techniques such as double-entry bookkeeping and recording of private financial transactions were becoming more widespread with the increase in literacy and numeracy, but calculation was not yet viewed as central to lifetime income. For example, the Medici family sought title through marriage and the church for their heirs, rather than continue investment in their well-known Medici bank (de Roover 1948) (an interpretation in contrast to Tarrow 2004).

According to historians of the period, "The 'rise of financial capitalism' for us is not a grand teleological process of inevitable modernization" (Padgett and McLean 2006, 1473).

IX.   Money as a Hybrid

Because money has a disciplinary dimension, the command of labor, it also can control the use of material resources and affect economic production. This constitutes a "hybrid" form, according to Latour (1993), which integrates human and natural/material contexts, violating the so-called "modern constitution," which separates nature and society. The intellectual separation of human and natural academic disciplines according to the "modern constitution" denies and obscures the instrumental use of human labor. Money is a "material anchor for a conceptual blend" (Hutchins 2005).

Money also crosses several "domains" (Poovey 1995, 1998), including family and church, as well as company and market. A methodology that integrates these various domains can provide insights into the related variation of institutional form across centuries and sectors (Padgett and Powell 2012). Like the "overlapping generations" models in economics, the "perpetual" form of the company and the state would not be possible without a relationship with family and human reproduction.

X.   Money and Value

Money as a representation of value affects values and forms of knowledge, as well as institutions and the organization of space and time. For Marx, self-ownership of the commodity labor power is a central institution of capitalism (Marx 1967, Vol. I, Ch. 6, 167–176). Money distinguishes the spaces and times in which labor is sold (the factory) and in which labor owns itself (the household). There is a connection between this dual role of labor and the projection of value onto the products of labor, or "commodity fetishism" (Marx 1967, Vol. I, Ch. 1, Section 4, 71–83). With the separation of use value and exchange value, exchange value becomes *value* in itself, symbolized by money. Money seems to grow, to expand automatically, based on these relationships (Marx 1967, Vol. I, Ch. 4, 152–155).

Instrumental use of human beings is justified by the limited duration of this relationship, its contribution to productivity, and to the pleasure of the private "individual." The category of "ownership" divides subject from object; those who use have initiative and agency, compared with those who are useful by laboring according to instruction. Money becomes "value" itself, replacing and displacing the moral meaning of "values" (Stark 2011). Money as value itself appears neutral, merely useful, convenient, and objective, rather than carrying an implicit set of values, which provides the basis for the separation of normative and positive economics in mainstream economic literature.

XI. Individualism

The capacity of money to represent value in an abstract form can facilitate individualism and freedom (Seigel 2012), on the one hand, as well as alienation and isolation on the other (Polanyi 1944). At times, Simmel can appreciate both views.

> With this teleological web [of money and credit] we have reached the very pinnacle of the contradiction that lies in the drowning out of the end by the means: the growing significance of the means goes hand in hand with a *corresponding* increase in the rejection and negation of the end. And this factor increasingly permeates the social life of the people; it directly interferes with personal, political and economic relationships on a large scale and indirectly gives certain age groups and social circles their distinctive character. (Simmel 1978, 481; italics in original)

Individual self-expression as a value emerged in the Renaissance, with the shift from the anonymous craft person to the individual socially acclaimed genius, whether artist or investor (Greenblatt 1980; Seigel 2012; Siedentop 2014).

According to some theorists (Berlin 1958; Ryan 1979), individual empowerment is the greatest achievement of a modern market economy. According to Simmel, the possession of money facilitates the "extension of the self" (Simmel 1978, 326). "The personal element becomes more and more independent, the individual becomes capable of developing more independently" (Simmel 1978, 332). Weber sees the capital market as a "battle of man against man" (Weber 1978, Ch. II, Section 11, 93). Marx sees the individual money holder as obtaining social power (Marx 1967, Vol. I, Ch. 3, Section 3.a, 132–133).

Keynes acknowledges the importance of individualism in capitalism, but is somewhat ironic about its impact (Keynes 1964, 375–376, 378, 380–381). He is quite willing to have the state assume important aspects of economic decision-making.

There are protections for the individual in the liberal state, such as human rights and free speech (Davis 2011), as well as checks and balances. The realism of "the individual" can nonetheless be questioned. Examining the social meanings of property, Davis observes "we have never been individuals"

(Davis 2015, 90–91). Subjectivity is shaped by discourse (Brown, W. 2015, 70, 177) and individuals are interdependent (Mirowski 2013, 93-155). Marx notes the *de jure* equality of property owners, whereas Weber observes the differential power relations in modern economies (Weber 1978, Ch. 11, Section 1, 67–68; Section 11, 97; and Section 22, 137–140).

Even Simmel sees a potential for means ends reversal (Brown, W. 2015, 119; Simmel 1978, 481) such that money would increase in importance relative to the individual whom it presumably empowers.

XII. Summary

The approach in this work, which views money as a social institution, can be reconciled with money as facilitating individualism in the broader context of money as a symbol, disciplinary device, and tool of sovereignty. Money *represents* the system, even as it is owned or possessed by the individual. The power of the system is then often projected onto the symbol itself, a form of "fetishism," especially when money takes the form of a standard unit of precious metal. In this way, money is naturalized and its history disappears. In order to resurrect the possibilities of conscious institutional design, this history and function of money, as well as the related meanings and institutions, must be fully explored. These tasks will be considered in the remaining chapters.

References

Arthur, W. Brian. *Complexity and the Economy*. New York: Oxford University Press, 2015.

Arrighi, Giovanni. *The Long Twentieth Century: Money, Power and the Origins of Our Times*. New York: Verso, 1994.

Barkan, Joshua. *Corporate Sovereignty: Law and Government under Capitalism*. Minneapolis, MN: University of Minnesota Press, 2013.

Berlin, Isaiah. *Two Concepts of Liberty*. Oxford: Clarendon Press, 1958.

Blockmans, Wim. "Inclusiveness and Exclusion: Trust Networks at the Origins of European Cities," *Theory and Society*, Vol. 39, 2010, 315–326.

Brown, Peter. *The Ransom of the Soul: Afterlife and Wealth in Early Western Christianity*. Cambridge, MA: Harvard University Press, 2015.

Brown, Wendy. *Undoing the Domos: Neoliberalism's Stealth Revolution*. Brooklyn, NY: Zone Books, 2015.

Callon, Michel, Yuval Millo, and Fabian Muniesa (eds.). *Market Devices*. Oxford, UK: Blackwell, 2007.

Castells, Manuel. *The Rise of the Network Society*. Malden, MA: Blackwell, 1996.

Chandler, Alfred D. Jr. Scale and Scope: *The Dynamics of Industrial Capitalism*. Cambridge, MA: Belknap Press, 1990.

Christensen, Clayton M. *How Will You Measure Your Life?* New York: Harper Business, 2012.

Christophers, Brett. *Banking Across Boundaries: Placing Finance in Capitalism*. Oxford, UK: Wiley/Blackwell, 2013.

Davis, Ann E. *The Evolution of the Property Relation: Understanding Paradigms, Debates, Prospects*. New York: Palgrave MacMillan, 2015.

Davis, John B. *Individuals and Identity in Economics*. New York: Cambridge University Press, 2011.

De Roover, Raymond. *The Medici Bank: Its Organization, Management, Operations, and Decline*. New York: New York University Press, 1948.

Desan, Christine. *Making Money: Coin, Currency, and the Coming of Capitalism*. New York: Oxford University Press, 2014.

De Vries, Jan. *The Industrious Revolution: Consumer Behavior and the Household Economy, 1650 to the Present*. New York: New York University Press, 2008.

Emigh, Rebecca Jean. *The Undevelopment of Capitalism: Sectors and Markets in Fifteenth-Century Tuscany*. Philadelphia: Temple University Press, 2009.

Fauconnier, Gilles. *The Way We Think: Conceptual Blending and the Mind's Hidden Complexities*. New York: Basic Books, 2003.

Ferguson, Niall. *The Cash Nexus: Money and Power in the Modern World 1700–2000*. New York: Penguin Press, 2001.

———. *The Ascent of Money: A Financial History of the World*. New York: Penguin 2008.

Fox, David, Francois R. Velde, and Wolfgang Ernst. "Monetary History Between Law and Economics," in David Fox and Wolfgang Ernst (eds.), *Money in the Western Legal Tradition: From Middle Ages to Bretton Woods*. New York: Oxford University Press, 2016, 3–17.

Goetzmann, William N. *Money Changes Everything: How Finance Made Civilization Possible*. Princeton, NJ: Princeton University Press, 2016.

Greenblatt, Stephen. *Renaissance Self-Fashioning: From More to Shakespeare*. Chicago: University of Chicago, 1980.

Greif, Avner. *Institutions and the Path to the Modern Economy: Lessons from Medieval Trade*. New York: Cambridge University Press, 2006.

Habermas, Jurgen. *The Structural Transformation of the Public Sphere: An Inquiry into a Category of Bourgeois Society*. Cambridge, MA: MIT Press, 1989.

Hayek, Friedrich A. von. *Monetary Theory and the Trade Cycle*. New York: Harcourt Brace & Co., 1933.

Hodgson, Geoffrey M. *Conceptualizing Capitalism: Institutions, Evolution, Future*. Chicago: University of Chicago Press, 2015.

Howland, Douglas, and Luise White (eds.). "Introduction: Sovereignty and the Study of States," in *The State of Sovereignty: Territories, Laws, Populations*. Bloomington, IN: Indiana University Press, 2009, 1–19.

Hutchins, Edwin. *Cognition in the Wild*. Cambridge, MA: MIT Press, 1996.

———. "Material Anchors for Conceptual Blends," *Journal of Pragmatics*. Vol. 37, 2005, 1555–1577.

Hutchins, Edwin and Christine M. Johnson. "Modeling the Emergence of Language as Embodied Collective Cognitive Activity," *Topics in Cognitive Science*, Vol. I, 2009, 523–546.

Hutter, Michael. "Communication in Economic Evolution: The Case of Money," in Richard W. England (ed.), *Evolutionary Concepts in Contemporary Economics*. Ann Arbor, MI: The University of Michigan Press, 1994, 111–136.

Ingham, Geoffrey. *The Nature of Money*. Cambridge, UK: Polity, 2004.

Kahneman, Daniel. *Thinking, Fast and Slow*. New York: Farrar, Straus, and Giroux, 2011.

Kelly, John D. "Who Counts? Imperial and Corporate Structures of Governance, Decolonization, and Limited Liability," in Craig Calhoun, Frederick Cooper, and Kevin W. Moore (eds.), *Lessons of Empire: Imperial Histories and American Power*. New York: The New Press, 2006, 157–174.

Kelly, John D. and Martha Kaplan. *Represented Communities: Fiji and World Decolonization*. Chicago: University of Chicago Press, 2001.

_____. "Legal Fictions After Empire," in Douglas Howland and Luise White (eds.), *The State of Sovereignty: Territories, Laws, Populations*. Bloomington, IN: Indiana University Press. 2009, 169–195.

Keynes, John Maynard. *The General Theory of Employment, Interest, and Money*. New York: Harcourt, Brace, & World, 1964.

Latour, Bruno. *We Have Never Been Modern*. Cambridge, MA: Harvard University Press, 1993.

_____. *Reassembling the Social: An Introduction to Actor-Network-Theory (ANT)*. Oxford: Oxford University Press, 2005.

Locke, John. *Two Treatises of Government*. New York: Cambridge University Press, 1988.

Lopez, Robert S. *The Commercial Revolution of the Middle Ages, 950–1350*. Englewood Cliffs, NJ: Prentice-Hall, 1971.

Luhmann, Niklas. *Theory of Society*. Vol. I. Stanford, CA: Stanford University Press, 2012.

MacKenzie, Donald A. *An Engine, Not a Camera: How Financial Models Shape Markets*. Cambridge, MA: MIT Press, 2006.

Mahoney, James and Kathleen Thelen (eds.). *Explaining Institutional Change: Ambiguity, Agency, and Power*. New York: Cambridge University Press, 2010.

Mann, Geoff. "Poverty in the Midst of Plenty: Unemployment, Liquidity, and Keynes's Scarcity Theory of Capital," in *Critical Historical Studies*, Vol. 2, No. 1, 2015, 45–83.

Marshall, Alfred. *Money, Credit, and Commerce*. London: Macmillan & Co., 1923.

Marx, Karl. *Capital*. New York: International Publishers, 1967.

McKeon, Michael. *The Secret History of Domesticity: Public, Private, and the Division of Knowledge*. Baltimore, MD: Johns Hopkins Press, 2005.

McLean. Paul D. *The Art of the Network: Strategic Interaction and Patronage in Renaissance Florence*. Durham, NC: Duke University Press, 2007.

McLean, Paul D. and John F. Padgett. "Obligation, Risk, and Opportunity in the Renaissance Economy: Beyond Social Embeddedness to Network Co-Constitution," in Frank Dobbin (ed.). *The Sociology of the Economy*. New York: Russell Sage Foundation, 2004, 193–227.

McMahon, Darrin M. and Samuel Moyn (eds.). *Rethinking Modern European Intellectual History*. New York: Oxford, 2014.

Meister, Robert. *Political Identity: Thinking Through Marx*. Cambridge, MA: Basil Blackwell, 1991.

Mirowski, Philip. *More Heat than Light: Economics as Social Physics, Physics as Nature's Economics*. New York: Cambridge University Press, 1989.

Mirowski, Philip. *Never Let a Serious Crisis Go to Waste: How Neoliberalism Survived the Financial Meltdown*. London: Verso, 2013.

Moseley, Fred. *Money and Totality: A Macro-Monetary Interpretation of Marx's Logic in Capital and the End of the 'Transformation Problem.'* Leiden, Netherlands: Brill, 2016.

Padgett, John F. "The Emergence of Corporate Merchant-Banks in Dugento Tuscany," in John F. Padgett and Walter W. Powell (eds.), *The Emergence of Organizations and Markets*. Princeton, NJ: Princeton University Press, 2012a, 121–167.

_____. "Transposition and Refunctionality: The Birth of Partnership Systems in Renaissance Florence," in John F. Padgett and Walter W. Powell (eds.), *The Emergence of Organizations and Markets*. Princeton, NJ: Princeton University Press, 2012b, 168–207.

_____. "Country as Global Market: Netherlands, Calvinism, and the Joint-Stock Company," in John F. Padgett and Walter W. Powell (eds.), *The Emergence of Organizations and Markets*. Princeton, NJ: Princeton University Press, 2012c, 208–234.

_____. "Autocatalysis in Chemistry and the Origin of Life," in John F. Padgett and Walter W. Powell. *The Emergence of Organizations and Markets*. Princeton, NJ: Princeton University Press, 2012d, 33–69.

_____. "From Chemical to Social Networks," in John F. Padgett and Walter W. Powell (eds.), *The Emergence of Organizations and Markets*. Princeton, NJ: Princeton University Press, 2012e, 92–114.

Padgett, John F. and Christopher K. Ansell. "Robust Action and the Rise of the Medici, 1400–1434," *American Journal of Sociology*, Vol. 98, No. 6, May 1993, 1259–1319.

Padgett, John F. and Paul D. McLean. "Organizational Invention and Elite Transformation: The Birth of the Partnership System in Renaissance Florence." *American Journal of Sociology*, Vol. 111, No. 5, March 2006, 1463–1568.

Padgett, John F. and Walter W. Powell. *The Emergence of Organizations and Markets*. Princeton, NJ: Princeton University Press, 2012.

Pateman, Carole. *The Sexual Contract*. Stanford, CA: Stanford University Press, 1988.

Pincus, Steven C. A. *The Politics of the Public Sphere in Early Modern England*. Manchester, UK: Manchester University Press, 2007.

Polanyi, Karl. *The Great Transformation*. Boston: Beacon Press, 1944.

Postone, Moishe. *Time, Labor, and Social Domination: A Reinterpretation of Marx's Critical Theory*. New York: Cambridge University Press, 1993.

Poovey, Mary. *Making a Social Body: British Cultural Formation 1830–1864*. Chicago: University of Chicago Press, 1995.

_____. *A History of the Modern Fact: Problems of Knowledge in the Sciences of Wealth and Society*. Chicago: University of Chicago Press, 1998.

_____. "The Liberal Civil Subject and the Social in Eighteenth-Century British Moral Philosophy," *Public Culture*. Vol. 14, No. 1, 2002, 125–145.

_____. *Genres of the Credit Economy: Mediating Value in Eighteenth-and Nineteenth-Century Britain*. Chicago: University of Chicago Press, 2008.

Powell, Walter W. "Neither Market nor Hierarchy: Network Forms of Organization," *Research in Organizational Behavior*, Vol. 12, 1990, 295–336.

Quint, Thomas and Martin Shubik. *Barley, Gold, or Fiat: Toward a Pure Theory of Money*. New Haven, CT: Yale University Press, 2014.

Rogoff, Kenneth S. *The Curse of Cash*. Princeton, NJ: Princeton University Press, 2016.

Ryan, Alan (ed.). *The Idea of Freedom: Essays in Honour of Isaiah Berlin*. New York: Oxford University Press, 1979.

Santner, Eric L. *The Weight of All Flesh: On the Subject-Matter of Political Economy*. New York: Oxford University Press, 2016.

Searle, John R. *Making the Social World: The Structure of Human Civilization*. New York: Oxford University Press, 2010.

Seigel, Jerrold. *Modernity and Bourgeois Life: Society, Politics, and Culture in England, France, and Germany since 1750*. New York: Cambridge University Press, 2012.

Shaikh, Anwar. *Capitalism: Competition, Conflict, Crises*. New York: Oxford University Press, 2016.

Siedentop, Larry. *Inventing the Individual: The Origins of Western Liberalism*. Cambridge, MA: Harvard University Press, 2014.

Simmel, Georg. *The Philosophy of Money*. Boston: Routledge & Kegan Paul, 1978.

Smith, Adam. *An Inquiry into the Nature and Causes of the Wealth of Nations*. New York: Modern Library, 1994.

Soll, Jacob. *The Reckoning: Financial Accountability and the Rise and Fall of Nations*. New York: Basic, 2014.

Spruyt, Hendrik. *The Sovereign State and Its Competitors: An Analysis of Systems of Change*. Princeton, NJ: Princeton University Press, 1994.

Spufford, Peter. *Power and Profit: The Merchant in Medieval Europe*. London: Thames and Hudson, 2002.

Stark, David. "What's Valuable?" in Jens Beckert and Patrik Aspers (eds.), *The Worth of Goods: Valuation and Pricing in the Economy*. New York: Oxford University Press, 2011, 319–338.

Tarrow, Sidney. "From Comparative Historical Analysis to 'Local Theory': The Italian City-State Route to the Modern State," *Theory and Society*, Vol. 33, No. 3–4, June–August 2004, 443–471.

Tcherneva, Pavlina R. "Money, Power, and Monetary Regimes," *Levy Institute Working Paper, No. 861*, March 2016, Annandale-on-Hudson, NY.

Tilly, Charles. "Cities, States, and Trust Networks." *Theory and Society*, Vol. 39, No. 3/4, May 2010, 265–280.

Veblen, Thorstein. *The Theory of the Leisure Class: An Economic Study of Institutions*. New York: Modern Library, 1934.

Weber, Max. *The Protestant Ethic and the Spirit of Capitalism*. New York: Charles Scribner's Sons, 1958.

_____. *Economy and Society: An Outline of Interpretive Sociology*. Vol. I. Berkeley, CA: University of California Press, 1978.

Wennerlind, Carl. *Casualties of Credit: The English Financial Revolution 1620–1720*. Cambridge, MA: Harvard University Press, 2011.

Wickham, Chris (ed.). *Marxist History Writing for the Twenty-First Century*. London Academy Occasional Papers, 2007.

_____. *Medieval Europe*. New Haven: Yale University Press, 2016.

Wolff, Robert Paul. *Money Bags Must Be So Lucky: On the Literary Structure of Capital*. Amherst, MA: University of Massachusetts Press, 1988.

Wray, L. Randall (ed.). *Credit and State Theories of Money: The Contributions of A. Mitchell Innes*. Cheltenham, UK: Edward Elgar, 2004.

_____. "From the State Theory of Money to Modern Money: An Alternative to Economic Orthodoxy," in David Fox and Wolfgang Ernst (eds.), *Money in the Western Legal Tradition: From Middle Ages to Bretton Woods*. New York: Oxford University Press, 2016, 631–652.

Zelizer, Viviana A. *The Social Meaning of Money: Pin Money, Paychecks, Poor Relief, and Other Currencies*. Princeton, NJ: Princeton University Press, 1997.

2 Money as a Social Institution

I. Introduction

This chapter will review the framework of John R. Searle, primarily the notion of a status function declaration and the use of language to form other social institutions. Money is one example of a social institution that Searle uses, and in turn his framework is instructive for carefully delineating the social nature of money. Second, certain points in Searle's framework can benefit from further discussion, such as the background of consciousness and power. Regarding these points, the contribution of other theorists, such as Poovey, Foucault, and Taylor, will be considered. Finally, Searle relies importantly on language as the foundation of social institutions. The strengths and weaknesses of this approach will be considered.

Although Searle is not a historian of ideas, in the first paragraph of his recent book, *Making the Social World: The Structure of Human Civilization* (2010), he describes the larger context of the question he is addressing:

> How, if at all, can we reconcile a certain conception of the world as described by physics, chemistry, and the other basic sciences with what we know, or think we know, about ourselves as human beings? How is it possible in a universe consisting entirely of physical particles in fields of force that there can be such things as consciousness, intentionality, free will, language, society, ethics, aesthetics, and political obligations? (Searle 2010, 3)

That is, Searle is trying to bridge the two poles of the "modern constitution," natural science as distinct from social science, with the former having greater credibility in the description of truth (Latour 1993). Searle is trying to explain phenomena that we experience as "subjective," or located in an individual person's mind, in an objective manner (Searle 2010, 17–18; Wacquant 2013). He emphasizes the empirical verification and importance of "collective intentionality" (Searle 2010, 8, 42–60), shared common purposes that can be accomplished by cooperation and coordination by norms and roles for distinct groups of individuals. This collective intentionality is scalable and generative of new institutions (Searle 2010, 79, 86).

II.   Money as a Social Institution

Money can be defined as a material substance that is assigned certain functions by collective consent. That is, the functions of money are not intrinsic to gold or to silver, but are assigned by convention and often enforced by government authority. In a given country in a specific time period, members of that country understand and recognize the role that money plays and use it frequently to pay taxes, buy groceries, and spend their wages. In fact, members of that country may rarely think about the origin of money (Searle 2010, 140), but may use it to plan careers, vacations, and retirement over a long-term time horizon. Money is in "everybody's interest" (Searle 2010, 164).

> Many institutions like language and money are in pretty much everybody's interest ... [People] tend to think of them as part of the natural order of things, to be taken for granted in the same way they take for granted the weather or the force of gravity. I am not at all sure that a general understanding of how institutions are created and function would actually facilitate their functioning.... Institutions ... such as money and government tend to work best when they are taken for granted and not critically analyzed. (Searle 2010, 107)

Language is the foundation for all social institutions, according to Searle (Searle 2010, 84–89, 109–114). Further, there is an obligation, or "deontology," associated with the use of language (Searle 2010, 80–85). The meaning of a particular word evolves by use and social convention, and is commonly understood in a given period and country. If one uses the language improperly, this will be noted as one who is either ignorant or not credible. For Searle, the proper use of language involves a commitment, or "social contract," which obliges the speaker to speak the truth (Searle 2010, 62).

Although money is based on collective intentionality, its operation may lead to unintended outcomes. These "systemic fallouts," such as the Great Depression and financial bubbles, would be studied by social scientists to understand and to improve the operation of the institution. Otherwise, there is a risk of loss of confidence and a dilution of its deontological powers to impose conforming behavior (Searle 2010, 116–119).

A.   *Status Function Declaration*

Searle's concept of a "status function declaration" is a statement in language that can be documented, which assigns a specific function to a well-delineated object. This object then performs that function by the common understanding of the members of the given social group. Collective recognition can be observed by the utilization that is made of that object in the appropriate contexts of its use. The status function declaration often involves a public performance (Searle 2010, 12–15, 83, 109–115), and those present can serve as witnesses to the event.

For the statement to create a social institution, it needs to be supplemented by a nonlinguistic institutional reality, including the appropriate behavior and coordinated actions (Searle 2010, 28, 91–93, 109–114). That is, status function declarations need to be made and enforced by authoritative agencies and enacted by the relevant parties. For example, my husband and I may promise each other lifelong fidelity in private, but we are only recognized as spouses by the pronouncement of our pledge in public and by the issue of a formal marriage license by the state. In the context of money, I may declare Monopoly money as legal tender, but if I try to pay my bills with it, I risk going to jail for counterfeiting. On the other hand, if an authoritative group of individuals declares Bitcoin to be money and to describe its methods of operation, some individuals may find it useful to serve as money. Because money is conventional, there are possibilities for its creation and recognition by independent groups, such as local currency. On the other hand, most governments that had coinage historically or fiat money in a contemporary economy have a specific and well-recognized enforcement mechanism for its currency, whether precious metal or fiat. In the United States, for example, in the eighteenth and nineteenth centuries, there were competing currencies among the various state banks, a situation that was only resolved with the federal monopoly of money creation after the establishment of the Federal Reserve in 1913 (DeSan 2014; Livingston 1986).

B. The Gap

Searle assumes individual free will and consciousness (Searle 2010, 26–27, 40–41, 133–141). That is, for an institution to have a deontic power, it must be based on conscious choice within the context of a voluntary commitment. The promise to conform to institutional roles and norms is based, in turn, on collective intentionality, a goal or an outcome that is recognized and valued by the participants. For this sense of volition, Searle prefers the term the "gap" instead of "free will" because of its history and connotations. Searle admits of the possibility of the unconscious (Searle 2010, 31–32, 68–71), but sees institutions as grounded in conscious choice. In this sense, he is critical of Foucault's notion of "bio-power" (Searle 2010, 152–155), which presumes a form of social power that is beyond conscious choice or intention.

C. Background

The operation of these status function declarations depends upon certain items of background knowledge present in a given population about the proper context and role relations relevant to the operations of a given institution (Searle 2010, 31–32, 155–160). For example, the spouse in a household may give her child an allowance, but may not expect to be paid for her own services in the household, such as cooking and child care. Money is understood as appropriate in retail settings, as well as bill and tax payments, but not among relatives who share a household, except as occasional gifts. This same spouse would certainly expect to be paid a wage for work in a restaurant or in a child care facility. Although Searle recognizes that background assumptions and norms are particular to a specific time and place and can vary historically, he does not attempt to explain these variations systematically. His framework for political power, for example, is ostensibly a universal analysis, albeit with special conditions (Searle 2010, 164–173).

III.   Forms of Knowledge

Searle gives some attention to the background as part of his framework for explaining social institutions. But there is a possibility that forms of knowledge in a given period influence the self-understanding and consciousness of individuals, and so influence the structures of their institutions. For example, modern democracies may empower individuals to consent and legitimation as the foundation for collective intentionality, whereas premodern societies would have no such notion. Yet social institutions such as money, government, and property, as well as marriage, existed in premodern societies. Thus, do Searle's conditions of consciousness and free will apply only to modern society? Other social theorists have endeavored to analyze social institutions comparatively and historically, such as Foucault, Poovey, Anderson, and Taylor.

A.   *History of Sciences*

In the *Order of Things* (1970), Foucault analyzes Classical and Modern *epistemes*, giving considerable attention to economic ideas. The experience of money accumulated over a long period historically, along with various explorations of its nature (Foucault 1970, 180). The associated forms of knowledge also changed, along with the emergence of political economy and economics as a formal science (Poovey 1998, 2008).

For the sixteenth century, the central question was what substance made the best money (Foucault 1970, 168–169).

> With the coming of mercantilism ... wealth becomes whatever is the object of needs and desires ... If it was possible to believe that mercantilism confused wealth and money, this is probably because money for the mercantilists had the power of representing all possible wealth, because it was the universal instrument for the analysis and representation of wealth ... All wealth is *coinable*; and it is by this means that it enters into *circulation*. (Foucault 1970, 175; italics in original)

This inquiry led to the formulation of rules for the proper regulation of bullion, as well as exploration of the nature of gold and its possible synthesis via alchemy. In the eighteenth century there were ongoing debates about the nature of money, such as quantitative ratios of precious metals, as well as the quantities of commodities for which it could be exchanged, in addition to the rate of circulation (Foucault 1970, 182–185).

> To say that money is a pledge is to say that it is no more than a token accepted by common consent—hence, a pure fiction; but it is also to say that it has exactly the same value as that for which it has been given, since it can in turn be exchanged for that same quantity of merchandise or the equivalent. Coinage can always bring back in to the hands of its owner that which had just been exchanged for it, just as, in representation, a sign must be able to recall to thought that which it represents. Money is a material memory, a self-duplicating representation, a deferred exchange. (Foucault 1970, 181)

The challenge for the state was to maintain "the order of things" in terms of the power of the state and economic balance of payments (Foucault 1970, 187–189). The creation of value, whether by production or consumption, was also long debated (Foucault 1970, 191–200). The shift in perspective from exchange to production led to related changes in the structure of knowledge, as well as the introduction of time and historicity, according to Foucault (1970, 226–232, 250–263). A new understanding of production led to a mistrust of visible appearances and a sense of the limits of representation (Foucault 1970, 243–248). With this understanding of the limits of rational knowledge, there is a focus on positivism and "mathematicization" and attempts at synthesis by Kant and Hegel. Language receives a new focus, along with literature (Foucault 1970, 294–300, 381–384).

> The threshold between Classicism and modernity ... had been definitively crossed when words ceased to intersect with representations, and to provide a spontaneous grid for the knowledge of things. (Foucault 1970, 304)

There is a new unity discovered in the "science of man," who is the viewer of the painting, the agent for whom representations had been constructed, who produces and consumes the objects for exchange, and who uses language (Foucault 1970, 307–312).

> It is no longer their identity that beings manifest in representation, but the external relation they establish with the human being. The latter, with his own being, with his power to present himself with representations, arises in a space hollowed out by living beings, objects of exchange, and words ... man is designated – more, required – by them, since it is he who speaks. (Foucault 1970, 313)

The agent from whose perspective all objects are observed becomes himself the object of study. Yet seeing humankind as the source of knowledge also leads to complexities. "Man ... is a being such that knowledge will be attained in him of what renders all knowledge possible [and] revealing the conditions of knowledge" (Foucault 1970, 318–319). According to Foucault, two kinds of analysis then come into being: the study of the body and the history of human knowledge. But this study of "man" is also the source of what cannot be known (Foucault 1970, 322–328).

There were three models for the human sciences, based on biology, economics, and philology (Foucault 1970, 355–367). In these models, there was always a tension between function and norm, conflict and rule, signification and system, all relating to life, labor, and language. In the modern *episteme*, human sciences become possible (Foucault 1970, 348–373) when rationality understands its limit.

> We shall say, therefore, that a "human science" exists, not wherever man is in question, but where there is analysis—within the dimension proper to the unconscious—of norms, rules, and signifying totalities which unveil to consciousness the conditions of its forms and contents. (Foucault 1970, 364)

That is, there is also a place for the unconscious in modern self-awareness, but it is uneasily situated within the human sciences. Ultimately Foucault reasons that human sciences cannot be "science" due to the problem of reflexivity.

> It is useless, then, to say that the 'human sciences' are false sciences; they are not sciences at all … Western culture has constituted, under the name of man, a being who, by one and the same interplay of reasons, must be a positive domain of *knowledge* and cannot be an object of *science*. (Foucault 1970, 366–367; italics in original)

B.   Abstraction

The "science of man" may explore the nature of the viewer, the source of the *gaze* (Foucault 1970, 308), but the perspective is still from on high, like the view of the merchant surveying the objects with potential for exchange that may ultimately include all objects (Foucault 1970, 172–173).

> In order to ascertain each day the rule and mathematical proportions that exist between things and between them and gold, we should have to be able to contemplate, from the height of heaven or some very tall observatory, all the things that exist or are done on earth, or rather their images reproduced and reflected in the sky as in a faithful mirror. (Davanzatti [sic] as quoted in Foucault 1970, 172)

This perspective can constitute a comprehensive worldview that reveals the entrepreneur's eye for the next commodity and reflects the market imperative for expansion. That is, the merchant can consider the potential for exchange among all objects and all peoples, with "exchange" taking the form of a "totalizing narrative."

The experience of money helps to actualize a vision that makes all things capable of substitution for each other in a given quantitative proportion. Like the view revealed in Velazquez's painting, "*Las Meninas,*"

> The painter is turning his eyes towards us only in so far as we happen to occupy the same position as his subject. We, the spectators, are an additional factor. Though greeted by that gaze, we are also dismissed by it, replaced by that which was always there before we were: the model itself. But, inversely, the painter's gaze, addressed to the void confronting him outside the picture, accepts as many models as there are spectators; in this precise but neutral place, the observer and the observed take part in a ceaseless exchange. (Foucault 1970, 4–5)

Here the viewer of the painting is like any other viewer, a form of abstraction that treats all individuals alike. In the market, similarly, all commodities, all consumers, and all workers occupy the same position, a form of "ceaseless exchange." There is a relation of equality, as well as anonymity and depersonalization. This merchant's gaze is a form of objectification, in my view, of both humans and nature, which is also expressed in the "objective" forms of modern knowledge (Daston and Galison 2010) and "reifying abstractions" of the modern "social imaginary" (Poovey 2002).

C. Desire

In discussion of the role of money in symbolizing wealth, Foucault emphasizes the "desire" that makes objects valuable, hence counting as wealth (Foucault 1970, 175–180, 196–200). Whereas Smith and Ricardo emphasize the value of the commodity based on production, later Marginalists in the mid-nineteenth century postulated "utility," fixed in quantitative relation to the amount of commodities consumed (Mirowski and Plehwe 2009). In later work, Foucault (1978) postulates the production of "desire" as part of the power relations of "governmentality." If every individual can be presumed to have the same wants and needs, then the individual can be trusted with "self-government" (Poovey 1998, 144–213), in the sense of perpetual pursuit of "more," as modern economists assume axiomatically.

D. Political Theory

Foucault (1991) also considers the role of Machiavelli in developing the "reason of state." That is, "governmentality" is a set of practices that maintain the power of the state per se, rather than for the purposes of social welfare (Davis 2015a, 86–89). For Searle, "*the government is the ultimate institutional structure*" requiring legitimation, even with a monopoly on armed violence (Searle 2010, 160–164; italics in original); "politics" is a distinct form of institution that mediates conflict among groups, separate from the market and other institutions (Searle 2010, 170–171). Searle discusses "power" as the outcome of the operation of institutions, including the state (Searle 2010, 145–173). For him, one important source of power is reducing the awareness of options for action (Searle 2010, 147–149). Further, any exercise of power must be "intentional" to satisfy Searle's definition (Searle 2010, 150–151). Social pressure from background norms does not constitute "power" according to Searle's restriction of "the exactness constraint," which must identify who exercises power over whom specifically (Searle 2010, 152–160).

IV.   Money as a Type of Social Relationship

Extending Searle's discussion, money is a type of social relationship (Searle 2010, 56–57). That is, based on the meaning of coin or currency in common understanding, there is a sale of labor, commodities, or services in return for the capacity to purchase any other commodity on the marketplace. One view of this relationship is a convenience, a voluntary choice, simply in everybody's interest (Searle 2010, 107). Others see a form of power. Once market exchange is extended to include necessities and alternative forms of income are contingent upon work performance, there is a form of "coercion" involved (Marx 1967; Polanyi 1944). One must sell in order to buy, either oneself or another commodity desirable to others (Meister 1991).

The ability to buy and sell in increments accomplished by many people in a given period of time creates a sense of the "flow" of money, even though there are discrete steps in each exchange. The rate of circulation can be measured by how many times a given coin changes hands in a given time (Foucault 1970, 183–185). The money loaned to a merchant can return to the lender, but it accomplishes the "circulation" of objects, which change location among different users. Adam Smith mentions money as part of the "stock" of capital, focusing on the total amount of currency in a given economy, and counts it as part of its total of wealth, perhaps from the experience of livestock as an asset and milk as the "flow" of nourishment to its offspring (Smith 1994, Book II, Ch. 1, 302–309).

I propose that this social relationship influences other relationships and forms of knowledge (Kaye 2000, 2014). An increasing share of one's lifetime is occupied with getting and spending money. New forms of business enterprise are developed, along with new work relationships. New forms of the family emerge when land is available for sale instead of inheritance, and labor is no longer tied to employment in a specific field. New forms of the authority and the state emerge as well, and shifting borders and territories.

Like Searle's discussion of language (Searle 2010, 64–65), money is "generative." Once exchange is well established, the possession of coin or currency can be used to offer credit, or promises to pay at a fixed future date. As Smith understood, credit can be overextended, based upon promises that cannot be fulfilled, like one of Searle's "systemic fallouts."

Based on the experience of counting and calculating equivalences, money changers, merchants, business owners, and wealth holders realize the value of account books. This experience increases the importance of literacy and numeracy, increasing the value of education and the formalization of educational institutions. The importance of documentation and calculating can increase the importance of numbers as an indication of truth, and so influence the development of "political arithmetic" and the structure of scientific evidence (Poovey 1998).

Analysis of the composition of precious metal, as well as the methods of production of commodities and techniques of navigation, provide a prod to the development of science. Western navigation techniques differed from indigenous populations by the universal perspective (Hutchins 2005). In the early modern period, Galileo provided discoveries that changed the worldview even further, altering the understanding the role of the heavens in relation to earth and challenging religious knowledge (Biagioli, 2006).

In fact, the period of the Renaissance was a period of innovation (Padgett 2012, 125–127), changing institutions, knowledge, and the development of arts and sciences, as well as literature and political theory. The coalescence of many types of endeavors could have been spurred by the role of money and the experience of trade. This period was certainly preceded, if not caused by, the "Commercial Revolution" (Lopez 1971).

V.   Dialogue: Searle vs. Foucault

This analysis of the structure of modern knowledge provides the opportunity for a further contrast between the respective positions of Foucault and Searle (Searle 2010, 152–155). On the one hand, Foucault sees the sequence of *epistemes* and tries to explain their history. On the other hand, Searle glosses the notion of worldview, or "background," but retains the notion of intentionality, the collective agency, which is the origin of social institutions by means of language. Yet Searle himself does not address the social and cultural conditions in which collective intentionality can be recognized and understood, although he continues to argue for the importance of subjective states of consciousness in his own work.

A.   Agent | Structure

Although both Searle and Foucault can be understood as endorsing a view of the "social construction" of institutions, this term is interpreted very differently for each thinker. For Searle, "social construction" takes place by formal linguistic statements assigning functions to persons and objects by means of legitimate intentions shared among members of a given community. This consent is the voluntary choice of rational individuals, from whom all political authority ultimately derives (Searle 2010, 139–142, 164–167). For Foucault, individuals are shaped and influenced by the forms of knowledge in a given period, which vary historically. As Searle notes, Foucault emphasizes the "*normalizing* practices of society," which create "human subjects who can be administered" (Searle 2010, 152–155; italics in original). This "subject creation" (Kennedy 1991, 353, 360–361) is a form of power beyond individual consciousness, according to Foucault, and reduces awareness of options.

B. Representation

Searle posits language statements such as status function declarations, which can communicate speaker meaning and the "conditions of satisfaction" (Searle 2010, 29–30, 72–74). For example, the U.S. Constitution gives the federal government the power to declare the currency, a function that can be documented and evaluated by its citizens. It is clear when these conditions are not met and the statement is false. Similarly, an institution that is no longer functional to its citizens would collapse (Searle 2010, 164–166). The declaration makes public the speaker's intention and commits the speaker to perform certain functions, consistent with the declaration. The public recognition and consent to such performances is the "glue" for social institutions (Searle 2010, 89), which can create an institutional reality that would otherwise not exist, like money.

For Foucault, the threshold for the modern period was crossed "when words ceased to intersect with representations and to provide a spontaneous grid for the knowledge of things" (Foucault 1970, 304). In the transition from Smith to Ricardo and Malthus, labor was no longer the representation of value as defined in exchange, but labor was the source of value defined in the process of production (Foucault 1970, 250–263). Later propositions regarding value based on utility were also locating the source of value in another private sphere of consumption (Foucault 1970, 257), both "invisible" to exchange. The limits of representation are found in the confrontation with the unconscious and with history, where the modern categories of labor, life, and language became transmuted into desire, death, and law (Foucault 1970, 355–367, 374–378). The complexity of human sciences derives from the need to represent man to himself (Foucault 1970, 348–355). For Foucault, representations of value like money are appropriately subject to a critical analysis of its history.

C. Social Ontology

For Searle and his colleagues at the social ontology group at UC Berkeley, human societies are qualitatively different than the forms of representation, like numbers and symbols. There is an ongoing reflection on the nature of subject and object. For Searle, language and social institutions like money express the intentions of individuals, arranged collectively by consent. For Foucault, institutions shape individuals more or less beyond their control.

In describing the relationship between psychoanalysis and ethnology, Foucault notes

> At any given instant, the structure proper to individual experience finds a certain number of possible choices (and of excluded possibilities) in the systems of society; inversely, at each of the points of choice the social structures encounter a certain number of possible individuals (and others who are not)—just as the linear structure of language always produces a possible choice between several words or several phonemes at any given moment (but excludes all others). (Foucault 1970 380)

Like Searle's discussion of language, there is an implicit commitment to use of the proper word in order to convey meaning to one's listeners and readers. On the other hand, in Foucault's examination of the history of human sciences, language itself has been the object of study, according to abstract rules like linguistics, as a means of expression in literature, and as the instrument for unambiguous representation of discrete objects in the world. For Searle, there is a "double direction of fit," using language to describe the world and to create institutional realities that cannot otherwise be created (Searle 2010, 38–41).

D.   Possibilities of Knowledge

For Foucault, the limits of human sciences are reached in the unconscious and history (Foucault 1970, 355–373). For Searle, it is possible to explain all of "human civilization." The only dilemma is that, for all the carefully constructed framework of explanation, Searle concedes that institutions work best when their history and construction are not widely understood. This emphasis on collective intentionality then seems to rest without foundation. Even in a democratic society, it is best that "few, if any, of the important problems of life are determined by elections," including such issues as racial equality and abortions (Searle 2010, 172–173).

VI.   Other Theories of History

Foucault's genealogical method is unique among social historians, and Searle is more philosopher than historian. Other approaches to institutional history include Smith's four stages (Jones 2007, 149–153) and Marx's historical materialism (McCormick 2002; Wickham 2007). There are also important contributions from Critical Theory (McCormick 2002), drawing from Marx and Hegel, along with World Systems Theory (Arrighi 1994) and Polanyi's "double movement" (1944). Anderson (1991) and Taylor (2004) continue to believe in the "long march" towards individual freedom as the course of history. By contrast, historians of science see the influence of existing paradigms and values that can shape technology (MacKenzie and Keynes 1985; Noble 1977). As mentioned in Chapter 1, there is at present no consensus on methodology.

It is the objective of the present work, nonetheless, to study the evolution of money in historical and institutional contexts.

VII. Contradictions of Money

Understanding money as a social institution helps to analyze its contradictions. For Foucault, there was a dual perspective on money as early as the mercantile period and corresponding debates in that period between the "money-as-sign" faction and the "money-as-commodity" faction (Foucault 1970, 181, 191). Both of these debates focused on the coin itself—its metal composition as well as its stamp. What is not readily apparent in these debates is that the meaning of money is to be interpreted by human individuals in the process of their production and exchange. Whether the focus is on the interpretation of money as a sign or its precious metal weight, both are interpreted by human users in specific social institutional contexts. These contexts can be documented historically, the evidence of which is further examined next.

A. Rule-Governed | Arbitrary

As early as the mercantile period, there was considerable concern regarding the proper ratios of precious metals and the proper prices of commodities as indexed in these metals (Foucault 1970, 183–186). These proportions seemed able to govern the "flows" of bullion into and out of countries, as reflected in the balance of payments. There were also mercantile policies, which restricted these bullion flows in order to manage and enhance the "wealth of nations."

These quantitative ratios were managed by experts, who sought the appropriate rules from their experiences and observations. Similarly credit was managed quantitatively, in relation to the stock of gold of the Bank of England, which nonetheless had a tendency to overflow its bounds, with no apparent limits.

B. Personal | Impersonal

Money was understood as an abstract symbol, representing value, no matter which object was to be measured according to its standards (Foucault 1970, 169). Yet the coin was always signed and dated, with the image of the prince or the symbol of the state stamped on its sides. Like medals, there was a prestige component in the design and circulation of coins.

The privilege of coining money or issuing currency was managed by the state. In addition to an external ranking of currency by "confidence," there was an internal ranking of the individuals with the authority to manage money. That is, the bankers were personally in conversation with heads of state, often in confidential processes of decision-making, such as bankers' loans to kings in the late medieval period and "haute finance" in the nineteenth century (Polyani 1944).

C.   *Rational | Irrational*

As Searle suggests, the process of spending or loaning money was the subject of careful deliberation and voluntary choice. There was increasingly a calculation of the rate of return, and the return of an expansion of money over the amount of money loaned out. Further, it was important for the promise or "pledge" of credit to be "backed" by adequate collateral (Foucault 1970, 182). Yet for all the careful calculation and estimated returns over time, there are also repeated experiences of frenzy, "manias, panics and crashes" with historical repetition (Kindleberger 1989). Although money is the epitome of rationality, it is also the arena of the most contagious emotional states (Pocock 1975, 450–467).

D.   *Convenient | Coercive*

Searle posits money as a social institution because it is convenient, in "everyone's interest." Yet there are critics who deplore the "cash nexus" (Ferguson 2008) as well as the conditions of labor and debtor's prison, or market advocates who celebrate the powerful incentives related to competition. The calculation of return and the opportunity to accumulate then provide a measure of one's life, the provision for one's children, and the extent of an inheritance. The standards of measurement ultimately apply to competing individuals, not just objects for sale, making visible their "true worth" (Davis 2015b).

E.   *Centered | Distributed*

Money comes in increments, which can be the possession of individuals as their own private property. Yet the functions of money, such as the means of payment, express a relationship *among* individuals, without which it would have no meaning. Further, the functions of money, including the unit of account and store of value, are typically regulated by government— a form of central power. Although the choices and initiatives of individuals are important, the ultimate concept is the "wealth of nations," which calculates the summation and ultimate effect of all these individual actions. Money is social, like language, a form of the "social contract" (Searle 2010, 62).

F.   *Equilibrium | Growth*

The idea that financial balances must reach equilibrium is embedded in the notion of double-entry bookkeeping, as well as Classical economic ideas (Foucault 1970, 253–260). On the other hand, the notion that money must grow is embedded in the rights of money holders, and their capacity to loan funds at interest, although contested by medieval teachings regarding usury.

G. Form of Governance | Exception to Governance

Money can be considered a form of governance, which determines the use of material resources and labor in the production of commodities in market economies. The phrase "let the market decide" implies the notion that the market is a "steering mechanism," to which has been delegated many important decisions (Habermas 1989). The concept of "laissez faire" is the self-regulating market (Polanyi 1944), developed by the physiocrats (Foucault 1970, 183-188). This notion of market freedom enables private individuals to express their will and their individuality in the modern liberal tradition (Berlin 1958; Ryan 2012; Simmel 1978).

On the other hand, money is the exception to governance, considered in the "civic republican tradition," in which commerce and concerns with money can lead to a form of "corruption" (Pocock 1975). The citizen, in public deliberation in the polis, is the highest form of expression of humanity, according to this tradition (Siegelberg 2013). Machiavelli, the presumed first modern political theorist, was keenly aware of the impact of war finance on the political power of the oligarchy and its threat to the republic (Barthas 2009, 2010; Najemy 2014, 1155–1159). That is, the distinction between monetary and nonmonetary relations form an institutional divide with important moral boundaries (Sandel 2012). For some commentators, this distinction is typical of premodern/modern forms of society (Ryan), rather than an ultimate criterion of "human."

H. Rules | Discretion

As Searle has discussed, the typical form of a status function declaration is to assign specific functions to an object or symbol. Such an assignment of function by a respected authority becomes conventional. In the case of money, often the assignment is to designate in quantitative terms the relationship that guarantees value. For example, the precious metal content of a coin is accurately reflected in its face value, or a given paper currency is convertible to precious metal at a certain rate. Further, for paper credit, this promise to pay is denominated in a specific amount of currency to be conveyed at some specific future date. These promises help assure the value of the object or symbol and enable it to circulate among various users without question.

On the other hand, there are situations when such promises need to be revised, such as the recoinage debate in England in the period 1694–1696 (Vilar 1976, 216–221). There was not only the issue regarding the value of money; there was also public debate regarding the best means of resolution, involving such highly regarded persons as John Locke and Isaac Newton. Such conditions would often be likely to reveal the "problematic of representation" (Poovey 2008, 5–9), where the symbol is no longer automatically accepted for its referent. Such occasions can contribute to political unrest and financial instability, which in turn create questions regarding the credibility of the public authority itself. The methods by which such crises of confidence are resolved can have lasting impact on the political and economic stability of a given country, such as Spain's "curse of gold" in the seventeenth century (Poovey 2008, 161–165; Vilar 1976, 165–168).

I.   Static / Generative

Because of consistent rules of language and the constitution of social insti-tutions, institutions like money can also be "generative." That is, once a promise to pay is created and credible, this promise can circulate more widely than just between the original debtor and creditor, like the history of "bills of exchange." As another example, once insurance is accepted as a common practice, an increasing number of objects and probable circumstances can be insured. Financial institutions can develop with increasing division of labor and more complex interconnections, so-called financial innovations.

Other scholars have studied such generativity. For example, the role of lan-guage in the spread of "rights" draws upon Wittgenstein (Bowles and Gintis 1986, 154–166), including both property rights and human rights. The extension and spread of the logic of calculation and rationality draws upon Weber and Foucault (Brown 2015). The pursuit and intensification of pleasure, instead of management within moral bounds, is a feature of modern society (Cooper 2014).

VIII.   Economics as a "Genre of the Credit Economy"

The objectifying merchant's vision, which sees all objects of nature and human society as potential commodities, is reflected in the genre of modern econom-ics. The assumptions of the rational individual seeking "more," maximizing utility, is consistent with modern "liberal governmentality" (Poovey 1998). The form of economic writing makes visible the producer and consumer, the costs and prices, viewed as though from on high using abstract concepts. For example, Poovey notes that the double-entry bookkeeping system provided a form of surveillance that improved merchants' credibility (Kessler 2004, 2007; Poovey 1998, 29–33). Humans are agents following market signals in predict-able behavior, which can be modeled and influenced by the economist/expert, who himself represents the view of the whole, perhaps serving as advisor to the state. This type of analysis takes money for granted and does not study its history, or view money as a special type of writing. That is, money has become "naturalized" (Poovey 2008, 3–9). Economics writing is considered scientific, with abstract models verified by quantitative empirical tests, in contrast with literature, considered "fiction." By its abstract method and universal, ahistori-cal assumptions, modern economics forecloses consideration of alternative options, itself a form of power (Searle 2010, 149–150, 160).

In economics, the agency is often invisible, considered simply as "market forces." For example, the economic historian Pierre Vilar discusses Foucault discussing Davanzati (Vilar 1969, 13–14, 76–79, 189–191). Rather than see the unusual nature of the merchant's vision, Vilar merely interprets Davanzati's text as an early insight into the quantity theory of money—that is, the appropriate proportion between money and things. The focus is on the quantities, not the relationships. What is absent in Vilar's vision is the subject, the individual persons who make use of money and who wish to consume the commodities; the form is simply an equation in algebraic terms, which becomes "true" by definition. Whereas Vilar himself considers economic history and the history of theories of money as proper subjects of study, modern economists typically do not. The focus is not on the agents and their relationships, but on the abstract operation of the system, properly maintained in balance like a well-tuned machine. Modern economic studies typically do not study the dynamics of empires or the shifting legality of particular commodities, such as slaves and rum, or the long-term histories of institutions. In this sense, Vilar as a historian is unusual.

An economic "science," which can view all objects as substitutes for each other and can merely focus on the calculation of the appropriate rates of substitution, does not question the final purpose. This perspective enables a type of "flattening" with which objects become homogeneous equivalents by means of the right proportion of exchange. The abstract notions of maximizing "wealth" or "utility" provide the justification for destroying ancient civilizations and indigenous populations to extract gold and slaves as commodities. As Latour notes ironically, economics is a science of value without values (Latour 2013, 450).

IX. Both Words and Things? A Framework for the Explorations to Follow

Searle is careful to insist on the material dimension of the sign of the status function declaration for verification and validation. This physical reality is recorded in human brains as well as investing a concrete object with meaning and purpose, even if only a text or a computer file. The role of the material object may be particularly important in distributed cognition as well (Hutchins 2005; Hutchins and Johnson 2009). According to recent theorists, a form of "cognition" may be characteristic of chemical and biological processes as well as human consciousness (Padgett interview 2015).

Searle's goal is to explain social institutions in both their subjective and objective dimensions (Searle 2010, 17–18).

> Let us constantly remind ourselves that the whole point of the creation of institutional reality is not to invest objects or people with some special status valuable in itself but to create and regulate power relationships between people. (Searle 2010, 106)

Yet Searle is quite content to let certain institutions remain unexamined, such as money. This may lead to the social phenomenon of "value" to be assigned to an object such as precious metals, as if it were a characteristic of the object itself (Foucault 1970, 189). This tendency towards objectification of human relationships may in turn be reflected in the form of the human sciences, which result in "reifying abstractions" (Poovey 2002), such as money and "the economy" (Brown 2015, 81–82). These institutions, which are human inventions, apparently operate without human intervention, beyond the control of individuals (Searle 2010, 165–166). Searle's analysis ultimately rests on the power of legitimation to maintain support for long-lasting institutions, in spite of this uncritical pragmatic acceptance.

On the other hand, Foucault sees the conditions of possibility of the "science of man," which are historically contingent.

> Among all the mutations that have affected the knowledge of things and their order ... only one, that which began a century and a half ago and is now perhaps drawing to a close, has made it possible for the figure of man to appear ... If those arrangements were to disappear as they appeared ... then one can certainly wager that man would be erased, like a face drawn in sand at the end of the sea. (Foucault 1970, 386–387)

For Foucault, "man for human sciences is that living being who ... constitutes representations by means of which he lives, and on the basis of which he possesses that strange capacity of being able to represent to himself precisely that life" (Foucault 1970, 352). Is this self-representation a form of knowledge integrating both subject and object, a source of reflexivity and self-governance, or an objectification that lends itself to mechanical, reified models (Davis 2015a, 160–162; Foucault 1970, 303, 350–352)?

Money is ostensibly an object that has value, referring both to the coin and to the commodity for which it is exchangeable. These objects give no hint of the humans who make use of them and for whose benefit their exchange takes place. "Man" has disappeared in his own creation of the automatic market and the financial circuits, whose automaticity he celebrates, whose history he has forgotten, and by which he organizes his life.

The category of "money" can provide the example to be further explored in the following chapters, including the category itself, as well as the history of the associated institutions and the theories that explain its power and persistence.

References

Anderson, Benedict R. *Imagined Communities: Reflections on the Origin and Spread of Nationalism*. London: Verso, 1991.

Arrighi, Giovanni. *The Long Twentieth Century: Money, Power, and the Origins of Our Times*. London: Verso, 1994.

Barthas, Jeremie. "Machiavelli, from the Ten to the Nine: A Hypothesis Based on the Financial History of Early Modern Florence," in Diogo Ramada Curto, Eric R. Dursteler, Julius Kirshner, and Francesca Trivellato (eds.), *From Florence to the Mediterranean and Beyond: Essays in Honour of Anthony Molho*. Florence, Italy: Leo S. Olschki, 2009, 147–166.

———." Machiavelli in Political Thought from the Age of Revolutions to the Present," in John M. Najemy (ed.), *The Cambridge Companion to Machiavelli*. New York: Cambridge University Press, 2010, 256–273.

Berlin, Isaiah. *Two Concepts of Liberty*. Oxford: Clarendon Press, 1958.

Biagioli, Mario. *Galileo's Instruments of Credit: Telescopes, Images, Secrecy*. Chicago: University of Chicago Press, 2006.

Bowles, Samuel and Herbert Gintis. *Democracy and Capitalism: Property, Community, and the Contradictions of Modern Social Thought*. New York: Basic Books, 1986.

Brown, Wendy. *Undoing the Demos: Neoliberalism's Stealth Revolution*. Brooklyn, NY: Zone Books, 2015.

Cooper, Melinda. "The Law of the Household: Foucault, Neoliberalism, and the Iranian Revolution," in Vanessa Lemm and Miguel Vatter (eds.), *The Government of Life: Foucault, Biopolitics, and Neoliberalism*. New York: Fordham University Press, 2014.

Daston, Lorraine and Peter Galison. *Objectivity*. New York: Zone Books, 2010.

Davis, Ann E. *The Evolution of the Property Relation: Understanding Paradigms, Debates, Prospects*. New York: Palgrave MacMillan, 2015a.

_____. "The Process of Provisioning: The Halter for the Workhorse." *Journal of Economic Issues*, Vol. 69, No. 2, 2015b, 449–457.

DeSan, Christine. *Making Money: Coin, Currency, and the Coming of Capitalism*. New York, Oxford University Press, 2014.

Ferguson, Niall. *The Ascent of Money: A Financial History of the World*. New York: Penguin, 2008.

Foucault, Michel. *The Order of Things: An Archaeology of the Human Sciences*. New York: Pantheon Books, 1970.

_____. *The History of Sexuality*. Vol. I: An Introduction. New York: Pantheon Books, 1978.

_____. "Governmentality," in Graham Burchell, Colin Gordon, and Peter Miller (eds.), *The Foucault Effect: Studies in Governmentality*. Chicago: University of Chicago Press, 1991, 87–104.

Habermas, Jurgen. *The Structural Transformation of the Public Sphere: An Inquiry into a Category of Bourgeois Society*. Cambridge, MA: MIT Press, 1989.

Hutchins, Edwin. "Material Anchors for Conceptual Blends," *Journal of Pragmatics*, Vol. 37, 2005, 1555–1577.

Hutchins, Edwin and Christine M. Johnson. "Modeling the Emergence of Language as Embodied Collective Cognitive Activity," *Topics in Cognitive Science*, Vol. 1, 2009, 523–546.

Jones, Gareth Stedman. "Marx's Critique of Political Economy: A Theory of History or a Theory of Communism?" in Chris Wickham (ed.), *Marxist History-Writing for the Twenty-first Century*. New York: Oxford University Press, 2007, 140–157.

Kaye, Joel. *Economy and Nature in the Fourteenth Century: Money, Market Exchange, and the Emergence of Scientific Thought*. New York: Cambridge University Press, 2000.

_____. *A History of Balance, 1250–1375: The Emergence of a New Model of Equilibrium and Its Impact on Thought*. New York: Cambridge University Press, 2014.

Kennedy, Duncan. "The Stakes of Law, or Hale and Foucault!," *Legal Studies Forum*, Vol. 15, No. 4, 1991, 327–366.

Kessler, Amalia D. "Enforcing Virtue: Social Norms and Self-Interest in an Eighteenth-Century Merchant Court," *Law and History Review*, Vol. 22, No. 1, 2004, 71–118.

_____. *A Revolution in Commerce: The Parisian Merchant Court and the Rise of Commercial Society in Eighteenth-Century France*. New Haven, CT: Yale University Press, 2007.

Kindleberger, Charles P. *Manias, Panics, Crashes: A History of Financial Crises*. New York: Basic, 1989.

Latour, Bruno. *We Have Never Been Modern*. Cambridge, MA: Harvard University Press, 1993.

_____. *An Inquiry into Modes of Existence: An Anthropology of the Moderns*. Cambridge, MA: Harvard University Press, 2013.

Livingston, James. *The Origins of the Federal Reserve System: Money, Class and Corporate Capitalism 1890–1913*. Ithaca, NY: Cornell University Press, 1986.

Lopez, Robert S. *The Commercial Revolution of the Middle Ages, 950–1350*. Englewood Cliffs, NJ: Prentice-Hall, 1971.

MacKenzie, Donald A. and Milton Keynes (eds.). *The Social Shaping of Technology: How the Refrigerator Got Its Hum*. Philadelphia: Open University Press, 1985.

Marx, Karl. *Capital*. Vol. I New York: International Publishers, 1967.

Meister, Robert. *Political Identity: Thinking Through Marx*. Cambridge, MA: Basil Blackwell, 1991.

McCormick, John P. "A Critical versus Genealogical 'Questioning' of Technology: Notes on How *Not* to Read Adorno and Horkheimer," in John P. McCormick (ed.), *Confronting Mass Democracy and Industrial Technology: Political and Social Theory from Nietzsche to Habermas*. Durham, NC: Duke University Press, 2002, 267–294.

Mirowski, Philip and Dieter Plehwe (eds.). *The Road from Mt. Pelerin: The Making of the Neoliberal Thought Collective*. Cambridge, MA: Harvard University Press, 2009.

Najemy, John M. "The 2013 Josephine Waters Bennett Lecture: Machiavelli and History," *Renaissance Quarterly*, Vol. 67, No. 4, 2014, 1131–1164.

Noble, David F. *America by Design: Science, Technology and the Rise of Corporate Capitalism*. New York: Knopf, 1977.

Padgett, John F. "The Emergence of Corporate Merchant-Banks in Dugento Tuscany," in Padgett, John F. and Walter W. Powell. *The Emergence of Organizations and Markets*. Princeton, NJ: Princeton University Press, 2012, 121–167.

Padgett, John F. personal interview. State Archive of Florence, June 22, 2015.

Pocock, John G. A. *The Machiavellian Moment: Florentine Political Thought and the Atlantic Republican Tradition*. Princeton, NJ: Princeton University Press, 1975.

Polanyi, Karl. *The Great Transformation*. Boston: Beacon Press, 1944.

Poovey, Mary. *A History of the Modern Fact: Problems of Knowledge in the Sciences of Wealth and Society*. Chicago: University of Chicago Press, 1998.

_____. "The Liberal Civil Subject and the Social in Eighteenth-Century British Moral Philosophy," *Public Culture*. Vol. 14, No. 1, 2002, 125–145.

_____. *Genres of the Credit Economy: Mediating Value in Eighteenth- and Nineteenth-Century Britain*. Chicago: University of Chicago Press, 2008.

Ryan, Alan. *The Making of Modern Liberalism*. Princeton, NJ: Princeton University Press, 2012.

Sandel, Michael J. *What Money Can't Buy: The Moral Limits of Markets*. New York: Farrar, Straus, and Giroux, 2012.

Searle, John R. *Making the Social World: The Structure of Human Civilization*. New York: Oxford University Press, 2010.

Siegelberg, Mira L. "Things Fall Apart: J.G.A. Pocock, Hannah Arendt, and the Politics of Time," *Modern Intellectual History*, Vol. 10, No. 1, 2013, 109–134.

Simmel, Georg. *The Philosophy of Money*. Boston: Routledge & Kegan Paul, 1978.

Smith, Adam. *An Inquiry into the Nature and Causes of the Wealth of Nations*. New York: Modern Library, 1994.

Taylor, Charles. *Modern Social Imaginaries*. Durham, NC: Duke University Press, 2004.

Vilar, Pierre. *A History of Gold and Money, 1450–1920*. Atlantic Highlands, NJ: Humanities Press, 1976.

Wacquant, Loic. "Symbolic Power and Group-Making: On Pierre Bourdieu's Reframing of Class," *Journal of Classical Sociology* Vol. 13, No. 2, 2013, 274–291.

Wickham, Chris. "Memories of Underdevelopment: What Has Marxism Done for Medieval History, and What Can It Still Do?," in Chris Wickham (ed.), *Marxist History-Writing for the Twenty-first Century*. New York: Oxford University Press, 2007, 32–48.

3 The Economy as Labor Exchange Mediated by Money

I. Introduction

The essence of the capitalist economy is labor exchange. The abstractions, divisions, and disciplinary structures of the economy, nonetheless, make this insight seem highly improbable. This chapter will proceed to explore those aspects using the method of historical institutionalism to make that case regarding the core of the capitalist economy.

II. Money as a Tool of Abstraction

The term "abstraction" is used in many different ways in modern social science.

A. Logic and Science

The term "abstraction" is used in logic and science. Abstraction is part of the scientific method of induction, whereby the observation of a wide variety of concrete facts leads one to formulate a generalization that fits the empirical observations. Yet scientific studies suggest that it is difficult to separate induction from deduction; that is, scientific empirical observations are always informed by a theoretical orientation (Poovey 1998).

> All systematic knowledge systems require something like a leap of faith and ... all attempts to gather theory- and value-free data are marked by the very theoretical assumptions they seem to leave behind. (Poovey 1998, *xix*)

The attempts to develop a science of political economy led Adam Smith to *assume a system*, which these assumptions then help to create, by becoming a general guide to behavior—what Poovey calls "self-actualizing fictions" (Poovey 1998, 58–59; see also 66–91, 236–248). These abstractions are then "verified" by observed numbers, which reinforce the validity of the abstractions. This type of epistemology Poovey calls the "modern fact."

In the introduction to *The Wealth of Nations*, Adam Smith introduces the concept of "the annual labour of every nation" (Smith 1994, *lix*) and with observations regarding factory labor. He further develops the concept of "division of labor," which is difficult to observe, because it can occur across different branches of industry rather than in a single workshop. In the period of his observations, the late eighteenth-century Scotland, the system of factory production was not yet the norm. Yet he could observe the increase in productivity of labor from this practice and projected the benefits for the nation as a whole (Smith 1994, Book I, Ch. 1, 3, 7–11).

> It is the great multiplication of the productions of all the different arts, in consequence of the division of labour, which occasions, in a well-governed society, that universal opulence which extends itself to the lowest ranks of the people. (Smith 1994, Book I, Ch. 1, 12)

The category of "labour" is assumed by Smith, without exploration of its origin except to compare advanced nations with primitive ones. Smith's concern is to increase its productivity, a focus that remains paramount in modern capitalist economies. Smith is aware of the impact of the division of labor on the workmen, and so recommends the importance of public education (Smith 1994, Book V, Ch. I, Part III, Article 2, 839–846). For the science of political economy that Smith helps to found, the concept of labor is no longer a person, but an "input" into production measured by the hour of abstract labor.

B.   Abstract Labor in Capitalism

In capitalism, "abstract labor" has a specific form, generalized from the specific skills of individual workers. The performance of work at the workplace is also disciplined by management, such as the separation of mental and manual labor, and the scientific study, organization, and exact measurement of discrete steps of the production process. "Capitalism is a system of abstract, impersonal domination" (Postone 1993, 125).

> The technical subordination of the workman to the uniform motion of the instruments of labour, and the peculiar composition of the body of workpeople ... give rise to a barrack discipline, which is elaborated into a complete system in the factory.
>
> (Marx 1967, Vol. I, Ch. 15, Section 4, 423–424)

Extending Postone's analysis, abstract labor in capitalism is an expression of interdependence. Labor is undertaken solely for the purpose of obtaining the products of others. "'The social' [is] a realm of the interdependence grounded in the mediating role of labor ... [For] the liberal subject ... the equivalence of the exchanging subjects is posited in the form of their products, leaving the subjects of the exchange indifferent to one another ... Such subjects experience themselves as individuals opposed to the domain of social interdependence" (Sartori 2013, 114–115).

Although Postone sees labor itself as an abstract mediation (Postone 1993, 147–152), the position here is that money is the instrument of this mediation of abstract labor. Financial circuits are the means of integration of the social whole, and money is seen as valuable in itself, rather than labor. That is, the value of labor is represented by money.

The use of money is a form of abstracting, objectifying oneself (Postone 1993, 153–157), becoming an anonymous, homogenous individual, submitting oneself to the comparison with other workers, as judged from the employers' point of view, or comparison with other consumers. Others do the same, and this becomes a means of relationship, mediated within the system of money. As a worker, a portion of oneself is sold for a period of the day, as is others'. As a consumer, one purchases the embodied labor of others, which is abstracted and quantified by the money price.

Money has three forms of mediation of value. One form is to relate all exchanges to a common base, a concrete valuable object as reference for all others; a second form is to relate all exchanges to each other in a comprehensive self-referential system. "Value is constituted by the exchanges themselves, and takes on an objective quality by the regularity of its repetition, or what is commonly understood as the market price" (Kreitner 2010, 179). A third form is to derive the value referent in abstract labor, which is itself performed on an ongoing basis and provides an invisible, ever-shifting foundation for all exchanges (derived from Marx). A global disciplinary system can be founded on labor in an ongoing process. Such a foundation becomes invisible when money and politics become formally separated in financial institutions (Kreitner 2010, 187, 200, 202–208).

Labor as the third referent for a form of value is based on "abstract" labor specifically. This process of abstraction takes place on the labor market, under competitive conditions (where labor organizations have been undermined by state laws; Marx 1967, Vol. I, Ch. 28). Both Marx and Keynes are willing to assume a homogenous unit of abstract labor, in spite of the reality of concrete skills and skill differentials (Marx 1967, Vol. I, Ch. 7, Section 2, 188–190; 195–198; Vol. Ch. 8, 199–201; Keynes 1964, 41–44). For Marx, there is the added characteristic that living labor helps preserve the value of capital ("dead labor") (Marx 1967, Vol. III, Ch. 24, 399) and to add value (from surplus value).

C. Abstract System

This system of division of labor and a competitive labor market has been observed by Adam Smith. The additional feature of a Marxian approach is to generalize from the individual worker/firm employment relationship to the economic system as a whole. The entire system operates as a "totality" in which value production is represented by money, another abstract form that applies to the whole (Postone 1993, 152–157). Then competition among firms and workers in a market system is mediated by money, as a specific type of relationship or institution, which operates as a whole entity. That is, like language, money has no meaning for a single individual. This entire system exists as an institutional unit outside the influence of the individuals, a form of structure/agent dichotomy. The abstract representation of value by money then enables individual firms and workers to achieve certain powers of buying and selling, nonetheless, using a symbol that is universally recognized, like a common language. The use of money as an abstract representation of value then enables participants in the financial circuit and delineates the exchange of money from other, nonmonetary relationships. The requirement of access to cash also operates as a form of discipline for individual workers and firms, a type of system-wide imperative. Every person and relationship in such a system is influenced by the operation of markets and money, a form of both individual empowerment and coercion. Because these forms of money and labor are abstract and impersonal and operate beyond the individual's control, the system tends toward alienation (Postone 1993, 158–166).

D.   The Abstraction of Capital

Money is a form of representation of the social system to itself. The "wealth" of the nation is a form of representation of the power of the nation. It is a matter of public pride and prestige, as being the "first" among all nations on the earth. Yet this wealth is viewed in objectified form, viewed as a third person, separate from individual experience.

Adam Smith carefully reviews the specific aspects of "capital stock" in Book II of the *Wealth of Nations*. He mentions tools, laboring cattle, skilled workers, and money as well as land. He notes that the purpose of the "accumulation" of capital stock is to increase the division of labor and its productive power (Smith 1994, Book II, Introduction, 300–301). In Book II, Chapter 1 Smith expands the analysis, stating that "the intention of the fixed capital is to increase the productive power of labor" (Smith 1994, 311), which can only occur with the circulation of money (p. 307). There is a statement that sounds very much like "the division of labor is limited by the extent of the market," from an earlier chapter (Book I, Ch. III).

> As the accumulation of stock is previously necessary for carrying on this great improvement in the productive power of labour, so that accumulation naturally leads to this improvement. (Smith 1994, Book II, Introduction, 300)

The capital stock enumerated by Smith is first a set of tools for production. Then the stock is animated by the owner of that stock.

Every man of common understanding will endeavor to employ whatever stock he can command, in procuring either present enjoyment or future profit ... A man must be perfectly crazy who ... does not employ all the stock which he commands. (Smith 1994, Book II, Ch. 1, 309)

In one statement quoted earlier, the "fixed capital" itself has an "intention," whereas in the other, the owner has these intentions. Gradually the operation of the system as a whole "intends" to increase the productive power of labor as an objective. In this way, "capital" as a human agent is divided against other human agents for the purpose of increasing labor productivity by means of the circulation of money. In this way, Smith attributes human motives to an abstract system, which operates objectively while consisting of human behavior.

III.   The Process of Abstraction

Like Smith's analysis of capitalism, the structure of social science analyzes human behavior in an objective fashion. The social scientist is observing an "other." The social sciences are subject to the "modern constitution" (Latour 1993). That is, there is a common scientific method and a norm of "objectivity," but applied differentially to natural science and to humans, as the subject of social science. There is an absence of reflexivity, nonetheless, even as there is a vague awareness of the implications of the different topics of study—one's own species in contrast to other forms of nature. These abstract, objective social sciences help to shape perceptions of social institutions as objective, impersonal entities, with abstract rules.

The science of political economy was formalized by Adam Smith (Poovey 1998). Smith's notion of the division of labor is not obviously human, but a disciplined, discrete input at the workplace. The goal of capital is to reduce the need for labor by simplifying the tasks, even at the expense of the worker. The worker's time then becomes a standard metric for judging the efficiency of the firm in a competitive market. It is no longer the worker's own time, at his own discretion, but alienated at the workplace, at the employer's discretion, organized for profit. Political economy then becomes a tool of the state to increase the "wealth of nations." Academic disciplines and professions in turn developed means of standardizing methods of production and management of labor. For example, energy was standardized in units of measurement to help create the field of engineering (Russell 2014, 38–41). Even in this "dehumanized" form, Western science is considered one of the most progressive aspects of Western civilization (Tresch 2014, 156–157).

IV.   Problematic of Representation

Money represents the entirety of the economy. Money is a symbol that refers to other objects, like language. At times, however, there is a "problematic of representation" when there is some question about the accuracy or validity of this representation.

> I argue that representation *becomes* problematic ... only at certain times and under conditions that are historically and socially specific. A system of representation is experienced *as* problematic only when it ceases to work ... When the problematic of representation becomes visible ... this can have grave implications for a society's economic and political stability, for it can jeopardize the prevailing model of value, the conventions that facilitate trust, and the signs that convey creditworthiness. (Poovey 2008, 6)

The occasion of "manias, panics, and crashes" (Kindleberger 1989) are occasions when the "problematic of representation" becomes visible. At such times, economic experts resort to explanations of various types to restore confidence and to support existing systems of authority. These explanations often blame certain types of people as having an inadequate work ethic, insufficient creativity, too much fraud, or too little rational deliberation of the evidence or indicators. Resolving the crisis frequently means restructuring and reissuing debt, making new transformations and substitutions possible to restore "liquidity," if not "convertibility," and reinforcing discipline. Professional economic explanations would rarely attribute instability of economic performance to the "problematic of representation" itself.

V.   Capitalism as Labor Exchange

Economics as a discipline takes the economy as a machine, an automaton, to be analyzed in objective, quantifiable terms (Albritton 1999; Marx 1967, Vol. I, Ch. 15, 381, 419–420, 423, 436; Vol. III, Ch. 24, 395, 399; Mirowski 2002; Poovey 1998, 2002, 2008). Using economics terminology, the economy is unrecognizable as a human institution (Latour 2013; Nelson 2006). Economics, like most social sciences, analyzes the economy in functional terms, implicitly assuming the appropriate human behavior will be forthcoming in the present, which will maintain institutional rules to continue this routine operation. Such an assumption is itself functional, or "performative," making this regular performance more likely, even normative (MacKenzie 2006). Further, money, although clearly a social institution (Searle 2010), is often represented by gold (Goetzmann 2016; Shaikh 2016), a natural durable substance that is uniquely identifiable by purity conditions, and also useful in decorative arts and luxury goods, a symbol of status and wealth. The purpose of this chapter is to analyze the economy in human term, and to understand why this approach is so unusual. The underlying premise is that the economy is a social institution capable of being consciously redesigned by collective insight and deliberation (Davis 2015a).

There is considerable debate regarding the definition of capitalism (Hall and Soskice 2001; Hodgson 2014, 2015). The position explored here is that capitalism is essentially a labor exchange model, with labor as both a factor of production and a means of realization of surplus, with sales back to the household. Awareness of this foundation of the economy on labor exchange is obscured by the role of money as a medium of circulation (Postone 1993, 264–267), with production and distribution mediated by the firm via money flows, as well as the institutional and geographic separation of production from the household. The privileges of "capital" in production and financial institutions include mark up on unit labor costs or mark up on money loaned and the privilege of allocation of funds for reinvestment, luxury consumption, or hoarding. Money becomes the automatic "steering mechanism" (Polanyi 1944, 137–138; Postone 1993, 250–252) of the system and is considered valuable in itself. The outcomes include divisions of life by paid and unpaid work; uneven global development; and divisions among peoples, genders, and generations. In spite of the historically specific, evolving institutions that are unique to capitalism, the unit of analysis in mainstream economics is the abstract individual (Milonakis and Fine 2009).

The purpose of the capitalist economy is the expansion of surplus in monetary terms, often described as M – M'. In a closed economy based on labor exchange, the surplus can be increased by lowering the unit labor cost of wage goods by productivity increases (Marx 1967; Postone 1993, 289–291) and by increasing the price markup over unit labor costs for differentiated, branded products (Porter and Kramer 2011). The first is aided by technological, managerial, and scientific innovation, whereas the latter is aided by oligopoly in product markets. Competition can be avoided with increasing firm size and market share, whereas geographic expansion and branded product innovation slow the erosion of price margins. There is a "first mover" advantage," as well as ongoing competition, which may result in a "shake-out" of incumbents. Neoliberal public policies protect the surplus by limiting wages and taxes (Harvey 2005; Tabb 2012).

The financial circuit is based on individual households treated as private property. The individual workers are responsible for their own individual maintenance, including necessities and housing. There is partial public support to education, health, and infrastructure (Davis 2004). The individual worker is "free in a double sense," with the requirement to sell oneself for wages (Marx 1967, Vol. I, Ch. 6, 169; Ch. 26, 714). The reward is individual property and consumer choice. One's lifetime is nonetheless pledged to the labor market and the housing market and the financial market for old age provision. Based on this foundation, there is apparently little choice in the design of the economic system as a whole. Often property and markets are considered "natural" and so not amenable to change.

Recent economic trends express the limits of neoliberalism: labor productivity is approaching infinity with robots, AI, and 3D printing (Ford 2015); monetary policy is no longer effective in encouraging investment; fiscal policy is difficult due to resistance to taxes and government deficits in global bond markets; hypergeographic and sectoral mobility of capital with financialization and flexible supply chains are reducing employment and wages due to the race to the bottom, resulting in a lack of effective demand. There are low returns on incremental investment, and corporations hoard cash and buy back stocks, and central banks experiment with negative interest rates. Fundamentalist political movements and populism at both political extremes compete with despair and violence as responses to stagnation, mirroring the polarization before World War II (Polanyi 1944, 237–248; Judis 2016; Mishra 2017).

VI.   Simple Labor Exchange Model: Household Compared with Commodity Production

As Marx noted, the worker in capitalism is "free in a double sense"—mobile but also available for low wages, nearly "free," to the employer. There is, nonetheless, a freedom of choice of the specific employer, as Milton Friedman points out. The comparison of labor supply to home production and to factory production is a choice for the household (Braunstein, van Staveren and Tavani 2011; Kotz 1994; Quick 2016). This choice of labor supply can be based on real purchasing power, given the productivity differential between home and work.

A.   The Rise of the Factory

Historically, the rise of the factory enabled the wage worker to share the gains from increasing labor productivity. That is, with division of labor and mechanization, the factory was much more productive than household labor, where there was only gender and generational division of labor and simple technology.

The following numerical example can illustrate these relationships. Consider the production of a dress by a relatively skilled domestic worker with one sewing machine, cloth, and a pattern, compared with a global supply chain in textile production.

Assume that the household worker could produce one dress in an eight-hour working day.

Alternatively the same worker in the factory could produce one dress every ten minutes, or 48 dresses in one eight-hour working day, where the "factory" is a global supply chain across several countries with assembly in one location.

That is, the productivity of domestic labor, Q/L, is $1/8 = 0.125$. The productivity of the factory labor is 48/8 or 6.

Assume that the factory wage is such that the worker can purchase at least one dress with a day's wages, at a nominal price of \$80 per dress and a wage of \$10/hour, so that he is no worse off. That is, the minimum real wage for a day's labor in the factory is equal to a day's output in the household.

We may discuss the "same" output: the dress produced at home and a dress produced in a factory. Once factory production becomes well established, nonetheless, this "same" commodity becomes very distinct and differentiable.

Similarly, the "same" quantity of labor, measured in hours, is quite different qualitatively in the home and in the factory in terms of autonomy and discipline. Yet for the person, the worker, there is a potential trade-off, typically called the "labor supply function" in economics texts. Finally, as mass production of commodities becomes more general and the prices lower, households lose the requisite skills for home production. Bread, clothes, and even meals are no longer "homemade," a term that becomes a nostalgic advertising slogan. What had been "relationships" among household members and the community becomes "entertainment" provided by mass media to passive "viewers."

As long as the nominal wage relative to the price of the product is no greater than the productivity differential for the factory relative to the household, both the worker and the factory owner can be better off (Lazonick 1990, 333–352). The worker can achieve the same or better standard of living, and the factory owner can retain a share of the surplus, whether for reinvestment or demand for luxury goods. That is, the wage/price ratio must be less than or equal to the factory/household productivity differential.

In this case the hourly wage/price = \$10/\$80 <{productivity factory/ productivity household} = 6/0.125 = 48.

At the wage of \$10/hour and a price of \$80 per dress, the worker can buy the equivalent of his own domestic output. At a wage of \$480/hour, the worker would be able to purchase the entire factory output of the day, or \$3,840 (\$80 times 48 dresses per day). In this case the owner receives no benefit from the productivity differential in the factory. At a wage of \$1.67, all productivity gains go to the firm, and the worker needs to work for six days to buy the dress.

At any wage between \$10/hr and \$480/hr, both the owner and the worker are better off.

To generalize this analysis, it is necessary to specify a standard homogeneous product, the necessary wage good, the dress, Q, and the standard of time, hours, L, in either the household or the factory.

Q/Lh is the output Q, the dress, per hour of household labor.
Q/Lf is the output Q, the dress, per hour of factory labor.
W is the money wage per hour, L.
P is the price per unit of the standard output Q, the dress.

For the worker to be indifferent between household and factory labor in terms of real purchasing power, the real wage must equal 1.

1   $W \{1/(Q/Lh)\} / \{P/Q\} = \{W \, Lh/Q\} \{Q/P\} = 1$

That is, the {wage payment per unit of standard output}/{market price per unit of standard output} = 1, as shown in equation (1) above.

The rate of surplus value is equal to the total revenue of the firm minus the wage payment to the worker, divided by the wage payment to the worker, standardized to the length of the working day, L_{wd}, as shown in equation (2) below.

2    $\{P\ Q/Lf\ L_{wd} - WL_{wd}\}\ /\ WL_{wd}$

An increase in productivity, Q/Lf, enables the firm to increase the rate of surplus value, (2), or the rate of exploitation, while leaving the workers just as well off, as long as equation (1) holds. Equation (2) is in nominal terms, denominated by abstract monetary units, but is affected by real concrete productivity, Q/Lf, as well as the length of the working day, L_{wd}. This equation translates a day in the life of a working person into financial flows and production of surplus.

By canceling the L_{wd} terms, equation (2) resolves into a price markup over wages, as shown in equation (3) below.[1]

3    $\{P\ Q/Lf - W\}/W$

Equation (3) can be used to explore much of capitalist dynamics. First, as factory productivity rises, Q/Lf, more surplus is produced. Second, prices tend to fall with increases in labor productivity through the mechanism of capitalist competition. This gradual decline in prices gives an advantage to the "first mover" and introduces competition among firms in a race to maintain and increase productivity, or a "treadmill" (Postone 1993, 289–291). With the widespread oligopoly market structure of modern industry, this effect of competition is delayed and serves to maintain the production of surplus. Third, there is a tendency for wages to rise as productivity increases. This tracking has mostly ended since the 1970s, also serving to maintain surplus production (Shaikh 2016, 60, 730–731). For an analysis of the effect on profit rates, the costs of capital must be calculated, also by unit and by time period. The valuation of capital is much more ambiguous, whether by original costs, by projected future rate of return, or by market value.[2] The value of capital equipment also tends to fall as productivity in the capital sector increases, or by obsolescence in the face of new technologies. The value of capital also falls with a collapse of the business cycle.

B.   *Types of Technical Change: "Capitalist Technology"*

Both Smith and Marx conceptualize "capital" as the use of technology to improve labor productivity (Marx 1967, Vol. I, Ch. 14 Section 5; Ch. 15; Smith 1994, Book 2, Introduction; Ch. 2, 299–301, 310–312). The assumption of capital/labor substitution and automation pervades modern economics, as well as business and engineering. Labor productivity is measured across all industries and countries, with an implicit "race" for advances. Prospects for the growth of the system rely on continuous productivity improvements (Gordon 2016; Piketty 2014). We can define such an approach to technology as specifically "capitalist technology," which is implicitly "labor saving" and "capital cheapening" for the purposes of automation and control (Gordon, Edwards, Reich 1982; Noble 1977).

The irony of capitalist technology is that increasing investments in productivity and reductions of "necessary labor" tend to also increase the actual length of the working day (see equation (2) earlier). This increase in the working day is needed in order to offset the greater share of fixed costs with proportionally increased living labor (Marx 1967, Vol. I, Ch. 25). That is, instead of freeing labor, improved "capitalist technology" actually extends the working day. Further, the reductions in necessary labor to purchase wage goods also facilitate the increase in surplus as long as the working day remains the same or even longer. This tendency towards increasing productivity in wage goods leads to increases in "relative surplus value."

C.　*Equal Pay and Surplus Extraction*

A central aspect of Marx's analysis is the explanation that commodities can receive their exchange value according to "equal" rules, yet exploitation can take place. For labor sold on the market as a commodity, with its exchange value based on the labor time necessary for its own production, the wage is equal to the labor time for the production of necessities. The price of the commodity is equal to the (direct and indirect) labor time of production. The mediation of money[3] enables the productivity increment from factory production to be allocated to the entity with the greatest bargaining power, with the greatest potential for wage and price setting (Marx 1967, Vol. I, Ch. 6). With the enhancements of business collectives, such as corporations, and the prohibitions of labor collectives such as unions, the bargaining power is typically higher with the business entity. The length of the working day is similarly a battle between two "property owners": the worker and the factory owner.

> Between equal rights force decides. (Marx 1967, Vol. I, Ch. 10, 235)

In this case, the "equal" exchange of commodities via the circulation of money accomplishes the extraction of surplus value and sharing according to the rules of finance, that is the claim to a *pro rata* increment over the money loaned (Marx 1967, Vol. III, Ch. 21).

The labor process is under the control of the capitalist, and the product is the property of the capitalist (Marx 1967, Vol. I, Ch. 7, 184–185). The expenditure of labor time is measured in its quantitative aspect alone (Marx 1967, Vol. I, Ch. 7, 195; Ch. 8, 200–201), by its capacity to produce exchange value in the abstract, as long as the productivity is at least equal to the socially necessary labor time per commodity (Postone 1993, 287–291).

D.　*Real | Nominal Intermediation*

In the history of economic thought, there is great diversity of opinions regarding whether money matters. For the classical economists, money is a "veil" that does not affect "real" decisions. For Keynes (1964, 235), money matters, and the nominal rate of interest provides a threshold for real investment. For Marx, money is the medium for extraction of surplus value. *Only* because the firm is able to pay money wages and receive revenue from the sale of the product in money can the firm extract surplus from the employment of labor. That is, the nominal wage can compensate the worker and enable the purchase of the "same" product as he could produce at home. At the same time, the firm can express in money terms the exchange value of the commodity produced and gain the increment of surplus value by a "markup" over costs (equation (3) earlier). For Marx, this markup represents the productivity differential of the worker who is employed at the factory, where the productivity differential is due to cooperation, division of labor, and mechanization of production.

For Marx, there were interlocking circuits, $M - C - M'$ for the financial institutions and $C - M - C$ for the worker and his domestic consumption. Modern financial institutions manage the circular flow of money, as articulated by both Marx and Keynes, whereas the separate institution of the corporation manages the labor process and the marketing and sale of the product. There is an additional interface between the corporation and the financial institutions that manage access to credit and incremental investment in new and technologically innovative productive capacity. For Marx, the financial flows are necessary for the extraction and expansion of the surplus, while also intermediated with concrete production and consumption processes. It is the intermediation between money and real that enables the system to expand value, which is attributed entirely to money itself.

> Money as money is potentially self-expanding value and is loaned out as such ... It becomes a property of money to generate value. Thus we get the fetish form of capital and the conception of fetish capital. In $M - M'$ we have the meaningless form of capital, the perversion and objectification of production relations in their highest degree ... Capital is now a thing, but as a thing it is capital.
>
> (Marx 1967, Vol. III, Ch. 24, 392–393)

The advantages of money include homogenization, abstraction, and the discipline of the "bottom line" and the price tag. The disadvantages include the externalization of money as the abstract expression of value and the goal of the system toward increasing quantity, $M - M'$, apparently unrelated to the process of production. Such outcomes as hoarding and "financialization" result from the misunderstanding that money is the source of value. The possibility of financial crises also comes from this misunderstanding of money, or "fetishism," according to Marx.

E.   *The Liberal State*

There is a new form of the state based on the "liberal governmentality" of the self-interested individual (Poovey 1998, 2008). The assumption is that individuals pursue their utility primarily through an increasing standard of living. The legitimacy of the state is based on equal political representation of each citizen, with universal suffrage and separation of powers. There is a citizen "social contract" based on protection of property and debt repayment, as well as taxes and social insurance, denominated in legal tender. This model of the liberal state first emerged in England following the enclosure movement and the repeal of apprenticeship regulations and parish support of the poor. The so-called "liberal creed" assumed and enforced the "self-regulating market," supported by "*laissez faire*" economics (Polanyi 1944).

F. Externalities

The positive externalities of the division of labor and mechanization contribute to the production of social surplus. The negative externalities of the impact of waste disposal to the environment are not accounted for (Sachs 2015). Further, this analysis does not include the loss of autonomy by the household, as factory labor is often deskilled with less control over the process of design or production. The increase in productivity may increase the material standard of living, but the geographical and cultural separation of work and family may intensify the gender and generational division of labor, as well as alienation.

VII. The Institutions of Capitalism: The Public/Private Divide

The capitalist system is prone to divisions, in part due to the limits of the working day. That is, part of the day is spent in the factory and part in the household. The establishment of these divisions as "natural" is the challenge of economics expertise.

Habermas (1989) analyzes these divisions of modern society into "spheres": the public and the private spheres (Table 3.1).

These various spheres can be defined as follows. First, the private sphere is based on individual private property, including the firm and the household. Second, civil society is based on voluntary associations, including clubs, religious associations, and political parties. This is the realm of equal rights and free speech, including critique of the state. Finally, the state is the formal bureaucracy of the state apparatus, as well as the public officials serving in the

Table 3.1 Public/Private Divide

Private	Civil Society	State
Firm (*bourgeois*)	Critical press	Public officials
Household (*homme*)	Informed electorate (*citoyen*)	Bureaucracy

Adapted from Habermas 1989, 30

branches of executive, legislative, and judiciary. For some analysts, the private sphere is the realm of freedom (Berlin 1969). For Marx, these very divisions of society are a form of unfreedom and alienation. Complete human emancipation would dispense with the divisions and the limits of each sphere (Tucker 1978, 31–36, 41–46).

> Political emancipation is a reduction of man, on the one hand to a member of civil society, an *independent* and *egoistic* individual, and on the other hand, to a *citizen*, to a moral person. Human emancipation will only be complete when the real, individual man has absorbed into himself the abstract citizen ... when he has recognized and organized his own power as *social* power so that he no longer separates this social power from himself as *political* power. (Tucker 1978, 46; italics in original)

Markets and a modern capitalist economy require the divisions identified by Habermas, because markets and capitalism depend on individual private property, with rules determined and enforced by the state, and limits to the working day. The circulation of money is the only means of integration of the social whole, although in alienated form.

The importance of private property as a theoretical foundation of the state has been noted (Purdy 2010), as well as the influence on culture and values (Lamoreaux 2011; Ott 2011). Ironically, protecting the so-called private sphere may have facilitated the differentiation by class, social networks, and conspicuous consumption (Pak 2013). Much of the life of consumer society takes place in the realm of "civil society," such as conspicuous consumption (Veblen 1934) and expression of personal identity (Akerlof and Kranton 2010). Much of the flux of "identity politics" also occurs in the civil society, where an individual expresses a personal identity by association with a group. Each group claims "equality," even though the distinctive group identity is based on a differentiation. This ferment of activity and dialogue does not affect property rights in the private sphere unless laws are changed in the public sphere (such as *Roe v. Wade*, or equal pay laws, or nondiscrimination in private retail spaces in the Civil Rights Acts, or equal marriage laws).

For Marx, the "rights of man" treat him as an "isolated monad."

> The right of property is, therefore, the right to enjoy one's fortune and to dispose of it as one will ... capitalize: It is the right of self-interest ... It leads every man to see in other men, not the *realization* but rather the *limitation* of his own liberty.
>
> (Tucker 1978, 42, italics in original)

This view of the other as the limit to one's own liberty is characteristic of the competitive nation-state in a system of states, as well as in the individual property owner with respect to other owners.

The founding of the liberal/fiscal/military state with the U.S. Constitution of 1787 firmly established a strong central government and currency (Davis 2005, 187–188; Sylla, Wright, and Cowen 2009). As a result, the local municipality in the United States has ability to tax and spend, but not to produce, according to the patterns of federalism and the subordination of public municipalities to the state and federal government. Public municipalities, which had been independent corporations before the revolution, became administrative divisions of local government, whereas private business corporations became the agents of economic development (Wright 2014). This governance hierarchy and public/private divide based on the primacy of money is the opposite of the local autonomy necessary for resilient governance of the commons (Frug 2006; Ostrom 1990, 2010).

VIII. Monetary Circuit as a Means of Integration, Discipline, and Surplus Extraction

The financial circuit operates to maintain production, realization, and expansion of value, even while breaking the production and realization process into separable segments. The completion of the financial circuit then requires management, a function that appears to be accomplished by money itself. The time taken by each segment of production and realization is facilitated by money as a representation of value, holding its meaning over the time interval in which its specific quantitative equivalence, or "value," may well be at issue. This management of the financial circuit is accomplished by the central bank and financial institutions, mediating among the separate individual agents in the private sphere who do not recognize their contributions to the whole. There is consequently a "fallacy of composition" and a split in perspective between "micro" and "macro."

In order to obtain the daily and generational means of subsistence, the worker must offer his labor power as a commodity in the factory once the separation of home and production has taken place. The "flow" of his labor time is "compensated" by the "flow" of money in wages in the opposite direction, as illustrated in the typical textbook circular-flow diagram of the economy. Although money itself is often perceived as the active agent in the economy, the apparent movements of money are embedded in the life cycle of persons (Davis 2015b). In fact, the expenditures of human labor in the concrete production process are not "realized" until there is an exchange of money based on the price of the commodity. Money represents the abstract exchange value in contrast to the use value of the concrete labor in production. Competition among firms based on productivity and price serves in the process of disciplining and the "abstraction" of labor in terms of rendering labor as homogeneous. In turn, it is not possible to distribute the incomes to the factors of production until the exchange of money for product has taken place. The money payment is the validation of the entire process and the reason for which it takes place. The paycheck is the reward for the worker in terms of purchasing power and social status, and the sales revenue feeds the "bottom line" for the firm, without which its survival would be in question. The speed of the "flows" of money is even measured by the concept of "velocity," or "turnover." The abstract impersonal agent of "capital" appears alive because of the life activities of humans, organized in specific institutional structures according to the public/private divide (Davis 2015b; Postone 1993, 267–272). In fact the economy operates by impersonal rules of "equal" property, which appear to be beyond the control of any specific actor (Abdelal 2007; Marx 1967, Vol. I, Ch. 1, Section 4, 80–83; Ch. 3, Section 2.a, 112; Rodrik 2015; Stiglitz 2016).

IX. Public/Private Divide

Although individual private property is a founding principle of the liberal state, the financial circuits encompass both public and private property in an integrated whole. The operation of one aspect, the private sphere, is complementary with the public sphere. For example, taxes on private property flow as revenues to the state and enable the state to anticipate its future revenue for the purposes of borrowing. The state debt then constitutes the foundation of the financial system, which finances both public and private actors (Davis 2010, 2013c, 2017). State revenues then finance public goods, which support the private sector. Financial circuits, denominated in the national currency, are equally valuable in both private and public spheres, among workers and investors alike. In fact, the larger the circuit, the more participants and the more stable and liquid the currency and the financial assets.

Building on Marx's financial circuit, $M - C - M'$, and integrating Keynes, it is possible to develop a type of translation between the terminology of each one. The first part of the circuit is $M - C$ and represents production, in Keynes' terminology. The second part of the circuit, $C' - M'$, represents realization to Marx and consumption to Keynes. Typically, the production takes place in the factory, a separate institution, the firm, whereas consumption takes place in the household. Often there is a perceived gender differentiation between these two institutions, which helps to "naturalize" this separation of the working day according to time and place (Davis 2017; Pateman 1988). Further, Keynes defines "equilibrium" as the equality between production and consumption and recognizes a contingency by considering *ex ante* values compared with *ex post* values. Expectations may govern the scale of production, validated by expenditures that take place after the fact. In fact, there is an uncertainty regarding the extent to which these expectations will be fulfilled, which in turn determines whether debt incurred in the production process can be repaid. Given the inherent uncertainty, which is a structural feature of the system, the normalization of gender roles and consumer practices help to provide stability of the system as a whole. The uncertainty in actual profit compared with expected profit can be represented by shifts in the marginal efficiency of capital (MEC), which then helps to determine future investments. Expectations can shape outcomes in what can be called a "performative" dimension in Keynes.

It is interesting to reconcile Marx and Keynes, at least in terms of financial circuits. For Marx, the first step in circulation is the firm's initial borrowing, M, used to purchase commodities as factor inputs and to produce other commodities for sale representing more value than the inputs, M – C – C'. For Keynes this is production and the generation of incomes. The second step for Marx is the realization of the value of commodities by sales, C' – M'. That is, the circuit is not complete until the commodity's value has been "realized" by sales proceeds or total revenue. In Keynes' terms this second step is described as expenditures, usually summing the major types of spending: consumer, investment, government, and net exports. The expected *ex ante* value of production may not equal the *ex post* realization of sales, depending on the state of the market, income distribution, expectations, and portfolio choices in financial markets. A condition for "equilibrium" in production and calculation of gross domestic product (GDP) in any time period is the equality of income and expenditures, ex post. Keynes was fully aware that the process of reaching this equilibrium may generate some uncertainty of outcome, as well as statistical revision after the fact.

That is, there is a possible dichotomy between value in production and realization in sales proceeds. Market price of commodities can be expected at a certain level but realized at a different level. With his emphasis on the monetary aspects of the economy, Keynes can also introduce uncertainty of portfolio choice, holding cash or financial assets of various types, including corporate stocks, bonds, and commercial paper related to production. Money and other financial assets can become a store of value if conditions are not encouraging for investment in the present.

The complete financial circuit, M – C – M', integrates the two private spheres of firm and household. Following Smith, for Marx, only "productive" labor creates "value," but even for Marx, this value must be "realized" by purchases by the household. This "realization" is in service of the daily and generational reproduction of the labor force. Although this household labor does not create value, either for Marx or for GDP calculations, it is essential for the operation of the entire system. The encumbrance of debt by the household, for consumer durables, education, or housing, can help regulate a stream of future payments to form new types of securities, in addition to government debt, which anticipates future tax payments. Financial innovation has expanded the financial circuit beyond the purchase of commodities for daily consumption to much more complex types of financial relationships.

These financial relationships begin to encompass all stages of life, not just the working day, in spite of critique by commentators like Sandel (2012).

The importance of money as an integrating device comes to overshadow the individual worker and homemaker, whose work is represented by financial flows. And yet the structure of labor and the household has implications for the stability of finance, and vice versa (Cooper 2015). The awareness of the contribution of the individual is reduced, nonetheless, in the great institutional complex of the self-regulating economy. The importance of money in all of the activities of life, working, consuming, leisure activities, and acquisition of luxury products, embodies and represents the value of all of these activities. The purpose of human life becomes getting, spending, and saving money, reducing the perceived value of those lives. Under such conditions, the reification of money becomes natural, enabling money to reorganize production, consumption, life purposes, and the landscape of the earth.

Money as an integrating device represents daily and intergenerational reproduction, without which realization of the value of commodities by sales to the household would not be possible.

X.   Relationship of Money and the Social

The centrality of labor has been recognized in the classical school of economics, including Smith, Ricardo, and Marx. Variations in measurement of labor time are also noteworthy, such as the work of Postone. Once discipline is a fundamental characteristic of the labor market, abstract labor has a socially observable and measurable standard definition as socially necessary labor time (Postone 1993, 287–291), which is continually adjusted to account for improvements in overall productivity. In contrast, the society-wide improvements in science, engineering, and organization are called "historic time." These ongoing transformations are less related to direct labor input and more associated with scientific and technologically advanced production (Postone 1993, 291–298). These advances in "historic time" are often considered the assets of business corporations, with accumulated skills, technology, and organization, along with innovation, product differentiation, and distribution networks. In such a context, corporations appear to dominate the individual worker.

Postone also points out that the expression of value by means of labor time is unique to capitalism. That is, the role of labor and money would differ, according to various forms of society (Postone 1993, 398–399). If the form of representation, like money, affects the type of relationships and institutions of society, and vice versa, then it would be possible to reorganize these interconnections, as in Table 3.2 (another form of representation and type of validation).

If social sciences are implicated in the "objectification" of society, then reflexive critique of social science is also an important project.

Table 3.2 Money and Social Referents

Period	Money [Object/Symbol]	Referent	Type of economy
Premodern	Precious metal coin	Foreign trade; mercenaries	Craft and subsistence agriculture
Modern	Paper money with collateral in land, convertibility in precious metals	General purchasing power of resources and commodities	Industrial with wage labor force
Postmodern ("financialization")	Paper money is considered valuable in itself	Hierarchical exchange rate among national currencies	Knowledge/service/global
Information/Internet	Electronic money	Images and symbols	Virtual products (video games; virtual realities)
Artificial intelligence	Electronic records of all factors and products	All potential transformations, science and economic	Highly automated, with little direct labor

Notes

1 The formula in mainstream microeconomics for average profit is similar, $\{P - W/(Q/L_f)\}$, ignoring fixed costs. There is a similar equation for a two-sector economy (Minsky 1986, Ch. 7, 141–170).

2 Valuing capital is complex, including cost of production, enhancement of productivity, estimates of depreciation, and expected future returns, and is the subject of ongoing controversies (see Keynes 1964, Ch. 6 and Appendix, 52–75; Ch. 11, 135–146; Shaikh 2016, 243–256). There is also a circularity in the definition of capital: the quantity of capital is presumed to influence the interest rate, but measures of the quantity of capital also rely on the interest rate (Keynes 1964, 137, 140; Minsky 1986, Ch. 9, 213–218).

3 The explanation of surplus in Marx's analysis is incorrect in Seigel 2012, 299–303. Rather than the difference between abstract and concrete labor, surplus is the difference between the price of the commodity labor power, the value of daily necessities, and the value produced in a given working day. That is, surplus is the difference between the total value produced in a working day after subtracting the value of the wage, both expressed in money terms representing abstract labor. Postone's analysis discusses the dialectic between abstract and concrete labor as tending to increase productivity (Postone 1993, 298–306). Postone tends to see this dialectic as mediated by labor and different forms of time instead of mediated by money in the analysis offered here.

Bibliography

Abdelal, Rawi E. *Capital Rules: The Construction of Global Finance*. Cambridge, MA: Harvard University Press, 2007.

Acharya, Viral V., Matthew Richardson, Stijn Van Nieuwerburgh, and Lawrence J. White. *Guaranteed to Fail: Fannie Mae, Freddie Mac and the Debacle of Mortgage Finance,* Princeton, NJ: Princeton University Press, 2011.

Akerlof, George A. and Rachel E. Kranton. *Identity Economics: How Our Identities Shape Our Work, Wages, and Well-Being*. Princeton, NJ: Princeton University Press, 2010.

Albritton, Robert. *Dialectics and Deconstruction in Political Economy*. New York: Palgrave, 1999.

Alperowitz, Gar. *What Then Must We Do? Straight Talk about the Next American Revolution*. White River Junction, VT: Chelsea Green Publishing, 2013.

Arrighi, Giovanni. *The Long Twentieth Century: Money, Power, and the Origins of Our Times*. London: Verso, 1994.

Berlin, Isaiah. *Four Essays on Liberty*. London: Oxford University Press, 1969.

Braunstein, Elissa, Irene van Staveren, and Daniele Tavani. "Embedding Care and Unpaid Work in Macroeconomic Modeling: A Structuralist Approach," *Feminist Economics*, Vol. 17, No. 4, 2011, 5–31.

Brewer, John. *The Sinews of Power: War, Money, and the English State 1688–1783*. Cambridge, MA: Harvard University Press, 1988.

———. *Consumption and the World of Goods*. New York: Routledge, 1993.

Brockling, Ulrich, Susanne Krasmann, and Thomas Lemke (eds.). *Governmentality: Current Issues and Future Challenges*. New York: Routledge, 2011.

Caliskan, Koray and Michel Callon. "Economization, Part 1: Shifting Attention from the Economy Towards Processes of Economization," *Economy and Society*, Vol. 38, No. 3, 2009, 369–398.

Clack, Brett and Richard York. "Carbon Metabolism: Global Capitalism, Climate Change, and the Biospheric Rift," *Theory and Society*, Vol. 34, No. 4, 2005, 391–428.

Commission for the Measurement of Economic Performance and Social Progress. *Mismeasuring Our Lives: Why Doesn't GDP Add Up?* New York: New Press, 2010.

Cooper, Melinda. "Shadow Money and the Shadow Workforce: Rethinking Labor and Liquidity," *South Atlantic Quarterly*, Vol. 114, No. 2, 2015, 395–423.

Daston, Lorraine and Galison, Peter L. *Objectivity*. New York: Zone Books, 2010.

Davis, Ann E. "(De)Constructing Dependency: Institutional, Historical Perspectives of Welfare," *Review of Radical Political Economics*, Volume 36, No. 1, 2004, 37–51.

———. "Property and Politics in the Hudson Valley: Continuity and Change in the Corporate Form," in M. Oppenheimer and N. Mercuro (eds.), *Law & Economics: Alternative Economic Approaches to Legal and Regulatory Issues*, Armonk, NY: M.E. Sharpe, 2005, 131–160.

———. "The Discourse of Property: Continuity Within Transformation," in Terrence McDonough, Michael Reich, David M. Kotz, and Maria-Alejandra Gonzalez-Perez (eds.), CISC Working Paper No. 24, December 2006. *Growth and Crisis: Social Structure of Accumulation Theory and Analysis*, 403–425. Available online at http://www.cisc.ie/documents/00024ciscwp.pdf.

———. "Endogenous Institutions and the Politics of Property: Comparing and Contrasting Douglass North and Karl Polanyi in the Case of Finance," *Journal of Economic Issues*, Volume XLII, No. 4, 2008, 1101–1122.

———. "Marx and the Mixed Economy: Money, Accumulation, and the Role of the State," *Science & Society*, Vol. 74, No. 3, 2010, 409–428.

———. "Panglossian Economics: Critiques, Paradigms, Policies, and Politics," *Challenge*, Vol. 55, No. 6, 2012, 67–87.

———. "Bringing Politics Back In: Violence, Finance, and the State," *Journal of Economic Issues*, Vol. XLVII, No. 1, 2013a, 1–28.

———. "Panglossian Paradox: How Paradigmatic Purity Compromises Policy Effectiveness," *Forum for Social Economics* Vol. 42, No. 4, 2013b, 346–358. DOI: 10.1080/07360932.2013.769893.

———. "The New 'Voodoo Economics': Fetishism and the Public/Private Divide," *Review of Radical Political Economics*, Vol. 45, No. 1, 2013c, 42–58.

_____. *The Evolution of the Property Relation: Understanding Paradigms, Debates, Prospects*. New York: Palgrave MacMillan, 2015a.

_____. "The Process of Provisioning: The Halter for the Workhorse," *Journal of Economic Issues*, Vol. XLIX, No. 2, 2015b, 449–457.

_____. "Paradoxical Positions: The Methodological Contributions of Feminist Scholarship," *Cambridge Journal of Economics*, Vol. 41, No. 1, 2017, 181–201.

_____. "Contested Continuity: Competing Explanations of the Evolution of the Corporate Form," forthcoming in *Journal of Economic Issues*, June 2016.

Davis, John B. *Individuals and Identity in Economics*. New York: Cambridge University Press, 2011.

Dosi, Giovanni and Louis Galambos (eds.). *The Third Industrial Revolution in Global Business*. New York: Cambridge University Press, 2013.

Eichengreen, Barry. *Exorbitant Privilege: The Rise and Fall of the Dollar and the Future of the International Monetary System*. New York: Oxford University Press, 2011.

Epstein, Gerald A. (ed.). *Financialization and the World Economy*. Cheltenham, UK: Edward Elgar, 2005.

Falkowski, Paul G. *Life's Engines: How Microbes Made Earth Habitable*. Princeton, NJ: Princeton University Press, 2015.

Ferguson, Niall. *The Cash Nexus: Money and Power in the Modern World, 1700–2000*. New York: Basic, 2001.

_____. *The Ascent of Money: A Financial History of the World*. New York: Penguin, 2008.

Fligstein, Neil. *The Transformation of Corporate Control*. Cambridge, MA: Harvard University Press, 1990.

Ford, Martin. *The Rise of the Robots: Technology and the Threat of a Jobless Future*. New York: Basic Books, 2015.

Foucault, Michel. *The History of Sexuality*. New York: Pantheon, 1978.

Fraser, Nancy. "Contradictions of Capital and Care," *New Left Review*, Vol. 100, 2016, 99–117.

Frug, Gerald E. "The Legal Technology of Exclusion in Metropolitan America," in Kevin M. Kruse and Thomas J. Sugrue (eds.), *The New Suburban History*. Chicago: University of Chicago Press, 2006, 205–219.

Galison, Peter. *Einstein's Clocks, Poincare's Maps: Empires of Time*. New York: W.W. Norton, 2003.

Goetzmann, William N. *Money Changes Everything: How Finance Made Civilization Possible*. Princeton, NJ: Princeton University Press, 2016.

Goldman, Rebecca L., Barton H. Thompson, Gretchen C. Daily. "Institutional Incentives for Managing the Landscape: Inducing Cooperation for the Production of Ecosystem Services," *Ecological Economics*, Vol. 64, 2007, 333–343.

Goldstein, Robert J. "Greenwood in the Bundle of Sticks: Fitting Environmental Ethics and Ecology into Real Property Law," *Boston College Environmental Affairs Law Review*, Vol. 25, 1998, 347–428.

Gordon, David M., Richard Edwards, and Michael Reich. *Segmented Work, Divided Workers: The Historical Transformation of Labor in the United States*. New York: Cambridge University Press, 1982.

Gordon, Robert J. *The Rise and Fall of American Growth: The US Standard of Living Since the Civil War*. Princeton, NJ: Princeton University Press, 2016.

Graeber, David. *The Democracy Project: A History, A Crisis, A Movement*. New York: Spiegel & Grau, 2013.

Greenstein, Shane. *How the Internet Became Commercial: Innovation, Privatization, and the Birth of a New Network*. Princeton, NJ: Princeton University Press, 2015.

Greenstein, Shane, Martin Peitz, and Tommaso Valletti. "Net Neutrality: A Fast Lane to Understanding the Trade-Offs," *Journal of Economic Perspectives*, Vol. 30, No. 2, 2016, 127–150.

Groffman, Peter, et al. "Ecological Homogenization of Urban USA," *Frontiers in Ecology*, Vol. 12, No. 1, 2014, 74–81.

Habermas, Jurgen. *Legitimation Crisis*. Boston: Beacon Press, 1973.

———. *The Structural Transformation of the Public Sphere: An Inquiry into a Category of Bourgeois Society*. Cambridge, MA: MIT Press, 1989.

———. *Moral Consciousness and Communicative Action*. Cambridge, MA: MIT Press, 1990.

Hall, Peter A. and David Soskice (eds.). *Varieties of Capitalism: The Institutional Foundations of Comparative Advantage*. New York: Oxford University Press, 2001.

Hartog, Hendrik. *Public Property, Private Power: The Corporation of the City of New York in American Law, 1730–1870*. Chapel Hill, NC: University of North Carolina Press, 1983.

Harvey, David. *A Brief History of Neoliberalism*. New York: Oxford University Press, 2005.

———. *The Enigma of Capital and the Crisis of Capitalism*. New York: Oxford University Press, 2010.

Hess, Charlotte and Elinor Ostrom (eds.). *Understanding Knowledge as a Common: From Theory to Practice*. Cambridge, MA: MIT Press, 2007.

Hewitson, G. "Economics and the Family: A Postcolonial Perspective," *Cambridge Journal of Economics*, Vol. 37, 2013, 91–111.

Hippel, Eric Von. *Democratizing Innovation*. Cambridge, MA: MIT Press, 2005.

Ho, Karen. *Liquidated: An Ethnography of Wall Street*. Durham, NC: Duke University Press, 2009.

Hodgson, Geoffrey M. "What Is Capital? Economists and Sociologists Have Changed Its Meaning: Should It Be Changed Back?," *Cambridge Journal of Economics*, Vol. 38, 2014, 1063–1086.

———. *Conceptualizing Capitalism: Institutions, Evolution, Future*. Chicago: University of Chicago Press, 2015.

Hoff, Karla and Joseph E. Stiglitz. "Equilibrium Fictions: A Cognitive Approach to Societal Rigidity," *American Economic Review*, Vol. 100, No. 2, 2010, 141–146.

Howell, Martha C. *Commerce Before Capitalism in Europe, 1300-1600*. New York: Cambridge University Press, 2010.

Hsu, Angel, Yaping Cheng, Amy Weinfurter, Kaiyang Xu, and Cameron Yick. "Track Climate Pledges of Cities and Companies," *Nature*, Vol. 532, 2016, 303–306.

Ivanova, Maria N. "The Crisis of Home-Centered Consumer Capitalism in the United States," in Alan W. Cafruny and Herman M. Schwartz (eds.), *Exploring the Global Financial Crisis*. Boulder, CO: Lynne Rienner Publishers, 2013, 165–177.

Jackson, Kenneth T. *Crabgrass Frontier: The Suburbanization of the U.S.* New York: Oxford University Press, 1985.

Judis, John B. *The Populist Explosion: How the Great Recession Transformed American and European Politics*. New York: Columbia Global Reports, 2016.

Keynes, John Maynard. *The General Theory of Employment, Interest, and Money*. New York: Harcourt, Brace & World, Inc. 1964.

Kindleberger, Charles. *Manias, Panics, Crashes: A History of Financial Crises*. New York: Basic Books, 1989.

Konings, Martijn. "Rethinking Neoliberalism and the Crisis: Beyond the Re-Regulation Agenda," in Martijn Konings (ed.), *The Great Credit Crash*. New York: Verso, 2010, 3–30.

———. *The Development of American Finance*. New York: Cambridge University Press, 2011.

Kotz, David M. "Household Labor, Wage Labor, and the Transformation of the Family," *Review of Radical Political Economics*, Vol. 26, No. 2, 1994, 24–56.

———. *The Rise and Fall of Neoliberal Capitalism*. Cambridge, MA: Harvard University Press, 2015.

Kreitner, Roy. "The Jurisprudence of Global Money," *Theoretical Inquiries in Law*, Vol. 11, 2010, 177–208.

Krippner, Greta R. "The Financialization of the American Economy," *Socio-Economic Review*, Vol. 3, 2005, 173–208.

_____. *Capitalizing on Crisis: The Political Origins of the Rise of Finance*. Cambridge, MA: Harvard University Press, 2011.

Lamoreaux, Naomi. "The Mystery of Property Rights: A U.S. Perspective," *Journal of Economic History*, Vol. 71, No. 2, 2011, 275–306.

Lapavitsas, Costas. *Profiting Without Producing: How Finance Exploits Us All*. New York: Verso, 2013.

Latour, Bruno. *We Have Never Been Modern*. Cambridge, MA: Harvard University Press, 1993.

_____. "Why Has Critique Run Out of Steam? From Matters of Fact to Matters of Concern," *Critical Inquiry*, Vol. 30, No. 2, 2004, 225–248.

_____. *An Inquiry into Modes of Existence: An Anthropology of the Moderns*. Cambridge, MA: Harvard University Press, 2013.

Lazonick, William. *Competitive Advantage on the Shop Floor*. Cambridge, MA: Harvard University Press, 1990.

_____. *Business Organization and the Myth of the Market Economy*. New York: Cambridge University Press, 1991.

_____. "Stock Buybacks: From Retain-and-Reinvest to Downsize-and-Distribute." Washington, DC: Center for Effective Public Management at Brookings, April 2015.

Levy, Jonathan. "The Mortgage Worked the Hardest," in Michael Zakim and Gary J. Kornblith (eds.), *Capitalism Takes Command: The Social Transformation of Nineteenth-Century America*. Chicago: University of Chicago Press, 2012, 39–68.

LiPuma, Edward and Benjamin Lee. *Financial Derivatives and the Globalization of Risk*. Durham, NC: Duke University Press, 2004.

_____. "A Social Approach to the Financial Derivatives Markets," *The South Atlantic Quarterly*, Vol. 111, No. 2, 2012, 289–316.

MacKenzie, Donald A. *An Engine, Not a Camera: How Financial Models Shape Markets*. Cambridge, MA: MIT Press, 2006.

_____. *Material Markets: How Economic Agents Are Constructed*. New York: Oxford University Press, 2009.

_____ "The Credit Crisis as a Problem in the Sociology of Knowledge," *American Journal of Sociology*, Vol. 116, No. 6, 2011, 1776–1841.

_____. "Knowledge Production in Financial Markets: Credit Default Swaps, the ABX and the Subprime Crisis," *Economy & Society*. Vol. 41, 2012, 335–359.

MacKenzie, Donald A., Fabian Muniesa, and Lucia Siu (eds.). *Do Economists Make Markets? On the Performativity of Economics*. Princeton, NJ: Princeton University Press, 2007.

MacPherson, C. B. *The Political Theory of Possessive Individualism: Hobbes to Locke*. London: Oxford University Press, 1962.

_____. *Democratic Theory: Essays in Retrieval*. Oxford, UK: Clarendon Press, 1973.

Marx, Karl. *Capital*. Vol. I, II, III. New York: International Publishers, 1967.

Mazower, Mark. *Governing the World: The History of an Idea*. New York: Penguin Press, 2012.

McGirr, Lisa. *Suburban Warriors: The Origins of the New American Right*. Princeton, NJ: Princeton University Press, 2001.

Mehrling, Perry G. *The Money Interest and the Public Interest: American Monetary Thought, 1920–1970*. Cambridge, MA: Harvard University Press, 1997.

Milberg, William and Deborah Winkler. *Outsourcing Economics: Global Value Chains in Capitalist Development*. New York: Cambridge University Press, 2013.

Millo, Yuval. "Making Things Deliverable: The Origins of Index-Based Derivatives," in Michel Callon, Yuval Millo and Fabian Muniesa (eds.), *Market Devices*. Oxford, UK: Blackwell Publishing, 2007, 196–214.

Milonakis, Dimitris and Ben Fine. *From Political Economy to Economics: Method, the Social and the Historical in the Evolution of Economic Theory*. New York: Routledge, 2009.

Minsky, Hyman P. *Stabilizing and Unstable Economy*. New Haven: Yale University Press, 1986.

Mirowski, Philip. *More Heat than Light: Economics as Social Physics, Physics as Nature's Economics*. New York: Cambridge University Press, 1989.

_____. *Machine Dreams: Economics Becomes a Cyborg Science*. New York: Cambridge University Press, 2002.

Mishra, Pankaj. *The Age of Anger: A History of the Present*. New York: Farrar, Straus, and Giroux, 2017.

Moore, Jason W. *Capitalism in the Web of Life: Ecology and the Accumulation of Capital*. London: Verso, 2015.

Nelson, Julie. *Economics for Humans*. Chicago: University of Chicago Press, 2006.

Noble, David F. *America by Design: Science, Technology, and the Rise of Corporate Capitalism*. New York: Knopf, 1977.

North, Douglass C. and Barry R. Weingast. "Constitutions and Commitment: The Evolution of Institutions Governing Public Choice in Seventeenth-Century England," *The Journal of Economic History*. Vol. 49, No. 4, 1989, 803–832.

North, Douglass C., John Joseph Wallis, and Barry R. Weingast. *Violence and Social Orders: A Conceptual Framework for Interpreting Recorded Human History*. New York: Cambridge University Press, 2009.

Nussbaum, Martha C. *Creating Capabilities: The Human Development Approach*. Cambridge, MA: Harvard University Press, 2011.

Ostrom, Elinor. *Governing the Commons: The Evolution of Institutions for Collective Action*, Cambridge University Press, 1990.

_____. "Beyond Markets and States: Polycentric Governance of Complex Economic Systems," *American Economic Review*, Vol. 100, 2010, 641–672.

Ott, Julia C. *When Wall Street Met Main Street: The Quest for an Investors' Democracy*. Cambridge, MA: Harvard University Press, 2011.

Pak, Susie J. *Gentlemen Bankers: The World of J.P. Morgan*. Cambridge, MA: Harvard University Press, 2013.

Pateman, Carole. *The Sexual Contract*. Stanford, CA: Stanford University Press, 1988.

Paustian, Keith, Johannes Lehmann, Stephen Ogle, David Reay, G. Philip Robertson, and Pete Smith. "Climate-Smart Soils." *Nature*, Vol. 532, 2016, 49–57.

Phillips-Fein, Kim. *Invisible Hands: The Making of the Conservative Movement from the New Deal to Reagan*. New York: W.W. Norton, 2009.

Piketty, Thomas. *Capital in the Twenty-First Century*. Cambridge, MA: Harvard University Press, 2014.

Piore, Michael J. and Charles F. Sabel. *The Second Industrial Divide*. New York: Basic Books, 1984.

Polanyi, Karl. *The Great Transformation: The Political and Economic Origins of Our Time*. Boston: Beacon Press, 1944.

Pollin, Robert. *Greening the Global Economy*. Cambridge, MA: MIT Press, 2015.

Poovey, Mary. *Making a Social Body: British Cultural Formation 1830–1864*. Chicago: University of Chicago Press, 1995.

_____. *A History of the Modern Fact: Problems of Knowledge in the Sciences of Wealth and Society*. Chicago: University of Chicago Press, 1998.

_____. "The Liberal Civil Subject and the Social in Eighteenth-Century British Moral Philosophy," *Public Culture*, Vol. 14, No. 1, 2002, 125–145.

_____. *Genres of the Credit Economy: Mediating Value in the Eighteenth-and Nineteenth-Century Britain*. Chicago: University Press, 2008.

Porter, Michael E. and Mark R. Kramer. "Creating Shared Value: How to Reinvent Capitalism—and Unleash a Wave of Innovation and Growth," *Harvard Business Review*, January–February 2011, 63–70.

Postone, Moishe. *Time, Labor, and Social Domination: A Reinterpretation of Marx's Critical Theory*. New York: Cambridge University Press, 1993.

Purdy, Jedediah. *The Meaning of Property: Freedom, Community, and the Legal Imagination*. New Haven, CT: Yale University Press, 2010.

_____. *After Nature: A Politics for the Anthropocene*. Cambridge, MA: Harvard University Press, 2015.

Quick, Paddy. Personal conversation, May 2016.

Rodrik, Dani. *Economics Rules: The Rights and Wrongs of the Dismal Science*. New York: W.W. Norton, Inc., 2015.

Ruckelshaus, Mary, Emily McKenzie, Heather Tallis, et al. "Notes from the Field: Lessons Learned from Using Ecosystem Service Approaches to Inform Real-World Decisions," *Ecological Economics*, Vol. 115, No. 15, July 2015, 11–21.

Russell, Andrew L. *Open Standards and the Digital Age: History, Ideology, and Networks*. New York: Cambridge University Press, 2014.

Sachs, Jeffrey D. *The Age of Sustainable Development*. New York: Columbia University Press, 2015.

Sandel, Michael J. *What Money Can't Buy: The Moral Limits of Markets*. New York: Farrar, Straus, and Giroux, 2012.

Sartori, Andrew. "Global Intellectual History and the History of Political Economy," in Samuel Moyn and Andrew Sartori (eds.), *Global Intellectual History*. New York: Columbia University Press, 2013, 110–133.

Schor, Juliet. *Plenitude: The New Economics of True Wealth*. New York: Penguin, 2010.

_____. *True Wealth: How and Why Millions of Americans Are Creating a Time-Rich, Ecological Light, Small-Scale, High Satisfaction Economy*. New York: Penguin, 2011.

Schor, Juliet and Craig J. Thompson (eds.). *The Quest for Plenitude: Case Studies of the New Economy*. New Haven: Yale University Press, 2014.

Schumpeter, Joseph A. "The Crisis of the Tax State," in Richard Swedberg (ed.), *The Economics and Sociology of Capitalism*. Princeton, NJ: Princeton University Press, 1991, 99–140.

Searle, John R. *Making the Social World: The Structure of Human Civilization*. New York: Oxford University Press, 2010.

Seigel, Jerrold. *The Idea of the Self: Thought and Experience in Western Europe Since the Seventeenth Century*. New York: Cambridge University Press, 2005.

_____. *Modernity and Bourgeois Life: Society, Politics, and Culture in England, France, and Germany since 1750*. New York: Cambridge University Press, 2012.

Self, Robert O. "Prelude to the Tax Revolt: The Politics of the 'Tax Dollar' in Postwar California," in Kevin M. Kruse and Thomas J. Sugrue (eds.), *The New Suburban History*. Chicago: University of Chicago Press, 2006, 144–160.

Sen, Amartya. *Development as Freedom*. New York: Alfred A. Knopf, 1999.

Shaikh, Anwar. *Capitalism: Competition, Conflict, Crises*. New York: Oxford University Press, 2016.

Smith, Adam. *An Inquiry into the Nature and Causes of the Wealth of Nations*. New York: Modern Library, 1994.

Stiglitz, Joseph E. *Rewriting the Rules of the American Economy: An Agenda for Growth and Shared Prosperity*. New York: W.W. Norton, 2016.

Stiglitz, Joseph E. and Bruce C. Greenwald. *Creating a Learning Society: A New Approach to Growth, Development, and Social Progress*. New York: Columbia University Press, 2014.

Streeck, Wolfgang. *Buying Time: The Delayed Crisis of Democratic Capitalism*. New York: Verso, 2013.

Sylla, Richard, Robert E. Wright, and David J. Cowen. "Alexander Hamilton, Central Banker: Crisis Management During the U.S. Financial Panic of 1792," *Business History Review*, Vol. 83, 2009, 61–86.

Tabb, William K. *The Restructuring of Capitalism in Our Time*. New York: Columbia University Press, 2012.

Tollefson, Jeff. "Carbon-Aensing Satellite System Faces High Hurdles: Space Agencies Plan an Advanced Fleet, but Technical and Political Challenges Abound," *Nature*, Vol. 533, 2016, 446–447.

Tresch, John. "Cosmologies Materialized: History of Science and History of Ideas," in Darrin M. McMahon and Samuel Moyn (eds.), *Rethinking Modern European Intellectual History*. New York: Oxford, 2014, 153–172.

Tucker, Robert C. (ed.). *The Marx-Engels Reader*, 2nd ed. New York: W.W. Norton, 1978.

———. *Alone Together: Why We Expect More from Technology and Less from Each Other*. New York: Basic, 2011.

Veblen, Thorstein. *The Theory of the Leisure Class: An Economic Study of Institutions*. New York: Modern Library, 1934.

Wilson, Edward O. *Half-Earth: Our Planet's Fight for Life*. New York: W.W. Norton & Co., 2016.

Wright, Robert E. *Corporation Nation*. Philadelphia: University of Pennsylvania Press, 2014.

4 Long-Term History of Money and the Market

I. Introduction

Over the course of several centuries, the emergence of money and the market reshaped knowledge, the state, institutions, and the "production" of space (Harvey 2001). The term "revolution" has been used frequently to refer to these long-term changes: the Commercial Revolution (Lopez 1971), Financial Revolution (Dickson 1967), Scientific Revolution, Technological Revolution, and Industrial Revolution (Horn, Rosenband, and Smith 2010). The increasing use of money helped to symbolize and stabilize certain types of relationships, which then affected other related institutions in turn. The Renaissance in Northern Italy during the thirteenth to the sixteenth centuries was a singular place and time when many of these changes coalesced and reshaped the related institutions all at once. Perhaps it is useful to think of "money" as an institutional tool that reshaped many other related institutions. In this chapter we consider "money" as both a term and an institution, which also reshaped knowledge, a methodology developed in an earlier work (Davis 2015). It is important to note that money did not "cause" these related changes, but rather provided new capacities and practices, which led to cumulative changes in other institutions.

Many distinguished scholars have studied this period. Although Padgett, Powell, and McLean have made prodigious efforts and notable contributions to the literature of the changes in social forms, they retain a formalistic approach based on natural science—chemistry in this case. They tend to view humans as objects only, "brought to life" when there are considerations of biography for the purposes of reproducing specific social forms (Padgett and McLean 2006, 1470–1471, 1544, 1547). By viewing money as a social institution with its own rules, this chapter can analyze the impact of money on other social forms, including work organizations, as well as the family and the state. Most treatments of institutional change either omit money entirely or take money as an object in reified form. In this treatment, by contrast, money is a distinctive institution with continually evolving rules and with explicit, although changing, interfaces with other social institutions.

These authors analyze "flows" of people, analogous to biochemistry (Padgett and McLean 2006, 1468–1470, 1544). The metaphor of chemical catalytic processes and protein folding is useful, but more insight might be gained by seeing the "flows" as financial circuits, the "liquidity" of which is provided by money. To expand this alternative metaphor, money is the ocean and corporations are the sea-worthy vessels, and all relationships are altered in this new universal solvent.

That is, the use of money follows certain rules, which then reshape existing institutions. By examining the historical tendency for the increasing extent of the market and the increasing use of money as a means of payment, store of value, and unit of account, the emergence of money as a tool of power also changes the shape of the state as well as the family, knowledge production, and structure of space.

Building on insights of Poovey and Searle, as well as Padgett, Powell, and McLean, we focus here on central institutions, the key concepts and their interpretations, as well as the expertise which interprets and guides their development over time (Davis 2015).

One example is the historic role of lawyers and their guild in maintaining traditional canonical interpretations of Roman and common law. The lawyers gain authority and influence by means of their expert knowledge of existing rules, norms, and practices, but may adjust them to new situations on behalf of their clients, while maintaining their own power in the process (Martines 1968). Another example is the emerging role of merchants, bankers, notaries, money changers, and accountants, who become a new set of powerful experts. As cities and states gain experience in the production and circulation of coin and merchants gain experience in expansion of long-distance trade and the development of credit instruments, their expertise is more valued and their role in governing institutions expands, further reshaping the reliance on their unique specialization. Other persons and groups who are affected by these new instruments may join to form a new coalition or group, which further defends and expands the use of money and credit. Existing forms like "corporations," which are already well known, accepted, and part of legitimate governance (Najemy 1982), may be adapted to new uses, like companies and merchant courts.

II. Coinage

Coinage emerged before the Christian era. Numismatic accounts describe issuance of coin by rulers, first to collect tribute, and then to facilitate tax payments (Davies 1994; Grierson 1975; Stahl 2000). The phenomenon of coinage, rather than direct exchange of ingots or bullion, indicates a symbolic function. Often coins are dated and "sealed" with the image of the ruler and specified by territory. This use of "writing" on coins (Poovey 1998) serves to personalize the issuer, contrary to the usual notion of money as abstract, symbolic, and impersonal. This suggests that coinage is part of a projection of power of the ruler. The authority of the ruler attests to the quality of the coin, and the circulation of the coin helps accrue power to the ruler (Ferguson 2001). The motivation for coinage by medieval communes and monarchs included prestige and political ambition, often in imitation of an earlier coin, such as the gold Roman *solidus* (Lopez 1956, 225, 236–240; Vilar 1976, 30–31). Global movements in coin and bullion were influenced by mining, trade, and conquest (Richards 1983).

For the medieval state, the mint had two distinct, and often opposing, functions: to provide a medium of exchange and a source of revenue for the fisc. Coinage also served to enhance the "prestige and renown of the rulers ... coinage was the one emanation of official authority that virtually every subject would experience in a personal and physical way" (Stahl 2000, 99). The "politics of monetary policy" involved a diverse constituency, including merchants, speculators, money changers, bankers, salaried workers, officials, mintmasters, and weighers, as well as wealthy families (Stahl 2000, 112–125).

Spufford places emphasis on the increase in the production of coin after the fall of the Roman Empire. Types and quantities of coin are documented (Spufford 1988, Appendix III, 415–422, for mining activities, mint production, and money stock estimates).

> The increase in the supply of money may not have been directly a cause of the late medieval commercial revolution, but it was a necessary precondition for it. (Spufford 2002, 59)

Feudalism was the result of a shortage of coin, in his view (Spufford 1988, 7, 16). Carolingian mints provided some additional coin, with centralized control under Charlemagne (Spufford 1988, 42–48). Subsequent fragmentation of authority led to local control of mints (Spufford 1988, 55–57, 105). In the medieval period, the dominant gold coins were the *bezant*, from Byzantium, and the Muslim *dinar* (Vilar 1969, 30–35).

City-states were prominent in the issue of coin as early as the thirteenth century in Italy. Genoa received a charter from the Emperor Conrad II to coin money in perpetuity in 1138 (Tracy 2003, 23). Silver coin of common weight and value were issued in Pisa in the 1220s, followed in the 1230s by Siena, Lucca, Florence, and Arezzo; England, in 1257; Perugia in 1259; and Rome in 1270 (Blomquist 1987, 320, 322; Davies 1994, 144; Goldthwaite 2009, 28, 48–57, 609–614; Lopez 1956, 235–236, 238). Even though there was a common money of account, the actual coins were recorded in notarial documents with city of origin identified (Blomquist 1994, 341). Frederick II had minted his own gold coin, the *Augustalis*, in imitation of the Roman imperial prerogatives (Walker 1983, 29). Mints of gold coin in Tuscany arose in the 1250s due to conflict between the pope and the empire, as well as increase in trade, first in Genoa, Florence, and then Lucca (Blomquist 1987; Goldthwaite 2009, 49; Lopez 1956, 229–230). Gold from mines in Africa had been a traditional resource for coinage in the Muslim trade of the high middle ages and was imitated by crusader coins until prohibited in 1250 by papal edict (Walker 1983, 30–31, 39–40, 44). The death of Frederick II in 1250 also provided an opportunity for a new coin from the merchant city-states. The rapid shift in control of the Mediterranean from Muslim to Christian enabled the increased access to bullion in sufficient scale (Walker 1983, 33, 45–46).

Unlike Venice, the guilds in Florence had a role in the mint (Edgcumbe 1906, 566-573). The florin was issued by the Commune of Florence in 1252 (Edgcumbe 1906, 172). "The Florentine *fiorino d'oro* became the most widely sought and the most valued coin in the money markets of the West and beyond for the next two and a half centuries" (Blomquist 1987, 317; italics in original). Although the gold coin of Venice, the ducat, appeared later in 1284, it maintained its hegemony for 500 years because of the strength of its position in world trade (Lopez 1956, 236–237; Richards 1983, 11).

The rise of coinage available from mints and mines in Europe provided the foundation for the rise of trade in the thirteenth century. Long-distance trade in turn provided the scale necessary for further division of labor in the founding of companies, banks, and stock markets (Spufford 1988, 251–263), where a quantitative change enabled a qualitative one. Lords took the initiative to convert feudal obligations into money, and they could maintain an advantage in periods of inflation by changes in the form of the contract (Spufford 1988, 242–245; 2002, 64–65). The state could also squeeze peasants by levying taxes in money.

There were benefits of seigniorage (Munro 1972, 21–23, 25–27) and international competition for bullion (Munro 1972, 32). There was a pattern of a drain of coinage from West to East due to Western demand for Eastern luxury goods and spices and a continual balance of payments deficit in the period of 1000–1500, in spite of gains made during the Crusades of the thirteenth century (Attman 1981, 13–18; Walker 1983, 39–42).

There was a change in attitudes toward money (Spufford 2002, 57–58). Resources came to be judged in terms of the money they could bring (Spufford 1988, 245–246). There was also a change in attitudes toward lending, with prohibitions of usury circumvented (Spufford 1988, 259). Money payments provided the foundation for a reorganization of government, no longer based on land and the associated obligations (Spufford 2002, 63–64).

There was a change in the division of space, with the merchant "fondaco" established in foreign cities to facilitate trade (Spufford 1988; 136, 146; 2002, 20–21, 352–353, 393–395; Walker 1983, 45–46). These special sites for conducting trade were also known as merchant "nations" (Gelderblom 2013, 17, 22–25), for their city-state of origin. In contrast to the merchant "nations" (Gelderblom 2013, 17, 22–25; Padgett 2012a, 126–129, 133, 135–139, 137, 143; Spufford 2002, 20–21, 24, 50–52, 312, 352–353, 393–395), the Hanseatic League established a *kontor* in Bruges (Cecchini and Pezzolo 2012, 102–104; Munro 1972, 104–105). The rise of the bourse followed to allow for the further centralization of trade, regardless of the place of origin (Spufford 2002, 50–52).

The commutation of feudal ties to rent in the twelfth century (Spufford 1988, 242–245) provided the foundation for geographic mobility. Nobles could relocate near the court, in the process forming capital cities, where the increase of the market provided for further division of labor (Spufford 2002,

63, 74–75, 84–85, 88–93). The increase in money incomes provided the basis for the market for luxury goods. There was a subsequent monetization of the rural economy, with the provision of food and resources from the hinterland (Spufford 2002, 95–106).

With the increase in the use of money, there were also opportunities for experiences of abstraction. For example, there were "moneys of account" (Carter and Goldthwaite 2013, 124, 131; Goldthwaite 2009, 57, 488; Lane and Mueller 1985; Padgett and McLean 2011, 14; Walker 1983, 41–42, 45), which helped to mediate between the large varieties of coin. Personal account books were kept in the third person (Carter and Goldthwaite 2013, 125). There was offsetting of equal values of commodities and coin (Carter and Goldthwaite 2013, 129; Goldthwaite 2009, 458–462). There was no adding up to assess total wealth in a given period (Carter and Goldthwaite 2013, 133, 139; Goldthwaite 2009, 58–60; Poovey 1998, 41–65), except by the state in the Catasto of 1427 (Padgett and McLean 2011, 4). Double-entry bookkeeping expressed the social relationship of the writer to the firm (Padgett and McLean 2011, 14–15). Rather than adding up an accumulation of financial assets, there was investment in land, dowries, companies, and public securities. The role of money was different in this period—without a monopoly of currency by the state, without a large wage labor force, with hereditary constraints on the market for land, without routine identification of what constitutes "property" and commodities by centralized legal and judicial institutions. There was a tendency to mix personal and company accounts, as well as credit, partly due to the role of credit in constituting an elite status and the importance of dowries in extension of credit (McLean and Gondal 2014).

> Clearly, name, reputation, and connections were more central in the generation of commercial credit in the fifteenth-century Florence than was asset security. (Padgett and McLean 2011, 8)

The transition from an economy in which money had a minor role to one in which it was "the measure of all things" took place during the "long thirteenth century" (Spufford 1988, 240–245; 2002, 65). The increasing dominance of money was due to the ongoing changes in banks, companies, and forms of governance, as well as geography of settlement patterns (Spufford 2002, 93–94, 389–390) and technology of transportation. In addition to trust and familiarity, the expansion of financial markets depended on a foundation in law and the courts (Epstein 2006, 240–245; Munro 2000).

In spite of its material form, the importance of money is based on social institutions.

> The mechanics that make money useful are in the society rather than in the money itself. Alone on a desert island, we would find a dollar bill to be practically worthless … It is amazing that the socially sanctioned production of a simple material object can result in a material anchor

that radically reorganizes social practice, with dramatic consequences for human culture generally. (Fauconnier and Turner 2002, 202–203)

The use of money as coin facilitated the abstraction of a general relationship of exchange. The material manifestation of coin gave a concrete sense of the experience of exchange, along with the availability of a wide variety of valuable commodities for consumption. With this social experience of abstraction came greater confidence and the spread of norms of exchange and legal enforcement mechanisms. The presence of rudimentary forms of credit facilitated liquidity and the extension of credit, which then facilitated the development of yet further innovations in credit instruments.

III. Emerging Political and Religious Perspectives

The political strategy of nation-states was influenced by the role of coin and bullion (Stern and Wennerlind 2014). The use of bullion to pay soldiers was an important motive for mercantilism.

In later mercantilist writings, one often finds this "war-chest" argument for acquiring bullion: that "treasure is the sinews of war." (Munro 1972, 12)

Strategies to economize on bullion included bills of exchange and deposit banking (more common among the Italians) as well as debasement of coinage (Munro 1972, 15–23; 2012). An early form of monetary policy was the development of export and import charges to acquire bullion and granting of monopoly privileges to the Staple Company in 1363 (Munro 1972, 36–41) and the Merchants Adventurers in 1421 (Munro 1972, 68–69). The English Parliament prohibited the export of all forms of precious metals, including gold and silver, in the form of bullion or coin, from 1364 to 1663 and maintained the ban on the export of English coin until 1819 (Munro 2012, 2–3).

Ideas regarding legitimate financial practices also changed in this period. Bills of exchange were used to circumvent prohibitions on usury (Carter and Goldthwaite 2013, 157–159). The *censo* was exempted from usury prohibition in 1569 (Carter and Goldthwaite 2013, 162–164), along with the Monte di Pieta (Carter and Goldthwaite 2013, 164–171). Government securities such as the Monte Commune in Florence in 1222 (Najemy 2006a, 139–141, 169–70) and in the 1340s were exempt from usury charges. The papacy in the late fifteenth century, when consolidating control over its territory, issued *luoghi*, interest-bearing certificates, transferable in a secondary market, with no fixed duration (Carter and Goldthwaite 2013, 169–173).

IV. Changes in Corporate Form

In the medieval and early modern period, the corporate form was important for innovations in governance (Davis 2015, 69–81), which included the church, commune, guild, company, and bank, as well as the liberal state based on mobile financial property. The commune as a cooperative collective institution was an "ideal type." The opening for its emergence in the early modern period was provided by the Investiture Controversy between the pope and the Holy Roman Emperor (Wickham 2015, 9, 15–18). There were chartered cities in the Low Countries as early as 1066 (Blockmans 2010, 317–318). Merchant guilds were formed for mutual protection as early as 1072 (Blockmans 2010, 318–319). The "corporation" was one of the most important innovations in Western political theory (Epstein 2006, 242–245).

A. Church, Guild, and Commune

The corporate form originated in the Church, a body separate from the individuals who compose it, with infinite life, discrete rules of operation, and insignia to represent its separate identity (Davis 2015, 69–70; Epstein 2006, 243–244; Padgett 2012a, 122–124, 139–140, 141–142). Padgett proposes that the church was an active agent in the recruitment of merchant partnerships into its operation, not just providing a metaphor of the corporation, to facilitate the financing of the Crusades and ultimately affected the form and role of the family (Padgett 2012a, 124–127, 140–144). The so-called Italian Crusades conducted by the pope against the Holy Roman Empire required funding in advance of collection of tithes. Tuscan banks from Lucca, Siena, and Florence provided this financing, in return for dispensation and for authority for collection of revenues (Padgett 2012a, 129–133). The Papal State provided an early model for public finance, with concentrated immediate needs for dispersal, and with long-term, geographically dispersed revenue sources. The model of the "corporation" was available from the church itself and from family and military organizations. A model of a central bank office with dispersed branches developed in this context, replacing the merchant caravans at regional fairs. The "camera," first referring to the pope's bedroom, was later transferred to the context of the state legislative bodies (Padgett 2012a, 129).

The Champagne Fairs, beginning in 1127 (Spufford 2002, 48–50, 134–136, 144–149, 161–163; Gelderblom 2013; Blockmans 2010, 320–321), were an important innovation in financial exchange. Fairs were organized by Genoa in Besancon, France, in 1535, which provided an integrated capital market to process Spanish silver and to provide gold for the payment of mercenaries for Spain's many wars (Pezzolo and Tattara 2008). There was a special currency of account, the *Scudo di Marco*, and a short-term fixed exchange rate on a form of bill of exchange, the *pactum de ricorsa*, enforced by Genoese authorities according to Genoese law that avoided the prohibition on usury. Competition among city-states facilitated the development of mercantile practices (Gelderblom 2013). Customs duties from trade were an important source of fiscal revenue in this period (Cecchini and Pezzolo 2012, 108–109).

Other corporate forms developed rapidly, such as the craft guild and the political party. The corporate form of the craft guilds (Cohn 1980; Epstein

2006, 2013; Najemy 1982) had an important role in urban government in Flanders after 1302 (Blockmans 2010, 321–322), as well as in Padua, Bologna, Rome, Milan, and Florence (Najemy 1979, 57). "Guild republicanism first became a reality in Florence during the 1290s" (Najemy 1979, 58). Florence is unique among other leading city-states like Genoa and Venice for the strong corporate guild system, as well as patrilineage (Padgett and McLean 2006, 1545–1547). Political parties were another form of organization, related to conflicts between the pope and emperor, the Guelfs and the Ghibellines (Blockmans 2010, 322–323; Padgett 2012a, 129–133; Tracy 2002, 39-41), and between elite factions competing for electoral supremacy (Padgett and Ansell 1993).

B.   Business Partnerships

There were new forms of business organization, such as the partnership, as well as *colleganza* and *commenda* contracts (Spufford 2002, 22–25, 43; Trivellato 2009a) and merchant *nazione* (Goldthwaite 2009, 108–109). The "corpo" was the amount of capital initially advanced by the partners in a company (Padgett 2012a, 122, 125; Spufford 2002, 22–25). Dowries were used as "start-up capital" (Padgett 2010, 389), and partnerships were modeled on the marriage contract (Padgett and McLean 2006, 1519–1521).

The "partnership system" as a new organizational form, with limited liability, resembling a "holding company," and double-entry bookkeeping emerged in 1383 (Padgett 2012b, 173–174, 192–201; Padgett and McLean 2006, 1465–1466, 1476). Padgett attributes this change in form to political challenges surrounding the *Ciompi* rebellion in Florence in 1378, the war with the papacy, the decline in business in Europe at the same time, and the consolidation of newly wealthy bankers into the elite in Florence. From a corporate guild organizational form, there developed a more individualized entrepreneurial form, with financial controls based on new accounting techniques.

The causes of the *Ciompi* revolt include greater confidence in the articulation of grievances, as well as changes in the real value of wages (Cipolla 1982, 77–78; Cohn 1980). There was a peasant revolt of 1381 in England, as well as other parts of Europe (Cohn 2006).

C.   Merchant Monopoly Trading Companies

The first monopoly trading companies were the Staple Company in 1363 (Munro 1972, 38–41), the Merchants Adventurers in 1421 (Munro 1972, 68–69), and the Levant Company in 1581 (Attman 1981, 24–25). In addition to the use of monopoly privileges to control trade, there were also restrictions on the export of bullion, and the requirement of payment in-kind in wool (Munro 1972, 35–36; Padgett 2012a, 126, 133, 136).

> Mercantilist English law prohibited the export of precious metal from the kingdom, so loans to the English king had to be repaid in raw wool, coming

largely from monasteries ... The enormous consequence for the Florentine economy was the diversion of high-quality English wool exports from their original destination of Flanders to the newly developing textile industry of Florence. Florence thereby came to displace Flanders as the primary center for wool-textile production in Europe. (Padgett 2012a, 126)

D. Banks

As discussed above, banks emerged from the partnership system. The first banks were in Venice, Genoa, and Florence, developing from the Tuscan fairs (McLean and Padgett 2004; Padgett and McLean 2006, 1546; 2011, 44–45; Spufford 2002, 34–43).

The original Medici bank of Vieri di Cambio de' Medici was founded in 1349 (Padgett and McLean 2006, 1532–1533). The Florence branch of the Medici bank dealt extensively with shares of the Monte Commune (De Roover 1963, 236–237). Lorenzo drew large sums from the state (de Roover 1948, 364–365, 366–367; 1963). The Medici bank also benefited from papal relations, with the Rome branch consistently the most profitable (De Roover 1963, 40–41, 47–48, 55, 106–107, 199–202, 205–207, 210, 216–217, 370). The Rome branch had the highest outstanding debt of any Florence bank, yet its startup capital was zero. "Clearly, name, reputation, and connections were more central in the generation of commercial credit in fifteenth-century Florence than was asset security" (Padgett and McLean 2011, 8). After the Pazzi conspiracy, there was a backlash from the papacy, which served to weaken the bank (De Roover 1963, 221–222, 366). The Medici bank also made decisions based on political alliances rather than private business, such as opening the branch in Ancona to maintain the Sforza alliance with Milan (De Roover 1963, 59, 64, 70–71, 372). Alliances with other monarchs were important to maintain trade privileges and financial accounts (Najemy 2006, 116–117, 133–134).

The Medici bank was innovative and well managed in many respects. It was, however, a bank based on a family, and on occasion hired personnel based on family connections rather than merit. This pattern is evident in the promotion of Giovanni Tornabuoni, a brother-in-law of Piero, as well as in the succession of sons after Cosimo, whose talents and interests were not fully engaged in banking (de Roover 1961, 220, 358). Profits from the bank were often invested in expansion of the company with many new branches in the early years. Nonetheless the Medici family also valued patronage (politics and arts), purchase of land, marriage alliances, and positions in the papacy, rather than a strict focus on the original source of the family wealth (de Roover 1961, 5, 48, 59, 64, 70–71, 216, 218–224, 229, 361–363, 365, 368, 372).

In spite of the "compelling evidence for viewing late medieval Italy as the birthplace of modern capitalism ... political participation was, if anything, a more vital component of a life well led than was commercial enterprise" (McLean and Padgett 2004, 196–197). That is, "economic life *is* itself inherently a social sphere of life" (McLean and Padgett 2004, 193–194; italics in original). There was a "porous interpenetration, or *co-constitution* ... of economic and other social networks in early fifteenth-century Florence" (McLean and Padgett 2004, 193–194; italics in original).

E. Merchant Guild

A commercial innovation was the *Mercanzia* in early city-states. Founded in Florence in 1308, the *Mercanzia* represented the elite guilds and their special concerns with international trade. At various times, the *Mercanzia* was responsible for determining trade reprisals, naming the treasurer for the mint, resolving debt and bankruptcies, regulating new instruments of insurance, and issuing letters of credit (Astorri and Friedman 2005, 18–29). A similar institution was found in Bologna, Florence, Siena, Venice, Milan, Genoa, Lucca, and Verona (Astorri and Friedman 2005; Boschetto 2011, 227–228; Friedman 1998; Goldthwaite 2009, 109–114; Najemy 2006a; Ravid 1994).

"For the protection of their collective interests the international import-export merchants and bankers of the five major commercial guilds ... formed the *universitas mercatorum*, or *Mercanzia* ... The *Mercanzia*'s chief purpose was to prevent reprisals and enhance the security of Florentines 'throughout the world' by forcing Florentine merchants to honor their agreements and satisfy creditors (Najemy 2006a, 110). The *Mercanzia* functioned like a merchant court, beyond the specialization of the guilds and beyond the territory of Florence proper. During the bankruptcies of the 1343s, the *Mercanzia* was responsible for resolving the debts of the Peruzzi and Bardi banks (Najemy 2006a, 141–144). This powerful role of a guild-based institution may have alarmed the elite concerning the potential threat of guild republicanism (Najemy 1979, 61–65). In a later regime of 1382, the *Mercanzia* was used as a method of controlling the other guilds within the redesigned electoral process (Padgett and McLean 2006, 1505–1508).

F. Public Finance

The consolidation of public debt, the *monte commune*, was another innovation in public finance. Genoa was the first Italian city-state to consolidate public debt in 1149. Venice followed in 1262, Siena in 1287, Florence in 1343, and Lucca in 1370 (Munro 2003, 514–515; Tracy 2003, 20–24). There was a historical pattern in the particular form of finance. Most city-states with forced loans were republican, as opposed to voluntary floating loans from cities governed by signori, as in Milan (Munro 2003, 515). Seen as necessary to fulfill the duty of citizens to protect the commune, many theologians and jurists made exceptions to interest on public debt, because it was required for the public good (compared with voluntary loans and usury). Florentine shares were negotiable and transferable and were widely held by the population (Becker 1968, 157–159; Munro 2003, 516, 546).

Florence expenses as a commune were moderate until times of war, particularly for payment of mercenaries (Becker 1968, 151–152, 154–155; Molho 1971, 9–21). Taxes on trade and necessities provided the requisite funds until financing of territorial expansion required property taxation and forced loans (Najemy 2006, 118–123). Even so, public debt continued to increase, especially after 1315, requiring more direct forms of management.

Florence had a variety of taxes, including sales taxes and property taxes, starting from the thirteenth century. The Monte Commune of Florence was formed in 1343 by the third popular government to consolidate public debt (Becker 1968, 156; De Roover 1963, 22; Najemy 2006, 137–144; Zorzi 2004, 153). Sales taxes (gabelles) were levied on necessities like salt and grain and collected on other items at the gates of the city. Forced loans (prestanze) were levied on all citizens. Those who were able to pay in full received interest payments. Those unable to pay in full did not receive interest payments, converting these forced loans into a form of property taxes. The wealthy were given opportunities for restricted loans paying interest rates of 10 to 15 percent, with interest payments guaranteed by the assignment of the gabelles (Najemy 2006, 118–120). The ability to pay and the level of interest rates on the debt varied by period and type of government, with progressive property taxes and ceilings on interest rates most often characteristic of the popular governments. The catasto, a property tax introduced by the Albizzi government in 1427, was progressive (de Roover 1963, 21–28).

> The adoption of the catasto constituted one of the most significant enactments in the history of Florence … Niccolo Machiavelli, in a characteristically pithy statement, suggested that for the first time the Florentines had agreed to be ruled by impartial and unchangeable laws rather than by the arbitrary decisions of human beings. (Molho 1971, 81–83)

Qualifications for public office included complete payment of taxes, and often positive contributions to the public treasury as well (Herlihy 1991, 199, 212–213).

> By the 1350s, virtually every Florentine active in civic affairs was a large shareholder in the Monte … By 1380 there were some 5,000 Florentines holding Monte stock. This was perhaps one-twelfth of the population – a total approximating the propertied class of the polis … the state was indeed no mere abstraction. (Becker 1968, 158–159)

Tax farming was replaced by a communal bureaucracy in 1344 (Becker 1968, 161, 165). Tax levies on citizens of the city were often more favorable than those in the contado (Petralia 2000, 75–78, 81–82). In the early fourteenth century, there were plans to consolidate the administration and finance of the new territories (Zorzi 2000, 15, 18). Financial crises as well as rebellions in the mountains were the occasions for administrative change in Florence (Brown 2000, 35–36; Cohn 1999, 4–6; 2000, 204–206). Florence also taxed the clergy for military expenses, while the clergy recognized the sacred authority of the government of Florence, including the oversight of the oath of office and balloting procedures (Peterson 2000, 137–139, 142–143).

Public life began to cluster around the funded communal debt, until the officials of the Monte came to be numbered among the most influential and revered of the state's elected officers. Florence was well on the way to becoming a giant corporation in which the middling and affluent citizenry had invested a very substantial portion of their patrimony. (Becker 1968, 162, 245)

The consolidation of public debt may have served the population at large by providing a financially safe asset. Before 1340, the restricted loans provided a "secure and lucrative form of investment for the wealthy" as well (Najemy 2006, 120). In later years when the Monte itself was administered by its creditors, it may have operated in the interest of the ruling elite (Molho 1971, 63–68, 102–103, 110). As evidence of this concern, in 1420, there was a ban on speculators in Monte debt becoming members of that office (Molho 1971, 121–122). The fiscal crisis of the 1430s may have been an additional cause of the change in government in this period (Molho 1971, 183–192).

G. Joint Stock Corporation

Based upon and extending innovations by Italians in banking and finance, the Dutch Republic was able to develop the first joint stock company in 1602, the Dutch East India Company, or VOC, integrating the Dutch Reform Church, the federal system of provinces, and the company form in homologous corporate form (Padgett 2012c).

As voyages were extended in scale and time, the companies existed for longer periods (Gelderblom and Jonker 2004, 645, 648). With limited liability, there developed a secondary market in VOC shares, and speculative trades became more common (Gelderblom and Jonker 2004, 649, 653–654, 655–658). Because of liquidity of shares, they also served as collateral for loans with a decline in interest rates reflecting the increasing attraction of investment from beyond the Dutch Republic in this market (Gelderblom and Jonker 2004, 643, 659–660, 663–664). Experience with both public and private debt extended trust in paper credit and helped develop the financial market in Amsterdam.

In the Venice model, there was a public role in financing shipbuilding and trade ventures, with important military complementarities (Cecchini and Pezzolo 2012, 92, 93–95, 107–109). In contrast, in Florence, business partnerships were often formed by family (Cecchini and Pezzolo 2012, 99, 104). Banks were differentiated by function, domestic deposit, or gyro banks, allowing Florence to serve international banking (Padgett and McLean 2006, 1546) and Genoa and the Fuggers international bullion flows.

On the other hand, the Genoa model (Marsilio 2012) had a relationship with Spain as its "symbiotic empire." With Spain controlling territories, Genoa provided the financing of the empire (Dauverd 2015) in an innovative form of the *Casa Di San Giorgio* (Taviani 2015).

V. Family, Network, and Class

One form of public debt was the dowry fund. The public debt was funded and marriage was secured to stabilize the family by means of the *Monte Delle Doti* (Kirshner and Molho 1978; Molho 1971, 140).

> By transforming the communal government into the guarantor of the matrimonial alliances engineered by members of the Florentine ruling class, the dowry fund reflected, and at the same time sustained, the political hegemony of that class. (Kirshner and Molho 1978, 436)

Patrilineal families with a common name emerged from the post-*Ciompi* cooptation of *popolani* families into a new merchant/public servant elite (Padgett 2010, 393–395, 402–405), a mid-sixteenth-century phenomenon (Carter and Goldthwaite 2013, 181).

> With the rise of the large, unitary merchant-banks in the mid-1200s, however, international merchant-bankers became associated with popes and kings ... Successful bankers in unitary banks became noble-mimicking patrilineages through bringing sons and relatives into the bank and through purchasing property in their native city and its countryside ... Company *corpo* became family patrimony. It also integrated bankers into the ruling patriciate of their city. (Padgett 2012a, 127)

That is, new forms of work organization and trade had an associated impact on family and class.

VI. Changes in Space

First finance was central to the extension of trade. Then, with greater access to funds, there were more frequent wars, shifting the territorial boundaries of nations (Neal 2015, 109–124).

The shifting role of the urban center was apparent in its architecture and urban design. First, the family towers marked neighborhoods as defensive enclaves, then public spaces for the new republican government, followed by the formation of a new elite and their great palaces, and finally the Medici principate (Najemy 2006b, 19–20).

> Florence's spaces were both sites of political control and resistance and also loci of symbolic and ideological power ... The ritual, processional, and festive dimension of politics likewise existed in symbiotic relationship with city spaces ... The history of political space in late medieval and Renaissance Florence can be plotted through four broadly successive, but overlapping, phases. (Najemy 2006b, 19)

There was a reshaping and relocating of institutions in Renaissance Florence as exemplified by the "old" and "new" buildings, from guild republics to Medici palaces (Bargello, Mercato Centrale and Nuovo, Palazzo of Signoria, Palazzo Vechio, and Pitti Palazzo) (Najemy 2006b).

The classic evolution of the Western city can be viewed in response to the emergence of the market, from walled city and fortress on the hill, with the major distinction between urban and rural divisions of labor, with centralized functions in the city center, such as church and court. Then later, with the increasing division of labor, the marketplace became the city center. Further, there emerged hierarchies of cities in terms of centralization within regions (Gelderblom 2013, 4–5, 15, 19; Fujita, Krugman, and Venables 1999). Paris was redesigned to symbolize the center of the empire (Harvey 2003).

The geography of innovating cities is like a cigar shape or banana, as the locus of mercantile trade centers shifted from the urban centers from Northern Italy to the Low Countries to England (Arrighi 1994; Blockmans 1994, 218–228; Epstein 2006, 240–241, 252, 253–259; 2013, 26; Gelderblom 2013, 4–5, 10–18; Spufford 2002, 389–390).

VII.   Repurposing Institutions and Financial Innovations

Organizational design and governance also shifted. The role of trade extended horizontal connections, and the hierarchy of finance changed relationships within the firm and the city, as well as among cities.

For example, merchants extended relationships horizontally, across long-distance trade networks, and then vertically, gaining power within a given state by means of political party, and then through competition, reshaping the form of the states. The *Mercanzia* was a general form that emerged from the guild structure, with a specialized cross-cutting role, which then became hierarchical in relation to the craft guilds (Astorri and Friedman 2005; Najemy 1982; Padgett and McLean 2006, 1499, 1505, 1508).

Money as a governance system tends to emphasize hierarchy, given the advantages of spanning the horizon to select the best and most profitable opportunity and technology. For example, the diagram of the credit "network" in Florence has the international merchant banks at the top and the cloth retailers at the bottom (Padgett and McLean 2006, 1483; 2011, 9). There are also economies of scale in credit, with the increase in investment options and the diversification of risk. On the other hand, there is a horizontal dimension, with the scope of the population that uses a given currency increasing its liquidity, which makes an equal commitment to the financial promises, and which can validate a given form of credit. The form of the partnership system, like the holding company, gives more emphasis to the hierarchical dimension, with the transition of the entrepreneur to the financier with international contacts and networks (Padgett and McLean 2006, 1535–1539). There is also an internal management dimension, where factors and partners are held accountable to results based on double-entry bookkeeping (Padgett and McLean 2006, 1539–1543, 1547). With the development of the partnership system after 1382, the senior partners evolved from being "industry-specific entrepreneurs into being cross-industry financiers" (Padgett and McLean 2011, 31).

As another example of the impact of trade, the Low Countries were a center of trade throughout the early modern period. This enabled the Dutch Republic to build an entrepot function, especially after the blockade of Antwerp in 1585 (de Vries and Woude 1994, 134–139, 147–158, 362–376). As a result of the Bank of Amsterdam policies, a trade in money developed alongside the trade in commodities, along with market information provided by the *Price Courant* and specialized financial services, such as insurance and brokerage. The availability of alternative financial assets and international capital investment may have actually drawn funds away from productive investment in the Dutch economy to the role of *rentier* (Adams 2005).

VIII.   Changes in Knowledge and Ideas

The experience of self-government in the communes and city-states provided an opportunity to articulate governance principles. The opening for guilds occurred due to the large-scale factional struggles between the pope and the Holy Roman Emperor, which were also mirrored by the internal aristocratic factions between the Guelfs and the Ghibellines (Najemy 1982, 4–5). The search for a stable government rested on the articulation of legitimate principles, as well as the development of practices, such as the process of nominations of eligible citizens, random selection of incumbents to the executive council, and limited terms of office (Najemy 1982, 14–16). The original documents still preserved in the archives of Florence attest to the importance of these debates.

The term "guild republicanism" refers to the reliance on the guilds to model and to enforce fair principles of governance (Najemy 1979; 1982, 8–10).

A corporation was inherently the free creation of its members, acting voluntarily and in concert. The powers exercised in the name of the corporation were held to reside in the community of the members. The membership of the corporation, or a council representing the same, delegated those [powers] to elected heads, who served for limited terms and with the specific mandate to preside over the corporation, or to represent it, within the limits of its written constitution, according to the will of the majority, and for the common good of the community. (Najemy 1979, 56)

In the second half of the thirteenth century, with increasing population growth and migration, "wave after wave of new social and professional groups began to organize themselves in societies, confraternities, and guilds" (Najemy 1979, 56). Federations or unions of guilds, "representing coalitions of new or newly prominent social classes," were achieved in Padua, Bologna, Rome, Milan, and Florence in the thirteenth century (Najemy 1979, 57), with an increasing role in the government of the communes.

A formal role in the governance of Florence for the guilds was a subject of electoral debate in November 1292 and formalized in January 1293, with significant additional episodes in the 1340s and 1380s as well (Najemy 1979, 58–59, 61–67; 1982). The principles of guild republicanism could in principle be extended to include the minor guilds and to workers not yet organized into guilds. This challenge was expressed in the *Ciompi* rebellion of 1378 and represented a threat to the existing guild leadership, as well as the elite families.

The shift from guild corporatism to republican oligarchy was accompanied by a new set of ideas: the resolution of conflict between patrilineages and guilds resulted in "civic humanism" (Pagdett and McLean 2006, 1473, 1497–1499) or "discursive republicanism" (Baker 2014). From the response to this challenge, the ideas of civic humanism were developed, including the "abstract idea of a state that existed above parties and factions, and that derived its legitimacy from the express or implied consensus of its politically active citizens" (Najemy 1979, 53).

> Bruni grounded his new republicanism in the centralized sovereignty of the state and in the consensus of a broad, unified, and undifferentiated political class. (Najemy 1979, 70)

In this transition, the numbers of eligible citizens increased, while the formal corporate representation and deliberation was eliminated. In my view, the corporate form shifted to the level of the state, and the "equal" individual citizens replaced the idea of equal guilds in a federated republic. "Popular consent" was still the foundation of the "popular will" of the "whole people," but now expressed through a "general assembly" or "parlamento," rather than a federation of equal, autonomous guilds with direct representation in government (Najemy 1982, 267–268).

These representative institutions may have played a role in Europe's innovation of public debt. The important factor may have been an "open elite" where electoral institutions allowed the observation and training of candidates for office (Padgett and McLean 2011). On the other hand, representative assembly dominated by merchants may have assured creditors of their commitment (Stasavage 2015). Large territorial states learned from city-states, and in some cases relied on cities and towns within their territories for credit, such as France's reliance on royal rentes sur l'hotel de ville in 1522 for credit to the crown, and the Castile monarchy's reliance on 18 towns (Stasavage 2015, 11).

Money, like the *panopticon*, is a source of visibility and a technique of surveillance, especially with standardized accounting and financial control (Padgett and McLean 2006, 1467, 1473, 1542–1543).

IX.   Summary

There was a tipping point of succession of forms of the state, from religious, then secular self-governing communes, to hereditary monarch, to the mercantile and "liberal" state. The definition of the "liberal" state is based on the primacy of commerce and industry and the circulation of money as a token of power, as a means of mobilization of resources, both human and natural, and a means of accumulation.

Money is a tool of abstraction, increasingly accepted to facilitate trade. In turn, money has modified all other aspects of life, including work, family, geography, and governance. Using a historical approach, the long-term evolution of these complex systems can be better understood.

Bibliography

Adams, Julia. *The Familial State: Ruling Families and Merchant Capitalism in Early Modern Europe*. Ithaca: Cornell University Press, 2005.

Armstrong, Lawrin. "Usury, Conscience, and Public Debt: Angelo Corbinelli's Testament of 1419," in John A. Marino and Thomas Kuehn (eds.), *A Renaissance of Conflicts: Visions and Revisions of Law and Society in Italy and Spain*. Toronto: Centre for Reformation and Renaissance Studies, 2004, 173–240.

Armstrong, Lawrin and Julius Kirshner (eds.). *The Politics of Law in Late Medieval and Renaissance Italy*. Toronto: University of Toronto Press, 2011.

Arrighi, Giovanni. *The Long Twentieth Century: Money, Power, and the Origins of Our Times*. New York: Verso, 1994.

Astorri, Antonella and David Friedman. *The Florentine Mercanzia and Its Palace*. Firenze: Leo S. Olschki, 2005.

Attman, Artur. *The Bullion Flow between Europe and the East, 1000–1750*. Goteborg, Sweden: Kungl. Vetenskaps- och Vitterhets-Samhallet, 1981.

Baker, Nicholas Scott. *The Fruit of Liberty: Political Culture in the Florentine Renaissance, 1480–550*. Cambridge, MA: Harvard University Press, 2013.

_____. "Discursive Republicanism in Renaissance Florence: Deliberation and Representation in the Early Sixteenth Century," *Past and Present*, No. 225, 2014, 47–76.

Becker, Marvin B. *Florence in Transition. Vol. Two: Studies in the Rise of the Territorial State*. Baltimore, MD: Johns Hopkins University Press, 1968.

Biagioli, Mario. *Galileo, Courtier: The Practice of Science in the Culture of Absolutism*. Chicago: University of Chicago Press, 1993.

_____. *Galileo's Instruments of Credit: Telescopes, Images, Secrecy*. Chicago: University of Chicago Press, 2006.

Biagioli, Mario and Peter Galison. *Scientific Authorship: Credit and Intellectual Property in Science*. New York: Routledge, 2003.

Blockmans, Wim P. "Voracious States and Obstructing Cities: An Aspect of State Formation in Preindustrial Europe," in Charles Tilly and Wim P. Blockmans (eds.). *Cities and the Rise of States in Europe, A.D. 1000 to 1800*. Oxford: Westview Press, 1994, 218–250.

_____. "Inclusiveness and Exclusion: Trust Networks at the Origins of European Cities," *Theory and Society*, Vol. 39, 315–326, 2010.

Blockmans, Wim, Till-Holger Borchert, Nele Gabriels, Johan Oosterman, and Anne van Oosterwijk (eds.). *Staging the Court of Burgundy*: Proceedings of the Conference "The Splendour of Burgundy." London: Harvey Miller Publishers, 2013.

Blomquist, Thomas W. "The Second Issuance of a Tuscan Gold Coin: The Gold Groat of Lucca, 1256," *Journal of Medieval History*, Vol. 13, 1987, 317–325.

_____. "Alien Coins and Foreign Exchange Banking in a Medieval Commune: Thirteenth-Century Lucca," in *Journal of Medieval History*, Vol. 20, 1994, 337–346.

_____. *Merchant Families, Banking and Money in Medieval Lucca*. Burlington, VT: Ashgate/Variorum, 2005.

Boies, John and Harland Prechel. "Capital Dependence, Business Political Behavior, and Change to the Multilayered Subsidiary Form," *Social Problems*, Vol. 49, No. 3, 2002, 301–326.

Boschetto, Luca. "Writing the Vernacular at the Merchant Court of Florence," in William Robins (ed.), *Textual Cultures of Medieval Italy*. Toronto: University of Toronto Press, 2011, 217–262.

Brown, Alison. "Lorenzo, the Monte, and thex Seventeen Reformers," in Alison Brown (ed.), *The Medici in Florence: The Exercise and Language of Power*. Perth: University of Western Australia Press, 1992, 151–214.

_____. "The Language of Empire," in William J. Connell and Anrea Zorzi (eds.), *Florentine Tuscany: Structures and Practices of Power*. New York: Cambridge University Press, 2000, 32–47.

Brown, Peter. *Ransom of the Soul: Afterlife and Wealth in Early Western Christianity*. Cambridge, MA: Harvard University Press, 2015.

Butters, Humfrey C. "Conflicting Attitudes Towards Machiavelli's Works in Sixteenth-Century Spain, Rome and Florence," in John E. Law and Bernadette Paton (eds.), *Communes and Despots in Medieval and Renaissance Italy*. Burlington, VT: Ashgate, 2010, 75–87.

Carter, Tim and Richard A. Goldthwaite. *Orpheus in the Marketplace: Jacopo Peri and the Economy of Late Renaissance Florence*. Cambridge, MA: Harvard University Press, 2013.

Cecchini, Isabella and Luciano Pezzolo. "Merchants and Institutions in Early-Modern Venice," *Journal of European Economic History*, Vol. XLI, No. 2, 2012, 89–114.

Cipolla, Carlo M. *The Monetary Policy of Fourteenth-Century Florence*. Berkeley: University of California Press, 1982.

Cohn, Samuel Kline Jr. *The Laboring Classes in Renaissance Florence*. New York: Academic Press, 1980.

_____. *Creating the Florentine State: Peasants and Rebellion, 1348–1434*. New York: Cambridge University Press, 1999.

_____. "Demography and the Politics of Fiscality," in William J. Connell and Anrea Zorzi (eds.), *Florentine Tuscany: Structures and Practices of Power*. New York: Cambridge University Press, 2000, 183–206.

_____. *Lust for Liberty: The Politics of Social Revolt in Medieval Europe, 1200–1425: Italy, France, Flanders*. Cambridge, MA: Harvard University Press, 2006.

Dauverd, Celine. *Imperial Ambition in the Early Modern Mediterranean: Genoese Merchants and the Spanish Crown*. New York: Cambridge University Press, 2015.

Davis, Ann E. *The Evolution of the Property Relation: Understanding Paradigms, Debates, Prospects*. New York: Palgrave MacMillan, 2015.

Davies, Glyn. *A History of Money: From Ancient Time to the Present Day*. Cardiff, Wales: University of Wales Press, 1994.

De Roover, Raymond. *The Medici Bank: Its Organization, Management, Operation and Decline*. New York: New York University Press, 1948.

_____. *The Rise and Decline of the Medici Bank 1397–1494*. Cambridge, MA: Harvard University Press, 1963.

De Vries, Jan and Ad van der Woude. *The First Modern Economy: Success, Failure, and Perseverance of the Dutch Economy, 1500–1815*. New York: Cambridge University Press, 1994.

Dickson, P.G.M. *The Financial Revolution in England: a Study in the Development of Public Credit, 1688–1756*. New York: St. Martin's Press, 1967.

Edgcumbe, Staley. *The Guilds of Florence*. London: Methuen and Co., 1906.

Epstein, Stephan R. "Peasantries of Italy, 1350–1750," in Tom Scott (ed.), *The Peasantries of Europe from Fourteenth to the Eighteenth Centuries*. New York: Longman, 1998, 75–108.

_____. "The Rise of the West," in John A. Hall and Ralph Schroeder (eds.), *An Anatomy of Power: The Social Theory of Michael Mann*. New York: Cambridge University Press, 2006, 233–262.

_____. "Transferring Knowledge and Innovating in Europe," in Maarten Prak and Jan Luiten van Zanden (eds.), *Technology, Skills, and the Pre-Modern Economy in the East and West: Essays Dedicated to the Memory of S. R. Epstein*. Boston: Brill, 2013, 25–67.

Fauconnier, Gilles and Mark Turner. *The Way We Think: Conceptual Blending and the Mind's Hidden Complexities*. New York: Basic, 2002.

Feavearyear, A. E. *The Pound Sterling: A History of English Money*. Oxford, UK: Clarendon Press, 1931.

Ferguson, Niall. *The Cash Nexus: Money and Power in the Modern World, 1700–2000*. New York: Basic Books, 2001.

Friedman, David. "Monumental Urban Form in the Late Medieval Italian Commune: Loggias and the Mercanzie of Bologna and Siena," *Renaissance Studies*, Vol. 12, No. 3, 1998, 325–340.

Fujita, Masahisa, Paul Krugman, and Anthony J. Venables. *The Spatial Economy: Cities, Regions, and International Trade*. Cambridge, MA: MIT Press, 1999.

Gelderblom, Oscar. *Cities of Commerce: The Institutional Foundations of International Trade in the Low Countries, 1250–1650*. Princeton, NJ: Princeton University Press, 2013.

Gelderblom, Oscar and Joost Jonker. "Completing a Financial Revolution: The Finance of the Dutch East India Trade and the Rise of the Amsterdam Capital Market, 1595–1612," *The Journal of Economic History*, Vol. 64, No. 3, September 2004, 641–672.

Goetzmann, William N. *Money Changes Everything: How Finance Made Civilization Possible*. Princeton, NJ: Princeton University Press, 2016.

Goldthwaite, Richard A. *The Economy of Renaissance Florence*. Baltimore, MD: Johns Hopkins University Press, 2009.

_____. "The Practice and Culture of Accounting in Renaissance Florence," *Enterprise and Society*, Vol. 16, No. 3, 2015, 611–647.

Grierson, Philip. *Numismatics*. New York: Oxford University Press, 1975.

Haberlein, Mark. *The Fuggers of Augsburg: Pursuing Wealth and Honor in Renaissance Germany*. Charlottesville, VA: University of Virginia, 2012.

Harvey, David. *Spaces of Capital: Towards a Critical Geography*. New York: Routledge, 2001.

_____. *Paris, Capital of Modernity*. New York: Routledge, 2003.

_____. *Rebel Cities: From Right to the City to the Urban Revolution*. London: Verso, 2012.

Heere, Franz. *The Life and Times of the Fuggers*. Augsburg, Germany: Wibner-Verlag, 2009.

Herlihy, David. "The Rulers of Florence, 1282–1530," in Anthony Molho, Kurt Raaflaub, Julia Emlen (eds.), *City-States in Classical Antiquity and Medieval Italy*. Stuttgart, Germany: Franz Steiner Verlag, 1991, 197–222.

Horn, Jeff, Leonard N. Rosenband, and Merritt Roe Smith (eds.). *Reconceptualizing the Industrial Revolution*. Cambridge, MA: MIT Press, 2010.

Hunt, Edwin S. and James M. Murray. *A History of Business in Medieval Europe, 1200–1550*. New York: Cambridge University Press, 1999.

Hutchins, Edwin. *Cognition in the Wild*. Cambridge, MA: MIT Press, 1995.

_____. "Material Anchors for Conceptual Blends," *Journal of Pragmatics*. Vol. 37, 2005, 1555–1577.

Hutchins, Edwin and Christine M. Johnson. "Modeling the Emergence of Language as an Embodied Collective Cognitive Activity," *Topics in Cognitive Science*, 1, 2009, 523–546.

Ianziti, Gary. *Writing History in Renaissance Italy: Leonardo Bruni and the Uses of the Past*. Cambridge, MA: Harvard University Press, 2012.

Isenmann, Moritz. "From Rule of Law to Emergency Rule in Renaissance Florence," in Lawrin Armstrong and Julius Kirshner (eds.), *The Politics of Law in Late Medieval and Renaissance Italy*. Toronto: University of Toronto Press, 2011, 55–76.

Kirshner, Julius and Anthony Molho. "The Dowry Fund and the Marriage Market in Early Quattrocento Florence," *The Journal of Modern History*, Vol. 50, No. 3, 1978, 403–438.

Lane, Frederic C. *Venice: A Maritime Republic*. Baltimore, MD: The Johns Hopkins University Press, 1973.

Lane, Frederic C. and Reinhold C. Mueller. *Money and Banking in Medieval and Renaissance Venice: Coins and Moneys of Account*. Baltimore: Johns Hopkins Press, 1985.

Lantschner, Patrick. "Revolts and the Political Order of Cities in the Late Middle Ages," *Past and Present*, No. 225, 2014, 3–46.

Law, John. "Technology and Heterogeneous Engineering: The Case of Portuguese Expansion," in Wiebe E. Bijker, Thomas P. Hughes, and Trevor Pinch (eds.), *The Social Construction of Technological Systems: New Directions in the Sociology and History of Technology*. Cambridge, MA: MIT Press, 2012, 105–127.

Law, John E. *Venice and the Veneto in the Early Renaissance*. Burlington, VT: Ashgate/ Variorum, 2000.

Lopez, Robert Sabatino. "Back to Gold," *The Economic History Review*, Vol. 9, No. 2, 1956, 219–240.

Lopez, Robert S. *The Commercial Revolution of the Middle Ages, 950–1350*. Englewood Cliffs, NJ: Prentice-Hall, 1971.

Marsilio, Claudio. "The Genoese and Portuguese Financial Operators' Control of the Spanish Silver Market (1627–1657)," *The Journal of European Economic History*, Vol. XLI, No. 3, 2012, 69–84.

Martines, Lauro. *Lawyers and Statecraft in Renaissance Florence*. Princeton, NJ: Princeton University Press, 1968.

McLean, Paul D. and Neha Gondal. "The Circulation of Interpersonal Credit in Renaissance Florence," *European Journal of Sociology*, Vol. 55, No. 2, 2014, 135–176.

McLean, Paul D. and John F. Padgett. "Obligation, Risk, and Opportunity in the Renaissance Economy: Beyond Social Embeddedness to Network Co-Constitution," in Frank Dobbin (ed.), *The Sociology of the Economy*. New York: Russell Sage Foundation, 2004, 193–227.

Mensinger, Sara. "*Consilium Sapientum*: Lawmen and the Italian Popular Communes," in Lawrin Armstrong and Julius Kirshner (eds.), *The Politics of Law in Late Medieval and Renaissance Italy*. Toronto: University of Toronto Press, 2011, 40–54.

Molho, Anthony. *Florentine Public Finances in the Early Renaissance, 1400–1433*. Cambridge, MA: Harvard University Press, 1971.

_____. "The State and Public Finance: A Hypothesis Based on the History of Late Medieval Florence," in Julius Kirshner (ed.), *The Origins of the State in Italy, 1300–1600*. Chicago: The University of Chicago Press, 1995, 97–135.

Molho, Anthony, Diogo Ramada Curto, and Niki Koniodos (eds.), *Finding Europe: Discourses on Margins, Communities, Images* Ca. 13th–Ca. 18th Centuries. New York: Berghahn Books, 2007.

Muir, Edward. *The Culture Wars of the Late Renaissance: Skeptics, Libertines, and Opera*. Cambridge, MA: Harvard University Press, 2007.

_____. "Italy in the No Longer Forgotten Centuries," *I Tatti Studies in Italian Renaissance*, Vol. 16, No. 1/2, 2013, 5–11.

Munro, John H. "The Medieval Origins of the Financial Revolution: Usury, Rentes, and Negotiability," *The International History Review*, Vol. 25, No. 3, 2003, 505–562.

_____(ed.). *Money in the Pre-Industrial World: Bullion, Debasements and Coin Substitutes.* London: Pickering & Chatto, 2012.

Munro, John H. A. *Wool, Cloth, and Gold: The Struggle for Bullion in the Anglo-Burgundian Trade, 1340–1478.* Toronto: University of Toronto Press, 1972.

_____. "English 'Backwardness' and Financial Innovations in Commerce with the Low Countries, Fourteenth to the Sixteenth Centuries," in Peter Stabel, Bruno Blonde, Anke Greve (eds.), *International Trade in the Low Countries: Merchants, Organizations, Infrastructures.* Antwerp, Belgium: Garant Publishers, 2000, 105–168.

Najemy, John M. "Guild Republicanism in Trecento Florence: The Successes and Ultimate Failure of Corporate Politics," *The American Historical Review*, Vol. 84, No. 1, 1979, 53–71.

_____. *Corporatism and Consensus in Florentine Electoral Politics, 1280–1400.* Chapel Hill, NC: University of North Carolina Press, 1982.

_____ "The Dialogue of Power in Florentine Politics," in Anthony Molho, Kurt Raaflaub, Julia Emlen (eds.), *City-States in Classical Antiquity and Medieval Italy.* Stuttgart, Germany: Franz Steiner Verlag, 1991, 269–288.

_____. "Politics: Class and Patronage in Twentieth-Century Italian Renaissance Historiography," in Allen J. Grieco, Michael Rocke, Fiorella Gioffredi Superbi (eds.), *The Italian Renaissance in the Twentieth Century: Acts of an International Conference*, Florence, Villa I Tatti, June 9–11, 1999. Florence, Italy: Leo S. Olschki, 119–136.

_____. *A History of Florence, 1200–1575.* Malden, MA: Blackwell, 2006a.

_____ "Florentine Politics and Urban Spaces," in Roger J. Crum and John T. Paoletti (eds.), *Renaissance Florence: A Social History.* New York: Cambridge University Press, 2006b, 19–54.

_____. "Machiavelli Between East and West," in Diogo Ramada Curto, Eric R. Dursteler, Julius Kirshner, and Francesca Trivellato (eds.), *From Florence to the Mediterranean and Beyond: Essays in Honour of Anthony Molho.* Vol. 1. Florence, Italy: Leo S. Olschki, 2009, 127–145.

_____. "The 2013 Josephine Waters Bennett Lecture: Machiavelli and History," *Renaissance Quarterly*, Vol. 67, No. 4, 2014, 1131–1164.

Neal, Larry. *A Concise History of International Finance: From Babylon to Bernanke.* New York: Cambridge University Press, 2015.

Padgett, John F. "Open Elite? Social Mobility, Marriage, and Family in Florence, 1282-1494," *Renaissance Quarterly*, Vol. 63, No. 2, 2010, 357–411.

_____. "The Emergence of Corporate Merchant-Banks in Dugento Tuscany," in John F. Padgett and Walter W. Powell (eds.), *The Emergence of Organizations and Markets.* Princeton, NJ: Princeton University Press, 2012a, 121–167.

_____. "Transposition and Refunctionality: The Birth of Partnership Systems in Renaissance Florence" in John F. Padgett and Walter W. Powell (eds.), *The Emergence of Organizations and Markets.* Princeton, NJ: Princeton University Press, 2012b, 168–207.

_____. "Country as Global Market: Netherlands, Calvinism, and the Joint-Stock Company," in John F. Padgett and Walter W. Powell (eds.), *The Emergence of Organizations and Markets.* Princeton, NJ: Princeton University Press, 2012c, 208–234.

Padgett, John F. and Christopher K. Ansell. "Robust Action and the Rise of the Medici, 1400–1434." *American Journal of Sociology.* Vol. 98, No. 6, 1993, 1259–1319.

Padgett, John F. and Paul D. McLean. "Organizational Invention and Elite Transformation: The Birth of Partnership Systems in Renaissance Florence," *American Journal of Sociology*, Vol. 111, No. 5, 2006, 1463–1568.

_____. "Economic Credit in Renaissance Florence," *The Journal of Modern History*, Vol. 83, No. 1, 2011, 1–47.

Padgett, John F. and Walter W. Powell. *The Emergence of Organizations and Markets.* Princeton, NJ: Princeton University Press, 2012.

Peterson, David S. "State-Building Church Reform and the Politics of Legitimacy in Florence, 1375–1460," in William J. Connell and Andrea Zorzi (eds.), *Florentine Tuscany: Structures and Practices of Power.* New York: Cambridge University Press, 2000, 122–143.

Petralia, Guiseppe. "Fiscality, Politics, and Dominion in Florentine Tuscany at the end of the Middle Ages," in William J. Connell and Andrea Zorzi (eds.). *Florentine Tuscany: Structures and Practices of Power.* New York: Cambridge University Press, 2000, 65–89.

Pezzolxo, Luciano and Giuseppe Tattara. "'Una Fiera Senza Luigo': Was Bisenzone an International Capital Market in Sixteenth-Century Italy?" *Journal of Economic History*, Vol. 68, No. 4, 2008, 1098–1122.

Poovey, Mary. *A History of the Modern Fact: Problems of Knowledge in the Sciences of Wealth and Society.* Chicago: University of Chicago Press, 1998.

_____. "The Liberal Civil Subject and the Social in Eighteenth-Century British Moral Philosophy," *Public Culture.* Vol. 14, No. 1, 2002, 125–145.

_____. *Genres of the Credit Economy: Mediating Value in Eighteenth- and Nineteenth-Century Britain.* Chicago: University of Chicago Press, 2008.

Raccagni, Gianluca. *The Lombard League 1167–1225.* New York: Oxford University Press, 2010.

Ravid, Benjamin. "The Third Charter of the Jewish Merchants of Venice, 1611: A Case Study in Complex Multifaceted Negotiations," *Jewish Political Studies Review*, Vol. 6, No. 1–2, 1994, 83–134.

Reeves, Eileen. "Galileo, Oracle: On the History of Early Modern Science," *I Tatti Studies in the Italian Renaissance*, Vol. 18, No. 1, 2015, 7–22.

Richards, John F. (ed.). *Precious Metals in the Later Medieval and Early Modern Worlds.* Durham, NC: Carolina Academic Press, 1983.

Roe, Mark J. *Strong Managers, Weak Owners: The Political Roots of American Corporate Finance.* Princeton, NJ: Princeton University Press, 1994.

_____ (ed.). *Corporate Governance: Political and Legal Perspectives.* Cheltenham, UK: Edward Elgar, 2005.

Shapin, Steven and Simon Schaffer. *Leviathan and the Air-Pump: Hobbes, Boyle, and the Experimental Life.* Princeton, NJ: Princeton University Press, 1985.

Soll, Jacob. *The Reckoning: Financial Accountability and the Rise and Fall of Nations.* New York: Basic Books, 2014.

Spufford, Peter. *Money and Its Use in Medieval Europe.* New York: Cambridge University Press, 1988.

_____. *Power and Profit: The Merchant in Medieval Europe.* London: Thames and Hudson, 2002.

Stahl, Alan M. *Zecca: The Mint of Venice in the Middle Ages.* Baltimore, MD: Johns Hopkins University Press, 2000.

Stasavage, David. "Why Did Public Debt Originate in Europe?" in Andrew Monson and Walter Scheidel (eds.), *Fiscal Regimes and the Political Economy of Premodern States.* New York: Cambridge University Press, 2015.

Steensgaard, Niels. *The Asian Trade Revolution of the Seventeenth Century: The East India Companies and the Decline of the Caravan Trade.* Chicago: The University of Chicago Press, 1973.

Stern, Philip J. and Carl Wennerlind (eds.). *Mercantilism Reimagined: Political Economy in Early Modern Britain and Its Empire.* New York: Oxford University Press, 2014.

Storrs, Christopher. *The Fiscal-Military State in 18th-Century Europe.* Ashgate, 2009.

Taviani, Carlo. "An Ancient Scheme: The Mississippi Company, Machiavelli, and the Casa di San Giorgio (1407–1720)," in Emily Erikson (ed.), *Chartering Capitalism: Organizing Markets, States, Publics* in *Political Power and Social Theory*, Vol. 29. Bingley, UK: Emerald Group Publishing Ltd, 2015, 239–256.

T'Hart, Marjolein, Joost Jonker, and Jan Luiten van Zanden. *A Financial History of the Netherlands*. New York: Cambridge University Press, 1997.

Tracy, James D. *Emperor Charles V, Impresario of War: Campaign Strategy, International finance, and Domestic Politics*. New York: Cambridge University Press, 2002.

_____. "On the Dual Origins of Long-Term Urban Debt in Medieval Europe," in Marc Boone, Karel Davids, and Paul Janssens (eds.), *Urban Public Debts: Urban Government and the Market for Annuities in Western Europe (14th–18th Centuries)*. Turnhout, Belgium: Brepols, 2003, 13–24.

Trivellato, Francesca. "A Republic of Merchants?" in Anthony Molho, Diogo Ramada Curto, and Niki Koniordos (eds.), *Finding Europe: Discourses on the Margins*. New York: Berghahn, 2007, 133–158.

_____. *The Familiarity of Strangers: The Sephardic Diaspora, Livorno, and Cross-Cultural Trade in the Early Modern Period*. New Haven, CT: Yale University Press, 2009a.

_____. "Sephardic Merchants Between State and Rabbinic Courts: Malfeasance, Property Rights and Religious Authority in the Eighteenth-Century Mediterranean," in Diogo Ramada Curto, Eric R. Dursteler, Julius Kirshner, and Francesca Trivellato (eds.), *From Florence to the Mediterranean and Beyond: Essays in Honour of Anthony Molho*. Vol. II. Florence, Italy: Leo S. Olschki, 2009b, 625–648.

Vanheeswijck, Gido. "Does History Matter? Charles Taylor on the Transcendental Validity of the Social Imaginaries," *History and Theory*, Vol. 54, 2015, 69–85.

Vilar, Pierre. *A History of Gold and Money, 1450–1920*. Atlantic Highlands, NJ: Humanities Press, 1976.

Walker, Thomas. "The Italian Gold Revolution of 1252: Shifting Currents in the Pan-Mediterranean Flow of Gold," in Richards, John F. (ed.), *Precious Metals in the Later Medieval and Early Modern Worlds*. Durham, NC: Carolina Academic Press, 1983, 29–51.

Wennerlind, Carl. *Casualties of Credit: The English Financial Revolution, 1620–1720*. Cambridge, MA: Harvard University Press, 2011.

Wickham, Chris. *Sleepwalking into a New World: Emergence of Italian City Communes in the Twelfth Century*. Princeton, NJ: Princeton University Press, 2015.

Witt, Ronald G. *The Two Latin Cultures and the Foundation of Renaissance Humanism in Medieval Italy*. New York: Cambridge University Press, 2012.

Wright, Robert E. *Corporation Nation*. Philadelphia: University of Pennsylvania Press, 2014.

Zorzi, Andrea. "The 'Material Constitution' of the Florentine Dominion," in William J. Connell and Anrea Zorzi (eds.), *Florentine Tuscany: Structures and Practices of Power*. New York: Cambridge University Press, 2000, 6–31.

_____. "The Populo," in John M. Najemy (ed.), *Italy in the Age of the Renaissance, 1300–1550*. Oxford, UK: Oxford University Press, 2004, 145–164.

5   Money and the Evolution of Institutions and Knowledge

The purpose of this chapter is to illustrate the method of historical institutionalism with respect to money. That is, the concept of money is related to specific institutions and forms of knowledge, using the method articulated in the study of the category of property (Davis 2015).

I.   Money

Money is often treated as a natural substance whose role in human institutions merely evolved due to convenience. Once it is observed that money has taken many forms and has played many different roles historically—that is, money is discretionary—the specific institutional setting is relevant, as well as the politics of money.

The three aspects of money identified in Chapter 1—symbol, discipline, sovereignty—can be related to the corporate form. The definition of money offered here embodies the power of a corporation, just like a corporate seal can signify authoritative decisions and actions. With reference to a nation-state, money is the delegation of authority to obtain, transform, and sell property, according to legal norms and regulations in that state (Desan 2016; Pistor 2013). Because this delegation is general, the token of the corporate seal can be exchanged for all other forms of legal property, like a general equivalent representing the authority of the state. Quite literally, the first notes issued by the newly incorporated Bank of England in 1694 were affixed with the corporate seal (Feavearyear 1931, 115–117). At present, the currency of the United States is the liability of the Federal Reserve, another corporate body with powers delegated by the state.

The definition of credit is the allowance of the use of the corporate seal, or other symbol, by individuals who conform to designated criteria determined through specific financial institutions. The use of the corporate seal can commit the corporation to certain actions in the present and future, such as an exchange for commodities in the present and a contract for repayment of money loans (denominated in the corporate seal) with interest in the future.

Public credit is an "imaginary" concept, where members of the corporate body or the state can envision their collective future (Davis 2015, 124–126).

Although not universal, the notion of "shares" of a corporation was experienced early in Western culture, with the incorporated communes, cities and towns, city-states, and shipping partnerships of limited durations. The notion of credit in modern industrial economies is usually confined to access to funds for a specific term with payment of interest, allocated to an individual with collateral by a financial institution. The notion of public credit is the collective of all such individuals, managed by the set of financial institutions supervised by the state, as well as borrowing by the state itself (Maurer1999; 2003, 81).

II. Institutions

The use of money has been observed for millennia. There are many fine histories, as reviewed in Chapter 4 (Goetzmann 2016; Ingham 2004). According to Poovey, the loss of knowledge of this history aids in the abstraction of the functions of money and to its mystification (Poovey 2010), along with the absence of knowledge of the existence of alternatives (Poovey 2008, 171–218).

The position elaborated here is that the role of money changes with specific forms of the state. In turn, the form of the state is influenced by the development of money and finance. In particular, the role of money has changed with the emergence of the liberal state, from the tax and tribute model of the territorial state to the mobile property and credit model of the global trading state, in a context of other competing trading nations (Sassen 2006). The state, which has internalized its own finance by means of tax and credit operations on its own account, is the best environment for "market-oriented capitalism," according to Weber.

> The way in which political and hierocratic bodies provide for their corporate needs has very important repercussions on the structure of private economic activity. A state based exclusively on money contributions, conducting the collection of the taxes (but no other economic activity) through its own staff, and calling on personal service contributions only for political and judicial purposes, provides an optimal [environment] for a rational market-oriented capitalism. (Weber 1978, Vol. I, Part 1, Ch. II, section 39, 199)

It is possible to develop a history of financial forms, or genres (Poovey 2008), in relation to institutional context. See Table 5.1 for a suggestive sample.

What is often missing in histories of money is the source of authority. If money is a form of writing, according to Poovey, who has the authority to write? Who can sign the document, such as a bill of exchange or letter of credit? In the Medici bank, it was the partners or branch managers, who were ultimately supervised by the family members (De Roover 1948, 1963).

In the modern period, there is a hierarchy of money, with the highest-valued money being closest to the state (Mehrling 2011, 2013). In international

Table 5.1 Financial Assets

Type of financial asset	Historical context	References
Dowry fund	Florence thirteenth century; family clans;	Molho, 1971
Annuities, rentes	Guilds; city-republics	Munro 2013; Tracy 1985
Monte Commune	Italian city-states	Neal 2015
Indulgences	Church	Brown 2015
Bank deposits	Private bankers with branches	De Roover 1948, 1963
Bills of exchange	Long-distance trade	Neal 1990
Bank notes	Circulating paper currency	Andreades 1966
Insurance	Venice merchant trade; Liverpool slave trade	Baucom 2005; Leonard 2015
Corporate stocks	Amsterdam, London	Neal 2015
Futures contracts	Early nineteenth-century United States	Millo 2007

contexts, the hierarchy of money reflects proximity to the hegemonic country (Eichengreen and Hausmann 2005). That is, there may be an implicit power expressed in money and a related control over life and death (Baucom 2005, 2010; Wennerlind 2011).

According to Mehrling (2013), there is an "inherent hierarchy" of money in terms of ranking of international currencies in global financial markets, as well as particular money forms within a given country. Within a country, the ranking is constituted by the "safest" asset, the one with the least question regarding liquidity, or trading most easily at par. In his illustration (Mehrling 2013, 395), gold is the most liquid, followed by currency, deposits, and securities, respectively. These assets reflect the implicit ranking from money to credit. In a subsequent figure, the respective market makers are also identified, as well as the price of the relevant asset (Mehrling 2013, 400). Including a longer-term time perspective, one could also include the coin/bullion ratio, or the "mint ratio," which was adjusted by countries to manage the gold flow between countries (Kregel 2016). These relationships are illustrated in Table 5.2, modifying Mehrling's figures with Kregel's addition. The central position of the banking system is reflected in its double role between currency and deposits.

The important point is the need for continual transformation of form to maintain liquidity of each financial asset. Consequently, a "market maker" is necessary for each unique type of asset. These continual transformations

Table 5.2 Financial Assets and Financial Markets

Asset	Market Maker	Price
Bullion/coin	Mint	Mint ratio
Gold coin	Central bank	Exchange rate
⌈Currency	Banking system	Par
⌊Deposits		
Securities	Securities dealers	Interest rate
Derivatives	Shadow banking system	"Haircut"

reflect the liquidity of each asset and maintain the standard of value of each asset, reinforcing that liquidity. The requirement for continual transformation is stressed in Derman's account of the market for derivatives, where the question of value is potentially more questionable (Derman 2016, 222–228). If there were temporary deviations of market price from the fundamental value, there would be a riskless arbitrage to adjust the price immediately by assumption of the law of one price (Derman 2016, 211–217). In the case of derivatives, the emergence of a price from the active trading of market makers facilitates further trades and the ongoing modification/perfection of that price.

A.   Definition of the "Tax | Credit State"

The differentiating feature of the liberal state is the monetization of relationships of citizenship and governance, compared with the feudal and family state (Ruggie 1983, 1993). The liberal state includes concepts such as the fiscal/military state (Carruthers 1996, 16–17, 22, 83–89; Knights 2005, 13–15; Stern and Wennerlind 2014, 5) and the tax state (Braddick 1996, 12; Schumpeter 1991). The core concept is the mobile individual who is recognized as an owner of individual private property. The state is founded to recognize and to protect property by means of suffrage and representation in governance. The goal of the state is the "wealth of nations," in money terms. The function of defense is funded by the state, by means of public debt, which may also support other discretionary public goods. Major functions of the state are monetized, such as taxes and military, rather than based on custom and obligation, as the service of the knights and nobles to the lord under feudalism. There is formal representation of the population in the state by elections and public debate (Hawkins 2015; Knights 2005; Kwass 2000; Withington 2005).

> The first instantiation of what was to become the liberal state [included] the development of a 'legitimate' system of laws and regulations that privileged the owners of productive capital. (Sassen 2006, 101)

To emphasize this new form of the state, the term "tax/credit state" may be useful. That is, after the financial revolution in England, public credit became the key relationship of the state, for the tax payer and for the stock or bond holder, or *rentier*. The designation of specific taxes to finance the debt, and the guarantee by the public body of Parliament, is widely considered the foundation of the modern liberal state. The public body is now defined by a set of quantitative relationships, whether paying or receiving wealth, and the common purpose is the expansion of wealth. The principle of accounting for rates of return to wealth, and for the investment criteria for expanding rates of return, became the governing principle of both public and private spheres. The tax is the issue of greatest contention, defining the citizen's individual contribution and obligation to the state as a whole. The security of these taxes for all citizens nonetheless guarantees the ability to issue credit, the ability for designated individuals to acquire access to resources in the present, with the promise to create additional returns in the future, a share of which are due back to private lenders, managed in aggregate by the state's financial system.

From the monarch's public finances there emerged a representative state to manage the public finances, according to accounts of the Glorious Revolution in England (Pincus 2007, 2009). The public *fisc* is now a focus of civil society, its new center, along with the capital markets on which public and private debt is traded. The king's body has been replaced by a public body (Barkan 2013; Santner 2016), in a corporate form, but invisible and subject to suspicion. Private "property rights" becomes an immediate rhetorical strategy to limit public claims on so-called private property. Habermas' (1989) public sphere is concerned with taxes as well as stock prices, discussed in coffee shops near Exchange Alley. Public debt has become a financial asset, a form of financial property, which can serve as collateral, as well as a tax liability, and trades become more liquid with wider participation of the public over the course of the eighteenth century.

According to Polanyi (1944, 40–42, 57, 71, 74, 137–138, 223–225, 254–255), the "liberal creed" requires the separation of economics and politics in order to have a self-regulating market that operates like a machine. Freedom of property was the form in which this liberal creed was often justified.

> The separation of powers, which Montesquieu (1748) had meanwhile invented, was now used to separate the people from power over their own economic life. The American Constitution, shaped in a farmer-craftsman's environment by a leadership forewarned by the English industrial scene, isolated the economic sphere entirely from the jurisdiction of the Constitution, put private property thereby under the highest conceivable protection, and created the only legally grounded market society in the world. In spite of universal suffrage, American voters were powerless against owners. (Polanyi 1944, 250–226)

Rather than view politics as the highest expression of humankind in the "civic republican tradition" (Pocock 1975), private property was celebrated as freedom. The public sphere was represented by the image of taxes and interference with private property, rather than public capacity and civic engagement. That is, the tax state was considered intrusive and limiting freedom of property.

Double-entry bookkeeping became the central document, for individual, corporate, and national accountability (Goldthwaite 2015; Poovey 1998; Soll 2014). Personal journals and account books become popular for individuals aside from their businesses. At the workplace, the individual inscribes his own records, to be reviewed by the supervisor, and checked for accuracy, as a verification of merchant virtue as well as creditworthiness (Kessler 2007). The double-entry bookkeeping format documents relationships in terms of commodities and money flows at a point in time, connecting the individual and the business to others in a financial network of national and international scope. The totals of debits and credits verify the corporate existence in time and over time. Smith's "impartial spectator" could examine the account books to verify the veracity of the individual as well as the business. The "individual" begins to anticipate such surveillance and to conform to its demands as part of the division of labor and specialization of the market system.

Taxes and interest payments introduce a self-interested calculus into the relationship of citizen to state. That is, the role of the state, and its cost to the citizen, are weighed in quantitative terms, relative to the benefits received. The relationship of citizen to state becomes subject to a contingent calculus, rather than an absolute commitment and a form of identity and self-expression.

> Taxes not only helped to create the state. They helped to form it … The tax brings money and calculating spirit into corners in which they do not dwell as yet, and thus becomes a formative factor in the very organism which has developed it. (Schumpeter 1991, 108)

Public debt becomes the burden as well as the instrument of the state. The consolidation of public debt occurred first in the Italian city-states with the *Monte Commune*, beginning in Venice in 1262, Genoa in 1274, and Florence in 1345 (Neal 2015, 39–51; Pezzolo 2014, 296; Stasavage 2003; Tracy 1985), where the obligation for repayment was assumed by the corporate body of the commune. The corporate form of public debt continued to expand in capacity with the innovations in Genoa in 1407 (Marsilio 2013), along with early modern France in 1522 and the Habsburg Netherlands in 1537, as well as the Dutch Republic (Munro 2013). Secondary markets for public debt emerged first in Italian city-states, followed by Antwerp (1531), Frankfurt (1585), Amsterdam (1608), and London (1694), before the formal foundation of the London Stock Exchange in 1801 (Munro 2013, 236; Pezzolo 2014, 296–300; Shaikh 2016, 174). Stock markets arose in Amsterdam and London after the capital of the Dutch and English East India companies became permanent in 1609 and 1650, respectively. That is, rather than be able to withdraw their paid in capital by the original subscribers, the stock certificates themselves were traded based on ledgers maintained by the companies (Neal 1990, 9, 44–47). England was able to learn from earlier models of international bills of exchange and the corporate form, under pressure of war finance and with forced migrations of knowledgeable practitioners (Neal 1990, 5–14), where traders, brokers, and financiers were called "Lombards." Because of the guild-based model of the goldsmith bankers (Quinn 1997), the Bank of England was founded based on fractional reserve, rather than the central clearing role of the Bank of Amsterdam (Neal 2000; Quinn and Roberds 2007).

The incorporation of the public debt was a key step in making it "perpetual" (Quinn 2008). The foundation of the Bank of England in 1694 proceeded to develop this consolidation of public debt in the form of the corporate structure (Broz and Grossman 2004; Carlos and Neal 2011; Murphy 2009, 39–65; Neal 2000), with the debt/equity swap to achieve a funded public debt. That is, the Bank of England acquired the government debt as its capital stock, with interest payments guaranteed by Parliament, based on tonnage duties. In turn it was allowed to issue stock to subscribers and notes based on its capital stock. The Bank of England was a joint stock corporation, owned and managed by its shareholders (Andreades 1966). In its first charter of 1694, the Bank of England (BOE) did not receive a monopoly on note issue or perpetual existence, but acquired additional powers with charter renewals of 1697 and 1708, in exchange for additional loans to the government. The expansion of the role of the BOE emerged from the collapse of the South Sea Bubble, when it acquired additional assets of the failed South Sea Corporation. This debt workout from that first stock market bubble constituted the "'big bang' of finance capitalism in England" (Neal 2000, 128; 2015, 81–99). Nearly all of the funded debt of England was held by the "three sisters," the Bank of England, the East India Company, and the South Sea Company, in the first half of the eighteenth century (Broz and Grossman 2004, 56). Ultimately the capacity of the BOE to issue notes and stock facilitated the monetization of the public debt of England, as did the "consol," a form of perpetual public bonds first issued in 1723 (Neal 2000, 128; 2015, 73). The South Sea Company in England and the Mississippi Company in France were both variations on the corporate form operating to consolidate public debt—in this case based on the projected revenues of the slave trade and land sales in North American colonies (Goetzmann 2016, 332–342, 354–362; Neal 2012). Central banks, public debt, and capital markets became the norm for core industrial countries after 1815. That is, the Bank of England, the chartered monopoly joint stock corporations, and the public debt had gradually extended the time period of their charters, with the BOE becoming "perpetual" only by implicit assumption with the Bank Charter Act of 1844, with its "emergent role as monetary manager under the gold standard" (Broz and Grossman 2004, 50; Neal 2015, 191–197).

The creation of a long-term national debt also marked the beginning of a new relationship between the state and the public. (Murphy 2009, 43)

The corporate form of the chartered town or borough also facilitated the transition from a nonmonetary feudal economy to a monetized market-based economy. Associations such as guilds provided apprenticeships to train and socialize migrants, as well as provided access to citizenship privileges in the city governance structures and in Parliament (Withington 2005). That is, even as individuals became more mobile in the commercialized economy, there was a collective corporate structure to contain and manage their movements.

The corporate form, repurposed into a commercial entity, combined the collective nature of the medieval commune and guild with regular membership criteria and decision-making procedures. This commercial application developed with the extension of long-distance trade between the Italian city-states and the Middle East during the Commercial Revolution (Lopez 1971). The bank notes of the Bank of England even reflected the Italian heritage with the term *"compania"* (Andreades 1966, 73). The collective representation of individual members by means of corporate seal and representative official enabled the new form of the nation-state to combine commercial purposes with collective organization. The notes issued by the central banks and the stock issued by the corporations were forms of representation of the whole, utilized by individuals in trade and credit, to represent the whole comprised of mobile individual members. Thus, money can be considered a type of corporate seal, like notes and stocks, representing the whole, for commercial purposes. This corporate form was scalable and mobile, from individual businesses to nation-states, from territorial powers to colonial powers in the "new world." The "financial revolution" in England took off after several centuries of experimentation with financial innovations based on the corporate form, combined with expanding capital markets in corporate shares and public debt, along with a "financial symbiosis" between London and Amsterdam (Neal 2015, 72–109). In addition, the increasing capacity of the United Kingdom to project power across the globe based on its naval supremacy, to anticipate the riches of the slave trade, and to engage its citizens in the investment in its future contributed further to its financial development.

"The pressing demands for war finance ... led to financial innovations" (Neal 2015, 78), with numerous wars among Western European powers between 1688 and 1815 as well as financial crises (Neal 2015, 109, 119). The long-standing corporate form of the joint stock companies (Neal 1990, 44) enabled the consolidation of government debt and the expansion of state capacity. The state *fisc* was able to adapt the familiar double-entry bookkeeping form to monetize the productive capacity of the nation (Davis 2010, 2013). The Bank of England was able to issue notes that ultimately became the monopoly currency. By providing the convenience of a standard unit of account, means of payment, and a store of value, the state was able to expand the scale of the financial circuit, using its own fiat currency. By assigning a tax liability to the public, the state was able to provide the "real" foundation for the currency in terms of productive assets as well as human initiative to combine those assets into more valuable forms. The acceptance of this currency then provided legal

Table 5.3 Public Finance

Financial Genre	Public	Treasury/Central Bank
Taxes	Liability	Asset
Money	Asset	Liability

tender for payment of taxes and debt settlement, as well as a means of credit expansion to both the state and to the increasing numbers of corporations, as illustrated in Table 5.3. The expansion of scale increased liquidity and stability, further increasing the capacity for state debt. The ultimate limits to liquidity are the initiative and innovations of the public, as well as the concrete real resources at its disposal, not the quantity of the currency per se.

Even though the assets and liabilities cancel in a given time period (Mehrling 2012), the process of cancelling the liability creates production and generates incomes and assets throughout the system.

B. Historical Emergence of the Liberal State in England by Legislation

Ironically, the market was the creation of the state (Evans 2008; Howe 1984; Polanyi 1944, 139–140). A series of laws were passed regarding property rights and privileges that helped to create the "legal persona of the national bourgeoisie" (Sassen 2006, 96–110). See key examples here:

Monopoly Merchant Corporations
    Muscovy (1555), Merchant Adventurers, Staplers (Neal 1990, 44–54)
Property Laws
    Statute of Monopolies 1624
Land Laws
    Enclosure Movements (Sassen 2006, 102–104)
    Statute of Merton 1236
    First phase 1761–1780
    General Enclosure Act of 1801
Labor Laws
    Statue of Artificers 1563 (Polanyi 1944)
    Anti-Combination Laws 1769, 1799 (Hunt 1990, 54; Sassen 2006, 104–114)
    Elizabethan Poor Law 1598, 1601 (Hunt 1990, 30, 41; Withington 2005, 25–34)
    Restriction of Slave Trade 1807
    Abolition of Slavery 1833
    Poor Law Reform of 1834 (Evans 2008, 81–97)
Maritime Laws
    Navigation Acts of 1651 and 1663 (Koot 2011) and repealed in the 1840s
    Staple Acts

Corporation Laws
   Perpetual form of English East India Company (founded in 1600;
      permanent in 1650; Neal 1990, 9)
   Dutch East India Company 1602 (permanent in 1612; Goetzmann
      2016, 316–319)
   Hudson Bay Company 1670
   Royal Africa Company 1672
   Bank of England 1694 (rechartered in 1697, 1708, 1713; established
      with central bank functions in 1844) (Broz and Grossman 2004;
      Neal 2000, 123–128; 2015, 81–83, 191; Wennerlind 2011)
   Limited Liability in 1850s and 1860s
   General Incorporation Laws
   London Stock Exchange (Neal 2015, 171–177)
Governance Laws
   Revolution of 1688
   Triennial Election Act 1694
   Reform of 1832 (Sassen 2006, 105–106)
   Municipal Corporations Reform 1835
Banking Laws
   BOE 1694
   Perpetual British debt ("consols") 1720s
   Bubble Act 1720 and repealed in 1825
   Bank Charter Act of 1844
Free Trade
   Corn Law of 1815 (Rothschild 2001, 76–81; Evans 2008, 15–17)
   Corn Law Reform in 1846 (Sassen 2006, 105–106)
Gold Standard
   Restriction Act 1797–1821 (Poovey 2010, 333–335; Vogl 2015, 42–48)
   Resumption Act of 1819

The privileges of property owners helped to construct a "disadvantaged subject" as well, such as workers (Sassen 2006, 110–115). The Lockean "social contract" supported the rights of private property, including workers, but in fact Parliamentary legislation supported bourgeois property as a foundation of the system.

With the public–private divide in the mid-nineteenth century, the business corporation is clearly differentiated from the municipal corporation, with the latter subordinate to the former, reflecting the priority on the expansion of the "wealth of nations." The priority of the private business corporation over the public municipal corporation facilitated the expansion of the wealth, while permitting the state and municipal levels of government to facilitate property transfer and to lower transaction costs. The shift in role of local government, such as the parish in labor laws, facilitated the development of a mobile labor force in England, for example (Polanyi 1944). The privileging of the private business corporation as "property" in the Dartmouth Case in 1819 in the United States facilitated the accumulation of capital within the corporate form (Wright 2014).

C.   The Role of Money in the Liberal State

Money is the symbolic representation of the whole, while also considered to be individual private property. The function of money is to express a standard of value and to circulate property. Money and financial circuits link the key institutions of corporation, central bank, state, and household. That is, the division of labor cannot contribute to the "wealth of nations" unless there is an integrating device. Yet the presumed "invisible hand" of the market provides that integration. In fact, historically, there is a set of financial institutions that provide the management and coordination, such as the "visible hand" of "capital" represented by bankers and central banks. The constitution and operation of these financial institutions is the subject of political debate, such as the chartered joint stock corporations (Carruthers 1996), the BOE (Andreades 1966; Pincus 2007), the Bank of the United States (BUS) (Wright 2014), the U.S. Federal Reserve (FED) (Livingstone 1986) and the International Monetary Fund (IMF) (Eichengreen 1996).

Symbols are important for signifying the nation (Ruggie 1993, 157–160). Gold may have symbolized a national supremacy in trade, military, and technology, and thus result in a positive balance of payments to underscore its creditworthiness. In turn, creditworthiness is helpful in the expansion of public debt and financing of military power. A nation with such demonstrable success then can mobilize its citizens to further commitment to the state and its perpetual existence. Its public debt then becomes a store of wealth and a source of enrichment and civic pride. See Table 5.4 as an illustration of this evolution.

There are certain paradigms for the analysis of money. Two main paradigms are the currency and the Banking School (Mehrling 2012; Neal 2015, 144; Wennerlind 2011, 235–245), one focusing on the origins of credit by the initiative of the borrower and the state of the business cycle, and the other focusing on the quantitative restriction of credit to maintain discipline and quality. The various theories of money continually encountered the issue of the proper quantitative ratio between total assets and the money supply. Aristotelian views of money emphasized balance (Vogl 2015, 84–90), whereas the Hartlibian school (Wennerlind 2014) stressed the possible infinite expansion of credit. The Bank of England was based on coin, not land, as a result of political disputes among the Tories and Whigs (Carruthers 1996) and the victory of the "Currency School" over the "Banking School" (Andreades 1966, 270–294; Lapavitsas 1994; Marx 1967, Vol. III, 546–549). The Bank of England was charged with balancing the international gold standard and the convertibility of its notes, along with the provision of domestic credit, with the Bank Act of 1844 (Mehrling 2011, 18–23).

The gold standard was not a natural and perpetual global foundation of trade, established among major industrial countries only in the early 1870s (Eichengreen 1996, 18–25). Important determinants include the introduction of steam technologies of minting, gold discoveries in Australia and California, and the mint ratio compared with market price of silver and gold. Other factors include the role of Britain as a hegemonic power, enforcing trade and balance of payments, as well as the emergence of the Industrial Revolution. In the context of new markets in land, labor, and commodities, a common standard in precious metals enabled an international realization of gains in productivity from commodity production, which would require a more strict calculation of equivalence than would merchant trade, which relied on knowledge of markets by skilled traders.

Given the common understanding that gold is the natural substance of money, it is notable that the formal gold standard was only in operation for a specific historical period (Eichengreen 1996; Neal 2015). The "gold standard was introduced in order to remove the currency from politics" (Polanyi 1944, 202). Instead of self-regulating specie flow, "gunboats" were used to balance payments among countries and "to induce colonial peoples to recognize the advantages of trade" (Polanyi 1944, 207).

> With the international gold standard the most ambitious market scheme of all was put into effect, implying the absolute independence of [the] market from national authorities (Polanyi 1944, 217).

Eichengreen characterizes the gold standard as a "social construction," involvement in which commits the participating countries to abide by the "rules of the game" regarding balance of payments adjustments. In spite of its apparent automaticity, there is discretion to the central bankers, especially because most central banks in the nineteenth century were private. In exchange rate adjustments and economic crises, there was important collaboration among central bankers, as well as network externalities which helped to maintain the system (Eichengreen 1996, 28–35).

D. Development of Finance and Commodity Circuits

Due to the specialization of academic disciplines, finance is often considered a self-contained system, rather than focus on the regular circuits of commodities, which constitute the "real" dimension of the financial trades. Although the importance of money and financial institutions in the history of the fiscal military state is well known, (Davis 2015), the relation to commodity circuits is less well understood. That is, for regular financial flows to be coordinated and predictable, the commodity flows must first be well organized, as shown in Table 5.4 below. For example, the slave trade was well organized in Liverpool in the eighteenth century, allowing the development of bills of exchange and insurance as novel financial instruments (Baucom 2005, 39–41, 59–64, 83–92, 99–106; Goetzmann 2016, 336). There is a long history of trade and commercial institutions where one "spaces-of-flows" (Baucom 2005, 25, 37; 2009, 339) learns from the previous center. It is possible to discuss a long-term history of trade, with new centers, commodities, and financial instruments, with accumulating knowledge and organizational development.

Table 5.4 Development of Trade and Financial Assets

Phase (source)	Geography	Financial Asset	Commodity
Commercial Revolution (Lopez 1971)	Europe/Asia	Gold coin	Spices
City-states trade and finance (Arrighi 1994)	Mediterranean	Letter of credit; merchant bankers	Silks
Low countries (Tracey 1985)	Mediterranean; Baltic	Annuity; corporate stock; Bank of Amsterdam	Wool; cotton
England and slave trade (Beckert 2014; Bowen, Mancke, and Reid 2012; Armitage and Braddick 2009; Baucom 2005)	Atlantic	Insurance; bonds; corporate stock	Slaves; textiles
Industrial Revolution (Allen 2009; Mokyr 2017)	Europe/North America	Government bonds; corporate stock	Textiles

The financial circuits of letters of credit and insurance depended on the military power of chartered monopoly corporations to organize trade in a reliable pattern (Baucom 2005). That is, the aggressive reorganization of global trade in cotton in the seventeenth century, or "war capitalism," paved the way for the new form of the state and the Industrial Revolution in the late seventeenth and early eighteenth centuries (Beckert 2014, 29–55).

There is a development of the corporate form, as well, in a long-term perspective, as shown in Table 5.5.

That is, the original corporate forms—church, commune, and guild—were territorial, with representative governance and symbols, such as corporate seals. Membership in guilds was available for a fee, in addition to heredity and apprenticeship, with access to control rights based on a hierarchical system of authority based on skill. With the development of mobile corporate forms such as companies and merchant corporations, the integration with trade and finance was achieved, with the support of the state. The symbol of the corporation was the share of stock, which was transferable as a financial asset, with relation to the corporation as a collective but allocated to individuals, with the separation of ownership and control (Neal 1990, 8–9). The stock was a form of financial claim on the corporation, but no longer a type of membership with control rights. Capital markets operated separately from corporate governance, delegating control in exchange for liquidity, with legal support for the claims of external finance. Later, with learning from previous models, the territorial nation-state integrated both military and finance into a new form of

Table 5.5 History of Corporate Forms

Type of Corporate Form	Period	Type of Asset
Commune	Medieval	Coin
Church	Medieval	Coin and bank deposits
Guild	Early Modern	Commodity
County and province/ city-states	Early Modern	Public debt
Monopoly merchant corporation	Exploration	Stock
Central banks (BOE)	Industrial Revolution	Notes
Private Business Corporations	Industrial Revolution	Stock
Liberal Nation-State	Industrial Revolution	Notes, fiat currency

state: the liberal state. Institutions of finance and governance were centralized, with hierarchical relations with local governance units and priority to private business enterprises. The currency was the representation of the authority and sovereignty of that corporate form, the state, usable in access to, as well as control and alienation, of property. After World War II, this form became a core system of advanced industrial states, with a trading and developing periphery.

III. Cultures of Credit in the Liberal State

The origin of public debt in the city-states of twelfth- and thirteenth-century Italy is well-known (Arrighi 1994; Stasavage 2003). The emergence of the political "public sphere" in late seventeenth- and early eighteenth-century England was related to the exchange of information regarding the emerging capital market (Pincus 2007; 2009). There is a possibility that the emergence of public debt was also related to the new recognition of the importance of public opinion (Wennerlind 2011, 169–196). That is, debt was a collective commitment, and the mobilization of the community was an essential aspect in demonstrating creditworthiness. The development of secondary financial markets for circulation of public debt aided liquidity and the voluntary investment of funds in these "bonds." Such voluntary investments by the community were more sustainable than forced loans in earlier periods.

The willingness of the public to invest in the "future" required a certain tolerance for risk and a capacity to imagine the future (Baucom 2005, 65–72, 149–151). New genres such as the novel emerged in this period (Baucom 2005, 214–217) and theater (Goetzmann 2016, 349–351; Withington 2005, 44–46). New forms of media and knowledge accompanied this transformed awareness (Siskin and Warner 2009, 12–15) and a new role of the "public," as investors, beneficiaries, and agents/partners of the state. The understanding of the "imagination" as a concept may also have changed, from biological to social (Mitchell 2008).

This new importance of culture and imagination may be related to the form of labor in capitalism (Postone 1993, 148–155, 264–267). That is, abstract labor is mediated by money, a social convention, which is based on belief (Searle 2010). This mediation by money is also abstract, and the relationship among individuals is by means of money values, such as wages and luxury commodity goods, as signs of wealth and status. An appreciation of the status of the person by money and luxury commodities developed with the rise of the market (Howell 2010).

The "social imaginary" (Mitchell 2008; Taylor 2004) may be a form of the culture in capitalism, related to the abstract relationship of money to symbolize the relationship of abstract individuals into an impersonal collective. That is, individuals are protected in their private spheres and have no direct personal relationship. The abstract relationship expressed by media, like print, journalism, public broadcasting, and social media, may amplify and reinforce their symbolic relationships via consumer goods, or "commodity fetishism" (Postone 1993, 166–171, 224–225). There may also be a "credit fetish," in which the social relationships related to the establishment of credit are invisible (Wennerlind 2011, 199, 229–230, 245, 330 fn. 178).

As noted by Pocock, the collectively imagined future is a resource for public credit (Mitchell 2008). Perpetual corporations and perpetual bonds are traded on a financial market that imagines an infinite future. That is, the English East India Company and the British "consols" were made perpetual in the early eighteenth century (Murphy 2014, 266; Stern 2014, 182–183; Wennerlind 2011, 163). The financial trader can trade in "any time," according to his personal preferences and aversion to risk. That is, in addition to production time (Postone 1993, 286–306), there is a time specific to financial markets. Money and credit enable conceptualization of an infinite future, yet its ultimate "liquidity" is determined in the immediate present, by the forms into which any asset may be converted, preferably to "hard cash."

IV.   Knowledge

Ruggie quotes Michael Walzer as saying, "The state is invisible; it must be personified before it can be seen, symbolized before it can be loved, imagined before it can be conceived" (Ruggie 1993, 157; Sassen 2006, 80). The "social episteme" is Ruggie's term for the "epistemic" dimension of social life. Ways of "imagining and symbolizing forms of political community itself underwent fundamental change" in the transition from feudalism to capitalism (Ruggie 1993, 157–160, 169). John Searle refers to expressions in language, which are then embodied in roles and institutions, and constitute a "background" for knowledgeable performance in a given society (Searle 2010).

Once parliaments and legislatures are recognized as reflecting the will of the sovereign nation, the "rule of law" becomes sanctified as reflecting the public interest. The representation of the bourgeoisie in the British Parliament after the Reform of 1832 then embodied the protection of property as the public interest of the liberal state, to be taken as a neutral grounding of the judiciary (Sassen 2006, 62–65, 96–110). These imagined concepts then become documented and incorporated in professional expertise and academic institutions (Poovey 1998) and public norms.

Mitchell notes the connection between the financial revolution in England and the imagined communities of the state and the collective future (Mitchell 2014). He cites the role of Hume in developing the concept of the "founding convention," which normalized the role of imagination in the formation of society.

> Hume's account of the founding convention, by contrast, suggested that society was *speculative from the start*, for property, including property in land, emerged only as the consequence of collective "investment" in a future system. The founding convention worked (and continues to work) because each individual anticipates the future actions of his fellows: "the actions of each of us … are perform'd upon the supposition, that something is to be perform'd on the other part" … The "general sense of common interest" that underwrites the founding social convention is not generated out of past experience, but arrives from the future. (Mitchell 2014, 54; italics in original)

Another way to express this role of collective imagination is to make use of the metaphor of a corporate body. Money and credit require the actions of a collective, just like the value of a share of stock of a corporation, as a financial asset, requires the existence of that corporation. In the case of money and credit, however, the role of the collective has become invisible.

The typical form of knowledge also varied historically with forms of the state and credit as illustrated in Table 5.6 below.

Table 5.6 History of Knowledge

Form of the State	Form of Credit	Form of Knowledge
Hereditary monarchy	Coin (private bankers)	Church
City-states (Italy)	Public credit	Renaissance
Trading states (the Low Country)	Public corporation	Enlightenment
Liberal nation state (UK)	Central bank	Scottish Enlightenment; Royal Society (natural science)

Poovey suggests that abstraction is typical of Enlightenment thinking and the notion of the market as a system (Poovey 2010). Abstraction is necessary for the analysis of insurance, a typical Enlightenment practice. Like the integration of induction and deduction, the analysis of the concrete event and the development of the appropriate category are both part of the epistemology of the insurance contract, along with assessing the value of the insurance object (Baucom 2005, 39–41, 95–96, 99–109, 117).

V.   History of Monetary Theory

A detailed history of monetary thought is beyond the scope of this work. A rough periodization of monetary theories could be suggested in Table 5.7, nonetheless, based on the respective institutional priorities.

The debate between the currency and banking school is more appropriate for purposes A and B in Table 5.7, facilitating trade. That is, the quantity of money is controlled to manage its value, and the expansion of credit is also acknowledged by the role of banks. For the classical school, where value is produced by labor, with such theorists as Locke, Smith, and Marx, the relevant period and institution is C. For the preservation of value in financial assets, with relevance for Keynes and Fama, with a focus on the *rentier* or "portfolio society" (Davis 2009), the purposes of D and E are most relevant. For this period, Keynes assumes that there is a return to parting with the liquidity of money, and the work of Fama and Black/Scholes assumes that there is a return to risk relative to "safe assets" (Gorton 2016).

Table 5.7 History of Money Theories

Purpose	Source of Value	Institution	Financial Asset	Method
A. Trade	Equal value of exchange	City-states	Gold coin	Long-distance trade by partners
B. Trade	Equal value of exchange	Mercantile nation-states	Merchant credit	Expanding merchant corporations
C. Create value in production	Expand value by commodity production	Tax/credit state and Industrial Revolution	Value based on labor time of production	Endogenous expansion by production
D. Preserve value	Return to liquidity	Post-WWII state	Insured deposits	Global banks
E. Preserve value	Return to risk	Twenty-first-century hegemonic state	Derivatives; repos	Global equity and hedge funds

VI. Time

Several scholars suggest a connection between money and time (Baucom 2005; Galison 2003; Goetzmann 2016; Keynes 1964; Mitchell 2014; Pocock 1975; Postone 1993; Sewell 2012a and 2012b), along with other uses and functions of money (Poovey 2010). A broader perspective sees the view of time and history as part of the culture of a period, as in Table 5.8.

The assumption that infinite time exists and can be consistently measured is required for the operation of financial markets in spite of the philosophical variations noted earlier.

VII. Representation: Political and Economic

Building on the type of abstraction unique to capitalism (Sartori 2013, 111–113), the liberal state is based on property, with two forms of "representation: 1) political quantitative representation in formal governance institutions, with checks and balances; and 2) the abstract representation of labor and property in the form of money. This dual form of representation is facilitated by the public/private divide.

That is, in the first, as a citizen, the individual person has political rights in the public sphere, equal to other citizens. These are rights of suffrage, which are counted in certain proportions, depending on categories based on age and residence, if no longer property ownership, race, and gender (Kishlansky 1986; Knights 2005; Withington 2005). In the second, as a person, one is represented by money in the capacity to mediate one's own labor to acquire commodities. That is,

Table 5.8 Conceptions of Time

Approach	Resource
Civilizations	Pocock 1975
Classical Greece	Aristotle 1984
Christian	Weber 1958
Evolution	Darwin 1923
Infinite financial time; revolutionary time	Marx 1967
Standard time	Newton 1952
Financial market time	Black-Scholes; capital asset pricing model (Derman 2004, 2016; Ayache 2016)
Cosmological time	Einstein 2015
Ecological time	Purdy 2015; Bonneuil and Fressoz 2016

"abstract labor" was the peculiar characteristic of a society in which labor is generally undertaken as a means to acquire the products of others, with value serving as an impersonal and abstract mechanism of the distribution and coordination of particular laboring activities. (Sartori 2013, 112–113)

The means by which "value" serves as an impersonal distribution mechanism is as represented and mediated by money.

That is, there are two governing principles of the liberal state: representation of persons as citizens in official public bodies, and representations as property owners in financial circuits. These financial circuits accomplish three tasks: first, the persons represented are not recognizable in their human form; rather, the financial circuits appear to be automatic and beyond human control; second, the financial circuits serve to discipline individual behavior; third, there is an appearance that all persons are equal property owners, but in fact there are distinct rules with respect to property in labor and property in financial assets or "capital." These differences among types of property are eliminated in the sphere of circulation, which is mediated by money.

The liberal state takes organization forms that integrate these two forms of representation, while also keeping them apparently separate in the public/ private divide, the first mediated by human action and the second mediated by money, which is not apparently human. The corporate form was first used for governance in the Italian city-states of the twelfth century, but was adopted to a commercial form with the first chartered monopoly corporations in the sixteenth century (Mitchell 2015, 444). After some experimentation with competing types of sovereignty (Barkan 2013) during the colonial period, the public/private divide resolved the competing claims, based on the hierarchy of wealth accumulation. The role of corporations as a major form of property within the liberal state (Wright 2014) and the formation of fixed territories for nation-states were part of this resolution.

The capacity for money to integrate across these spheres is based on the role of the governance institutions in taxation and expenditures and the role of the private business corporation in managing financial flows, including production, distribution of commodities, and operation in capital markets. Money represents the disciplining and integrating device in the "bottom line" of corporations and the public budget of the government, managed by the central bank and debated in the "public sphere."

There are many theories of money, but no consensus about what money is. The highest levels of government, both national and international, are responsible for managing money in direct personal deliberations, yet financial institutions play no consistent role in monetary theory. Most institutional histories and studies of "property" and "money" are in separate fields and disciplines. The proposal here is to integrate these topics as part of understanding the political economy of capitalism.

VIII.   Contradictions of Liberalism

One of the contradictions of liberalism is the apparent mutual consistency with "freedom" and constraint, most famously during the eighteenth-century slave trade (Pettigrew 2013). The so-called freedom of the citizen in the liberal state is combined with various types of coercion and deprivation (Commons 1995; Mehta 1999). In spite of formal "democracy," citizens in advanced industrial countries feel powerless, even while celebrating the "invisible hand" of the market.

One reason for the contradictions of liberalism is the separation of rules of law for the "inside" citizen vis-à-vis the outsider/noncitizen (Beckert 2014, 38, 43, 78; Baucom 2005, 297–299; 2010, 337–350; Mehta 1999; Stern 2012). This was particularly true when English monopoly–chartered corporations were sovereign military powers in parts of India in the nineteenth century.

Another reason for this apparent anomaly is due to the form of "representation" in money, which is abstract labor and property, a key principle of the liberal state. By respecting property and by not inquiring into the nature of money, the so-called public sphere does not interfere with the automatic market of the private sphere. By leaving this form of representation in place, the role of labor is divided and constrained, to the point of the "prod of hunger" (Polanyi 1944). The so-called fetish of money and credit (Wennerlind 2011, 199, 229–230, 245) allows these disparate phenomena to remain separate in awareness, rather than linked by institutional construction. For example, the first permanent stock markets primarily traded government debt and the corporate stock of the Dutch and English East India Corporations (Baucom 2005, 37–38). That is, monopoly control of the slave trade was granted to chartered corporations in order to finance the public debt, in order to wage wars on the continent for hegemonic power for the liberal state of England. These dichotomies and disconnections persist in the twenty-first century (Baucom 2005, 145–148).

IX.   Methodology

The methodology proposed in this work is a long-term institutional history of money and the state. This contrasts with other approaches discussed later. First the New Institutional Economists assume that property is the foundation of the economic system, with a general and static definition of property. Second, another approach to the study of capitalism lists its characteristics, rather than study its emergence.

A.   *New Institutional Economics*

The principles of political economy from Adam Smith include property rights, individual freedom, self-regulating markets, and free trade (Cardoso 2014). This model of political economy may be useful compared with militarized trade for which the West has been recognized (Pomeranz 2000). The early model of Venice included public financing of armed convoys to accompany merchant shipping (Pezzolo 2014). Later merchant monopoly corporations like the Dutch East India Company and the English East India Company were also allowed to use force to establish colonies and trading routes. England established a publicly financed navy with monopoly shipping rights in order to maintain its control of the seas (O'Brien 2014). Tonnage duties in turn helped to finance the Bank of England, which then served as a model for the New East India Company and the South Sea Company in order to manage Britain's public debt. Customs duties from England's empire then provided a significant portion of the revenue for the state, from 20 percent to 30 percent over the period of 1696–1914, enabling it to avoid direct taxes on its citizens and to improve the legitimacy of the state (Daunton 2010, 30). Britain's dominance of global trade and military power then reduced the capacity of other nation-states to compete and to gain a similar share of revenues from trade and colonies.

Rather than one-time "credible commitments" accomplished in 1689, which were lauded by North and colleagues in the New Institutional Economics literature, one wonders whether the English model instead represents militarized monopoly control over trade and empire. For example, O'Brien emphasizes the experience of the English Civil War and centralized tax collection, as well as support for the Royal Navy and merchant marine, as leading to economies of scale in investments in trade and protection. Rising expenditures on the Royal Navy (O'Brien 2014, 370–373) were judged to yield benefits for economic development, and its tonnage exceeded that of European rivals after 1695. This relative strength of the Royal Navy may have assured investors regarding the viability of the public debt and the long-run development of the British economy as much as the Glorious Revolution of 1688 (O'Brien 2014, 362–363).

Other commentators have contributed to this debate as well (Coffman, Leonard, and Neal 2013). For example, Neal emphasizes the imitation of Dutch precedent as well as the model of the Italian city-states in the financial revolution in England (Neal 2015, 73–76, 108–109). Broz and Grossman (2004) emphasize the ongoing negotiation regarding the charters of the Bank of England and Parliament, rather than the one-time permanent resolution, which is implied by North and Weingast (1989) in their treatment of the Glorious Revolution. Murphy stresses the demands by investors, in addition to the top-down commitments of Parliament (Murphy 2009, 4; 2013a; 2013b). According to Munro (2013), the first financial revolution was in Habsburg, Netherlands, in 1537, rather than in England in 1688. Daunton discusses the trust in English public finance waning after the defeat of France in 1815 and requiring subsequent efforts to legitimize the state, including political reform and changing party composition (Daunton 2010, 29–38).

Rather than protecting property rights against the state, as in the New Institutional Economics formulation (North and Weingast 1989), the formation of the liberal state in England may reflect the bourgeoisie as a "novel legal persona" (Sassen 2006, 96), whose interests become the public interest as expressed in the actions of the state. Money is seen as the natural product of the market (Polanyi 1944) rather than the instrument of the state, because of the assumed separation of state from market in this literature. Rugggie's warning that "the intellectual apparatus by which we study fundamental change is itself implicated in a world that may be changing" (Ruggie 1993, 170) may be especially apt in an era of "financialization."

B. *History of Capitalism*

The definition of capitalism includes historically specific institutions, such as individual property rights protected by law, commodity exchange involving money, private ownership of the means of production used to produce commodities for profit, separation of household and factory, widespread wage labor, and financial institutions that provide credit (Hodgson 2015, 252–257; Rose-Ackerman 2017). First, in Marx's discussion property rights take a particular form—the product of the worker belongs to the capitalist (Marx 1967, Vol. I, Ch. 24, Section 1, 585). Further, unlike Marx, Hodgson mentions, but does not stress, the purpose of accumulation of money for its own sake as a driving force of the system. Aside from the so-called "General Law of Capitalist Accumulation" (Marx 1967, Vol. I, Ch. 25), there are the typical dramatic quotes, such as the following.

"Accumulate, accumulate! That is Moses and the prophets!" (Marx Vol. I, Ch. 24, Section 3, 595).

Money which can command interest becomes "capital" by means of the financial circuit, $M - C - M'$, or more simply $M - M'$ (Marx 1967, Vol. III, Ch. 21).

"Money ... may be converted into capital ... It produces profit ... it acquires an additional use-value, namely that of serving as capital" (Marx 1967, Vol. III, Ch. 21, 338).

"Capital manifests itself as capital through self-expansion" (Marx 1967, Vol. III, Ch. 21, 354).

If one defines capitalism as consisting of two essential features—mobile wage labor force and legitimacy of interest charges on money loans—then the emergence of capitalism occurred in the early nineteenth century. This timing is based on the emergence of the British consol, Neal's (2000, 2015) "big bang" of finance, along with the accumulated effects of the enclosure movement on residential patterns. Further, the Industrial Revolution built upon the global trade networks that had already been established from the sixteenth century, along with regular commodity circuits and instruments of money and credit. Energy sources and labor-saving devices were present in England (Allen 2009) to facilitate its productivity advantage in commodity production and trade.

The reorganization of human settlement patterns involved with enclosures and separation of household from factory required the authority of the state in a series of legislative acts, including formal representation in the legislature itself. The guarantee of a financial rate of return on government debt also required the "credible commitment" of the state, as well as state-managed financial institutions such as central banks. The legal protection of property was also required state action, as well as provisions for its ongoing redefinitions. That is, "free markets" in land, labor, and money required the action of the state, as argued by Polanyi (1944).

X.   Collective Intentionality

Ultimately the purpose of the study of institutional history is for a greater understanding of its long-term evolution. This study of human history must also bring reflexivity, an awareness of collective intentionality, as well as institutional resilience.

The flux in values can be observed as well, across the types of state, finance, and cultures. In the classical and medieval periods, money was condemned and merchants disrespected. At the end of the "long wave" of modernity in the contemporary period, money is highly honored and represents the highest purpose. Money enables the greatest individual freedom within the public/private divide of the liberal state, according to some. For others, these divisions prevent a vision of the whole. In a broader conception of collective communities, the ultimate purpose is open. The form of money and the state would then follow.

References

Allen, Robert C. *The British Industrial Revolution in Global Perspective.* New York: Cambridge University Press, 2009.

Andreades, A. *History of the Bank of England, 1640–1903.* New York: Augustus M. Kelley Bookseller, 1966.

Aristotle. *Politics.* Chicago: University of Chicago Press, 1984.

Armitage, David and Michael J. Braddick. *The British Atlantic World, 1500–1800.* New York: Palgrave MacMillan, 2009.

Arrighi, Giovanni. *The Long Twentieth Century: Money, Power, and the Origins of Our Times.* New York: Verso, 1994.

Ayache, Elie. "On Black-Scholes," in Benjamin Lee and Randy Martin (eds.). *Derivatives and the Wealth of Societies.* Chicago: University of Chicago Press, 2016, 240–251.

Barkan, Joshua. *Corporate Sovereignty: Law and Government under Capitalism.* Minneapolis, MN: University of Minnesota Press, 2013.

Baucom, Ian. *Specters of the Atlantic: Finance Capital, Slavery, and the Philosophy of History.* Durham, NC: Duke University Press, 2005.

———. "Financing the Enlightenment, Part Two: Extraordinary Expenditure," in Clifford Siskin and William Warner (eds.), *This is Enlightenment.* Chicago: University of Chicago Press, 2010, 336–356.

Beckert, Sven. *Empire of Cotton: A Global History.* New York: Alfred A. Knopf, 2014.

Bonneuil, Christophe and Jean-Baptiste Fressoz. *The Shock of the Anthropocene: The Earth, History and Us.* London: Verso, 2016.

Bowen, H.V., Elizabeth Mancke, and John G. Reid (eds.). *Britain's Oceanic Empire: Atlantic and Indian Worlds, c. 1550–1850.* New York: Cambridge University Press, 2012.

Braddick, Michael J. *The Nerves of State: Taxation and the Financing of the English State, 1558–1714.* Manchester, UK: Manchester University Press, 1996.

Brown, Peter. *The Ransom of the Soul: Afterlife and Wealth in Early Western Christianity*. Cambridge, MA: Harvard University Press, 2015.

Broz, J. Lawrence and Richard S. Grossman. "Paying for Privilege: The Political Economy of the Bank of England Charters, 1694–1844," *Explorations in Economic History*, Vol. 41, 2004, 48–72.

Cardoso, Jose Luis. "The Political Economy of Rising Capitalism," in Larry Neal and Jeffrey G. Williamson (eds.), *The Cambridge History of Capitalism. Volume I: The Rise of Capitalism: From Ancient Origins to 1848*. New York: Cambridge University Press, 2014, 574–599.

Carlos, Ann M. and Larry Neal. "Amsterdam and London as Financial Centers in Eighteenth Century London," *Financial History Review*, Vol. 18, No. 1, 2011, 21–46.

Carruthers, Bruce G. *City of Capital: Politics and Markets in the English Financial Revolution*. Princeton, NJ: Princeton University Press, 1996.

Coffman, D'Maris, Adrian Leonard, and Larry Neal (eds). *Questioning Credible Commitment: Perspectives on the Rise of Financial Capitalism*. New York: Cambridge University Press, 2013.

Commons, John R. *The Legal Foundations of Capitalism*. New Brunswick, NJ: Transaction Publishers, 1995.

Darwin, Charles. *On the Origins of Species by Means of Natural Selection*. London: Oxford University Press, 1923.

Daunton, Martin. "Creating Legitimacy: Administering Taxation in Britain, 1815–1915, in Jose Luis Cardoso and Pedro Lains (eds.), *Paying for the Liberal State: The Rise of Public Finance in Nineteenth-Century Europe*. New York: Cambridge University Press, 2010, 27–56.

Davis, Ann E. "Marx and the Mixed Economy: Money, Accumulation, and the Role of the State," *Science & Society*, Vol. 74, No. 3, July 2010, 409–428.

_____. "The New 'Voodoo Economics': Fetishism and the Public/Private Divide." *Review of Radical Political Economics*, Vol. 45, No. 1, March 2013, 42–58.

_____. *The Evolution of the Property Relation: Paradigms, Debates, Prospects*. New York: Palgrave Macmillan, 2015.

Davis, Gerald F. *Managed by the Markets: How Finance Reshaped America*. New York: Oxford University Press, 2009.

Derman, Emanuel. *My Life as a Quant: Reflections on Physics and Finance*. New York: John Wiley & Sons, Inc. 2004.

_____. "Remarks on Financial Models," in Benjamin Lee and Randy Martin (eds.). *Derivatives and the Wealth of Societies*. Chicago: University of Chicago Press, 2016, 199–239.

De Roover, Raymond. *The Medici Bank: Its Organization, Management, Operation and Decline*. New York: New York University Press, 1948.

_____. *The Rise and Decline of the Medici Bank, 1397–1494*. Cambridge, MA: Harvard University Press, 1963.

Desan, Christine. "Money as a Legal Institution," in David Fox and Wolfgang Ernst (eds.), *Money in the Western Legal Tradition: Middle Ages to Bretton Woods*. New York: Oxford University Press, 2016, 18–40.

Eichengreen, Barry. *Globalizing Capital: A History of the International Monetary System*. Princeton, NJ: Princeton University Press, 1996.

Eichengreen, Barry and Ricardo Hausmann (eds.). *Other People's Money: Debt Denomination and Financial Instability in Emerging Market Economies*. Chicago: University of Chicago Press, 2005.

Einstein, Albert. *Relativity: The Special and the General Theory*. Princeton, NJ: Princeton University Press, 2015.

Evans, Eric J. *Britain Before the Reform Act: Politics and Society, 1815–1832*, 2nd ed. New York: Pearson Longman, 2008.

Feavearyear, A. E. *The Pound Sterling: A History of English Money*. Oxford, UK: Clarendon Press, 1931.

Galison, Peter. *Einstein's Clocks, Poincare's Maps: Empires of Time*. New York: W.W. Norton, 2003.

Goetzmann, William N. *Money Changes Everything: How Finance Made Civilization Possible*. Princeton, NJ: Princeton University Press, 2016.

Goldthwaite, Richard A. *The Economy of Renaissance Florence*. Baltimore: Johns Hopkins University Press, 2009.

_____. "The Practice and Culture of Accounting in Renaissance Florence," *Enterprise and Society*, Vol. 16, No. 3, September 2015, 611–647.

Gorton, Gary. "The History of Safe Assets," Cambridge, MA: National Bureau of Economic Research Working Paper 22210, August 31, 2016.

Habermas, Jurgen. *The Structural Transformation of the Public Sphere: An Inquiry into a Bourgeois Category*. Cambridge, MA: MIT Press, 1989.

Hawkins, Angus. *Victorian Political Culture: "Habits of Heart and Mind."* New York: Oxford University Press, 2015.

Hodgson, Geoffrey M. *Conceptualizing Capitalism: Institutions, Evolution, Future*. Chicago: Universityof Chicago Press, 2015.

Howe, Anthony. *The Cotton Masters 1830-1860*. Oxford, UK: Clarendon Press, 1984.

Howell, Martha C. *Commerce Before Capitalism in Europe, 1300–1600*. New York: Cambridge University Press, 2010.

Hunt, E.K. *Property and Prophets: The Evolution of Economic Institutions and Ideology*. 6th ed. New York: Harper & Row, 1990.

Ingham, Geoffrey. *The Nature of Money*. Cambridge, UK: Polity, 2004.

Kessler, Amalia D. *A Revolution in Commerce: The Parisian Merchant Court and the Rise of Commercial Society in Eighteenth-Century France*. New Haven: Yale University Press, 2007.

Keynes, John Maynard. *The General Theory of Employment, Interest, and Money*. New York: Harcourt, Brace & World, 1964.

Kishlansky, Mark A. *Parliamentary Selection: Social and Political Choice in Early Modern England*. New York: Cambridge University Press, 1986.

Knights, Mark. *Representation and Misrepresentation in Later Stuart Britain: Partisanship and Political Culture*. New York: Oxford University Press, 2005.

Koot, Christian J. *Empire at the Periphery: British Colonists, Anglo-Dutch Trade, and the Development of the British Atlantic, 1621-1713*. New York: New York University Press, 2011.

Kregel, Jan. "Financial Stability and Secure Currency in a Modern Context," Levy Institute Working Paper No 877. Annandale-on-Hudson: Bard College, November, 2016.

Kwass, Michael. *Privilege and the Politics of Taxation in Eighteenth-Century France*. New York: Cambridge University Press, 2000.

Lapavitsas, Costas. "The Banking School and the Monetary Thought of Karl Marx," *Cambridge Journal of Economics*, Vol. 18, No. 5, 1994, 447–461.

Leonard, A. B. "Reassessing the Atlantic Contribution to British Marine Insurance," in D'Maris Coffman, Adrian Leonard and William O'Reilly (eds.), *The Atlantic World*. New York: Routledge, 2015, 513–530.

Livingston, James. *Origins of the Federal Reserve System: Money, Class, and Corporate Capitalism, 1890–1914*. Ithaca, NY: Cornell University Press, 1986.

Lopez, Robert S. *The Commercial Revolution of the Middle Ages, 950–1350*. Englewood Cliffs, NJ: Prentice-Hall, 1971.

Marsilio, C. "Genoese Finance, 1348–1700," in Gerard Caprio Jr. (ed.), *Handbook of Key Global Financial Markets, Institutions and Infrastructure*. Boston: Elsevier, 2013, 123–132.

Marx, Karl. *Capital*. Vol. I–III. New York: International Publishers, 1967.

Maurer, Bill. "Forget Locke? From Proprietor to Risk-Bearer in New Logics of Finance," *Public Culture*, Vol. 11, No. 2, 1999, 365–385.

_____. "International Political Economy as a Cultural Practice: The Metaphysics of Capital Mobility," in Richard Warren Perry and Bill Maurer (eds.), *Globalization Under Construction: Govermentality, Law, and Identity*. Minneapolis, MN: University of Minnesota Press, 2003, 71–98.

Mehrling, Perry. *The New Lombard Street: How the Fed became the Dealer of Last Resort*. Princeton, NJ: Princeton University Press, 2011.

_____. "Three Principles for Market-Based Credit Regulation," *American Economic Review: Papers & Proceedings*, Vol. 102, No. 3, 2012, 107–112.

_____. "The Inherent Hierarchy of Money," in Lance Taylor, Armon Rezai, and Thomas Michl (eds.), *Social Fairness and Economics: Economic Essays in the Spirit of Duncan Foley*. New York: Routledge, 2013.

Mehta, Uday Singh. *Liberalism and Empire: A Study in Nineteenth-Century British Liberal Thought*. Chicago: University of Chicago Press, 1999.

Millo, Yuval. "Making Things Deliverable: The Origins of Index-Based Derivatives," in Micel Callon, Yuval Millo and Fabian Muniesa (eds.), *Market Devices*. Oxford, UK: Blackwell Publishing, 2007, 196–214.

Mitchell, Robert. "'Beings that Have Existence only in ye Minds of Men': State Finance and the Origins of the Collective Imagination," *The Eighteenth Century*, Vol. 49, No. 2, 2008, 117–139.

_____. *Sympathy and the State in the Romantic Era: Systems, State Finance, and the Shadows of Futurity*. New York: Routledge, 2014.

Mokyr, Joel. *A Culture of Growth: The Origins of the Modern Economy*. Princeton, NJ: Princeton University Press, 2017.

Molho, Anthony. *Florentine Public Finances in the Early Renaissance, 1400–1433*. Cambridge, MA: Harvard University Press, 1971.

Munro, J. H. "Rentes and the European 'Financial Revolution,'" in Gerard Caprio Jr. (ed.), *Handbook of Key Global Financial Markets, Institutions and Infrastructure*. Boston: Elsevier, 2013, 235–249.

Murphy, Anne L. *The Origins of English Financial Markets: Investment and Speculation before the South Sea Bubble*. New York: Cambridge University Press, 2009.

_____. "Demanding 'Credible Commitment': Public Reactions to the Failures of the Early Financial Revolution," *Economic History Review*, Vol. 66, No. 1, 2013a, 178–197.

_____. "The Financial Revolution in England," in Gerard Caprio, Jr., *Handbook of Key Global Financial Markets, Institutions and Infrastructure*. Boston: Elsevier, 2013b, 85–94.

_____. "Financial Markets: The Limits of Economic Regulation in Early Modern England," in Philip J. Stern and Carl Wennerlind (eds.), *Mercantilism Reimagined: Political Economy in Early Modern Britain and Its Empire*. New York: Oxford University Press, 2014, 263–281.

Neal, Larry. *The Rise of Financial Capitalism: International Capital Markets in the Age of Reason*. New York: Cambridge University Press, 1990.

_____. "How It All Began: The Monetary and Financial Architecture of Europe During the First Global Capital Markets, 1648–1815." *Financial History Review*, Vol. 7, No. 2, 2000, 117–140.

_____. *"I Am Not Master of Events": The Speculations of John Law and Lord Londonderry in the Mississippi and South Sea Bubbles*. New Haven, CT: Yale University Press, 2012.

_____. *A Concise History of International Finance: From Babylon to Bernanke*. New York: Cambridge University Press, 2015.

Newton, Isaac. *Mathematical Principles of Natural Philosophy*. Chicago: Encyclopedia Britannica. 1952.

North, Douglass C. and Barry R. Weingast. "Constitutions and Commitment: The Evolution of Institutions Governing Public Choice in Seventeenth-Century England." *The Journal of Economic History*, Vol. 49, No. 4, 1989, 803–832.

O'Brien, Patrick Karl. "The Formation of States and Transitions to Modern Economies: England, Europe, and Asia Compared," in Larry Neal and Jeffrey G. Williamson (eds.), *The Cambridge History of Capitalism. Volume I: The Rise of Capitalism: From Ancient Origins to 1848*. New York: Cambridge University Press, 2014, 357–402.

Pettigrew, William A. *Freedom's Debt: The Royal African Company and the Politics of the Atlantic Slave Trade, 1672–1752*. Chapel Hill, NC: University of North Carolina Press, 2013.

Pezzolo, Luciano. "The *Via Italiana* to Capitalism," in Larry Neal and Jeffrey G. Williamson (eds.), *The Cambridge History of Capitalism. Volume I: The Rise of Capitalism: From Ancient Origins to 1848*. New York: Cambridge University Press, 2014, 267–313.

Pincus, Steven. "The State and Civil Society in Early Modern England: Capitalism, Causation and Habermas's Bourgeois Pubic Sphere," in Peter Lake and Steven Pincus (eds.), *The Politics of the Public Sphere in Early Modern England*. Manchester, UK: Manchester University Press, 2007, 213–231.

_____. *1688: The First Modern Revolution*. New Haven, CT: Yale University Press, 2009.

Pincus, Steven and Alice Wolfram. "A Proactive State? The Land Bank, Investment and Party Politics in the 1690s," in Perry Gauci (ed.), *Regulating the British Economy, 1660-1850*, Burlington, VT: Ashgate, 2011, 41–62.

Pistor, Katharina. "A Legal Theory of Finance," *Journal of Comparative Economics*, Vol. 41, 2013, 315–330.

Pocock, J.G.A. *The Machiavellian Moment: Florentine Political Thought and the Atlantic Republican Tradition*. Princeton, NJ: Princeton University Press, 1975.

Polanyi, Karl. *The Great Transformation: The Political and Economic Origins of Our Time*. Boston: Beacon Press, 1944.

Pomeranz, Kenneth. *The Great Divergence: China, Europe, and the Making of the Modern World Economy*. Princeton, NJ: Princeton University Press, 2000.

Poovey, Mary. *A History of the Modern Fact: Problems of Knowledge in the Sciences of Wealth and Society*. Chicago: University of Chicago Press, 1998.

_____. *Genres of the Credit Economy: Mediating Value in Eighteenth- and Nineteenth-Century Britain*. Chicago: University of Chicago Press, 2008.

_____. "Financing Enlightenment, Part One: Money Matters," in Clifford Siskin and William Warner (eds.), *This is Enlightenment*. Chicago: University of Chicago Press, 2010, 323–335.

Postone, Moishe. *Time, Labor, and Social Domination: A Reinterpretation of Marx's Critical Theory*. New York: Cambridge University Press, 1993.

Purdy, Jedediah. *After Nature: A Politics for the Anthropocene*. Cambridge, MA: Harvard University Press, 2015.

Quinn, Stephen. "Goldsmith-Banking: Mutual Acceptance and Interbanker Clearing in Restoration London," *Explorations in Economic History*, Vol. 34, 1997, 411–432.

_____. "Securitization of Sovereign Debt: Corporations as a Sovereign Debt Restructuring Mechanism in Britain, 1694–1750," Department of Economics, Texas Christian University, Fort Worth, TX, 2008.

Quinn, Stephen and William Roberds. "The Bank of Amsterdam and the Leap to Central Bank Money," *American Economic Review*, Vol. 97, No. 2, 2007, 262–265.

Rose-Ackerman, Susan. "A Review of Geoffrey M. Hodgson, *Conceptualizing Capitalism: Institutions, Evolution, Future*," in *Journal of Economic Literature*, Vol. 55, No. 1, 2017, 182–190.

Rothschild, Emma. *Economic Sentiments: Adam Smith, Condorcet, and the Enlightenment*. Cambridge, MA: Harvard University Press, 2001.

Ruggie, John Gerard. "Review: Continuity and Transformation in the World Polity: Toward a Neorealist Synthesis," *World Politics*, Vol. 35, No. 2, 1983, 261–285.

_____. "Territoriality and Beyond: Problematizing Modernity in International Relations," *International Organization*, Vol. 47, No. 1, 1993, 139–174.

Santner, Eric L. *The Weight of All Flesh: On the Subject-Matter of Political Economy*. Oxford University Press, 2016.

Sartori, Andrew. "Global Intellectual History and the History of Political Economy," in Samuel Moyn and Andrew Sartori (eds.), *Global Intellectual History*. New York: Columbia University Press, 2013, 110–133.

Sassen, Saskia. *Territory, Authority, Rights: From Medieval to Global Assemblages*. Princeton, NJ: Princeton University Press, 2006.

Schumpeter, Joseph A. "The Crisis of the Tax State," in Richard Swedberg (ed.), *Joseph A. Schumpeter: The Economics and Sociology of Capitalism*. Princeton, NJ: Princeton University Press, 1991, 99–140.

Searle, John R. *Making the Social World: The Structure of Civilization*. New York: Oxford University Press, 2010.

Sewell, William H. Jr. "Economic Crises and the Shape of Modern History," *Public Culture*, Vol. 24, No. 2, 2012a, 303–327.

_____. "The Capitalist Epoch," Presidential Address, Social Science History Association, 2012b.

Shaikh, Anwar. *Capitalism: Competition, Conflict, and Crises*. New York: Oxford University Press, 2016.

Siskin, Clifford and William Warner, "This Is Enlightenment: An Invitation in the Form of an Argument," in Clifford Siskin and William Warner (eds.), *This Is Enlightenment*. Chicago: University of Chicago Press, 2009, 1–36.

Soll, Jacob. *The Reckoning: Financial Accountability and the Rise and Fall of Nations*. New York: Basic Books, 2014.

Stasavage, David. *Public Debt and the Birth of the Democratic State*. New York: Cambridge University Press, 2003.

Stern, Philip J. "Company, State, and Empire: Governance and Regulatory Frameworks in Asia," in H. V. Bowen, Elizabeth Mancke, and John G. Reid (eds.), *Britain's Oceanic Empire: Atlantic and Indian Ocean Worlds, c. 1550–1850*. New York: Cambridge University Press, 2012, 130–150.

_____. "Companies: Monopoly, Sovereignty, and the East Indies," in Philip J. Stern and Carl Wennerlind (eds.), *Mercantilism Reimagined: Political Economy in Early Modern Britain and Its Empire*. New York: Oxford University Press, 2014, 177–195.

Stern, Philip J. and Carl Wennerlind (eds.). *Mercantilism Reimagined: Political Economy in Early Modern Britain and Its Empire*. New York: Oxford University Press, 2014.

Taylor, Charles. *Modern Social Imaginaries*. Durham, NC: Duke University Press, 2004.

Tracy, James D. *A Financial Revolution in the Habsburg Netherlands: Renten and Renteniers in the County of Holland, 1515–1565*. Berkeley, CA: University of California Press, 1985.

Vogl, Joseph. *The Specter of Capital*. Stanford, CA: Stanford University Press, 2015.

Weber, Max. *The Protestant Ethic and the Spirit of Capitalism*. New York: Charles Scribner's Sons, 1958.

_____. *Economy and Society*. Edited by Guenther Roth and Claus Wittich. Vol. I and Vol. II. Berkeley: University of California Press, 1978.

Wennerlind, Carl. *Casualties of Credit: The English Financial Revolution, 1620–1720*. Cambridge, MA: Harvard University Press, 2011.

Withington, Phil. *The Politics of Commonwealth: Citizens and Freemen in Early Modern England*. New York: Cambridge University Press, 2005.

Wright, Robert E. *Corporation Nation*. Philadelphia: University of Pennsylvania Press, 2014.

6 Fetishism and Financialization

I. Introduction

It is possible to apply the method of historical institutionalism to money, extending the analysis of property (Davis 2015). That is, the central concept is "money," which is operationalized by a specific set of institutions and interpreted by a specific body of knowledge. This related institutional complex then varies historically and can be traced by documenting institutional practices and knowledge production. The particular analysis in this chapter builds on Marx, Keynes, Postone, and Minsky, with reference to recent trends in the global economy. The objective is to interpret money as a historically specific institution with changing functions and meanings, rather than a discrete "natural" object that is historically invariant. Consistent with Marx's notion of the "fetishism of money," there is a trend in modern monetary theories from viewing money as a representation of value to an intrinsically valuable asset itself, with implications for the operation of the system.

II. Marx's View of Money: Representation of Value and Instrument of Accumulation

One of Marx's most important analytical concepts is money. In the famous Chapter 1 of Volume I of *Capital*, Marx introduces money as the abstract *representation* of social labor time in commodity production. Workers are not aware of their role as part of the whole of social labor in any given time period or location (Marx 1967, Vol. I, Ch. 1, Section 4, p. 73). The whole of social labor is only represented by the total value produced by employment in a given period, measured by the market value of total production, or gross domestic product in modern terminology. Workers do not feel a relationship with other individual workers based on their collective role in social production, what Marx calls the "fetishism of commodities" (Gordon 2016).

In Vol. I, Ch. 3, Marx discusses money as an abstract expression of the value of commodities, or unit of account, in Section 1, and as a means of payment in Section 3. It is as a means of payment that money acquires the form of "hard cash" (Marx 1967, Vol. I, Ch. 3, Section 1, 103, and Section 3b, 138; Vol. III, Ch. 32, 515–517). Because credit is elastic in the banking system, cash is often short, especially in a crisis (Marx 1967, Vol. III, Ch. 30, 490–493). The circulation of commodities is not based on the quantity of money, but on the expression of value in an independent form (a critique of the Quantity Theory of Money is developed in Vol. I, Ch. 3, Section 2, 120–124; see also Vol. III, Chs. 28, 33, and 34). Whether gold or paper (fiat currency), the symbolic role of money is sufficient as a measure of value until payment must be made (apart from the clearinghouse function of canceling offsetting debts). Money as the "universal commodity" becomes the subject of all contracts, and the specific form of money as cash is required for settlement.

> In so far as actual payments have to be made, money does not serve as a circulating medium, as a mere transient agent in the interchange of products, but as the individual incarnation of social labour, as the independent form of existence of exchange-value, as the universal commodity … and the universal subject-matter of all contracts. (Marx 1967 Vol. I, Ch. 3, Section 3b, 138; Vol. I, Ch. 3, Section 3b, 140).

In the form of a means of payment, money becomes a *tool* of abstraction and accumulation, a "universal money" necessary for settling international accounts (Marx 1967, Vol. I, Ch. 3, Section 3c). That is, money is an abstract symbol of value, whose origin is not widely understood, but it is also a *means* of accumulation, or a "technology of power" (Arrighi 1994, 15). In this context, the history of "primitive accumulation" (Marx 1967, Vol. I, Part VIII, Ch. 26) provides certain groups with the social power of further accumulation, as well as concentration and centralization through the financial system. Capital accumulation is backed by the force of the state (Marx 1967, Vol. I, Ch. 31, 751).

> The credit system, which has its focus in the so-called national banks and the big money-lenders and usurers surrounding them, constitutes enormous centralization, and gives to this class of parasites the fabulous power, not only to periodically despoil industrial capitalists but also to interfere in actual production in a most dangerous manner. (Marx 1967, Vol. III, Ch. 33, 544–545)

Once production is separate from consumption, or labor from ownership of the means of production and the product, there is a time lapse between production and realization, which is bridged by money as a unit of account and as a means of payment. "The appearance of the two equivalents, commodities and money, at the two poles of the process of sale, has ceased to be simultaneous" (Marx 1967, Vol. I, Ch. 3, Section 3b, 136). The use value of the commodity to the consumer becomes separate from the exchange value of the commodity to the producer and appears only as a "double" (Marx 1967, Vol. I, Ch. 3, Section 3b, 108, 134, 136). which becomes a potential contradiction in an economic crisis. The apparent self-expansion of value is due to activities of humans, contrary to appearances, manifested in "flows of money" (Marx 1967, Vol. I, Ch. 3, Section 2a and 2b, 103–124).

This aspect of money as an *instrument* or a "technology" (Goetzmann 2016) is important for firms, who can acquire means of production and purchase the commodity labor power. Further, money is a *method* of homogenization and abstraction of commodities and labor, by means of workplace discipline and competition in product and labor markets. It is also an important means of payment for workers who can purchase the means of subsistence. The financial system is organized by the state to restrict access to credit to those who are capable of repayment with interest (Rousseau 2016). Circulation of the financial token of a particular state is a technique to extend the scale of circulation, increase the speed of turnover, and increase its power among competing capitalist states. In this context, the state control of public credit becomes a means of extension of the power of the state.

Although the historical origin of credit is from long-distance trade and from the self-defense of Italian city-states, the modern liberal state has internalized the credit mobilization and allocation function in partnership with financiers and merchants (Arrighi 1994). That is, the modern liberal state issued debt repayable with future tax revenues in the form of public bonds. These bonds became the center of public credit, as "safe assets" of commercial banks, and later as collateral for "shadow banking" (Gabor and Vertergaard 2016). Regulation of access to credit is a state function, to assure creditworthiness and to provide a backstop. Public bonds are the most liquid asset and are guaranteed by the state as a whole.

Money becomes a tool of abstraction of social life as well. The level of income and wages provides a metric for social status by which individuals evaluate each other (Meister 1990) and provides the foundation of individual competition (de Vries 2008). The level of compensation provides a platform of individual competition in the labor market, where one tends to see one's own value in terms of the comparative wage payment (Frank 2010). The quality of a product is presumably measured by its price (leading to an upward-sloping demand curve for a "Giffen" good). Housing is segregated by income level (and other forms of social status), which then influences life chances by access to schooling and social networks. Even ecological assets are measured in money terms, in the form of "ecosystems services" (Daily 1997).

III.   Capital as Totality

When the purpose of commodity production becomes the expansion of value, per se, "the possessor of money becomes a capitalist" (Marx 1967, Vol. I, Ch. 4, 152) and the expansion of value appears automatic, as if "money begets money" (Vol. I, Ch. 4, 155; Vol. III, Ch. 21, 345; Ch. 24, 391–399). The holder of money seems to have social power himself.

> Just as every qualitative difference between commodities is extinguished in money, so money, on its side, like the radical leveler that it is, does away with all distinctions. But money itself is a commodity, an external object,

capable of becoming the private property of any individual. Thus social power becomes the private power of private persons. (Marx 1967, Vol. I, Ch. 3, Section 3a, 132).

While consisting of the production of specific commodities by specially trained workers employed by competing firms, the capitalist system operates as a whole. The value produced by the aggregate employment is measured at the macro level, coordinated in some mysterious fashion by Smith's "invisible hand." That mystery for Marx consists of the value produced by direct labor consisting of the value of the commodity and represented in external form by money (Vol. I, Ch. 3, Section 2b, 116).

> But how are gold and silver distinguished from other forms of wealth? Not by the magnitude of their value ... but by the fact that they represent independent incarnations, expressions of the *social* character of wealth ... It is faith in the social character of production which allows the money-form of products to assume the aspect of something that is only evanescent and ideal. (Marx 1967, Vol. III, Ch. 35, 573–574; italics in original)

The concrete institutional coordination of the system is then conducted by corporations, financial institutions, and central banks by means of money. There is a division of labor between production and finance capital (Marx 1967, Vol. III, Ch. 21), and bankers become the "representatives of social capital" (Marx 1967, Vol. III, Ch. 32, 368). The whole of the system remains elusive and vaguely manifested by the abstract notion of "capital" (Postone 1993, 152–157, 183–185, 271, 319–321, 349–352).

> Marx's category of capital refers to an alienated, dualistic structure of labor-mediated relations in terms of which the peculiar fabric of modern society, its abstract form of domination, its historical dynamic, and its characteristic forms of production and of work can be understood systematically. For Marx, capital, as the unfolded commodity form, is the central totalizing category of modern life. (Postone 1993, 352)

The financial circuit, $M - C - M'$, is the abstract expression of the operation of capital as self-expanding value. As the system becomes well established, money appears to expand of itself, in the form $M - M'$, a "pure fetish form" (Marx 1967, Vol. III, Ch. 24, 391–393).

> Interest as such expresses precisely the existence of the conditions of labour as capital, in their social antithesis to labour, and in their transformation into personal power vis-à-vis and over labour. It represents the ownership of capital as a means of appropriating the products of the labour of others. But it represents this characteristic of capital as

something which belongs to it outside the production process and by no means is the result of the specifically capitalist attribute of this production process itself. Interest represents this characteristic not as directly counterposed to labour, but rather as unrelated to labour, and simply as a relationship of one capitalist to another. (Marx 1967, Vol. III, Ch. 23, 382)

IV.   Equality of Property Owners vs. Two Distinct Types of Property

A key element of Marx's analysis is the difference in outcomes of the exchange capital and labor, even though all property owners are treated equally (Marx 1967, Vol. I, Ch. 6, 176). That is, all property consists of access to concrete use value and receives its exchange value in circulation based on the embodiment of socially necessary living labor time. For the commodity labor power, the employment in actual production is the use value, and the exchange value is the labor time necessary for its own reproduction. The difference is surplus value (Vol. I, Ch. 6). For capital, the concrete use value is the legal capacity to organize and/or employ labor in the production of commodities, and the exchange value is a legal claim to the share in surplus produced (Vol. III, Chs. 21 and 23). That is, both capital and labor appear as commodities, subject to the same rules that determine use and exchange value. The appearance of money as a claim to an increment, M – M', and the appearance of the capacity of money to expand itself, makes money appear as the source of value. Marx contrasts these appearances compared with the underlying social relations.

> These reasons for compensation which enter the distribution of surplus-value as determinants are distorted in a capitalist's mind to appear as bases of origin and the (subjective) justification of profit itself. (Marx 1967, Vol. III, Ch. 23, 383).

That is, there is an ideological role for the claim to a share of the surplus by money capital. There is a danger in this view, nonetheless, which may tend towards a declining rate of investment when an apparent option for financial returns exists with less "risk" than production of commodities.

> The individual capitalist has a choice of making use of his capital by lending it out as interest-bearing capital, or of expanding its value on his own by using it as productive capital ... [but] if an untowardly large section of capitalists were to convert their capital into money-capital, the result would be a frightful depreciation of money-capital and a frightful fall in the rate of interest. (Marx 1967, Vol. III, Ch. 23, 377–378)

There is an ambiguity in the measure of capital as well. Marx differentiates between the technical and the "organic" composition of capital, where the first is the physical mass of machinery and the second is the reflection of the cost of production of that machine. There is also ongoing concentration and centralization of competing firms (Marx 1967, Vol. I, Ch. 25, Section 2, 621–628). In terms of credit, Marx considers this a form of "fictitious" capital, which relies on calculation of present value (Marx 1967, Vol. III, Ch. 25, 400–413; Ch. 29, 463–475).

V. The Role of the State with Respect to Money

Designation of currency is a function of the state (Marx 1967, Vol. I, Ch. 3, Section 2c, 124–129). Each state maintains the circulation of its distinct token of money (Davis 2010; Polanyi 1944). There is currency competition among competing nation-states (Cohen 2015) and currency hierarchies (Eichengreen and Hausmann 2005).

The state is responsible for managing and integrating the "capitalist totality," as well as defining and enforcing the divisions among specific institutional forms, such as individual private property and wage labor. Both state and markets are constituted by "status function declarations" (Searle 2010), which assign functions to certain categories of persons. Key categories such as "property" and "money" are related to the totality of capitalism (Postone 1993, 216–225). These functions are often symbolized in documents or other types of writing, including money (Poovey 1998). The definitions and institutions of money and the state are mutually reinforcing and so elicit "performances," which maintain and enhance these institutions (MacKenzie 2006).

For example, the formation of the joint stock corporation was both a legal and a political process (Davis 2009, 64–67), involving "other people's capital" (Marx 1967, Vol. III, 436–441). As merchant guilds evolved into business companies, there was a removal of labor from membership to form the modern business corporation. The attack on guilds and constraints on labor organization as "monopolies" in the early modern period reduced labor's bargaining power, with some support from the Factory Acts (Marx 1967, Vol. I, Ch. 10, 278–302; Ch. 28, 734–741; Smith 1994). The exclusion of workers from the corporate organization, the guild, helped establish the institutional base for the process of commodification of labor, along with mechanization and use of science in aid of capital (Marx 1967, Vol. I, Ch. 15, 371–507; Ch. 24 Section 4, 605). Over time, finance became the dominant purpose of the corporation, within an infinite time perspective. Stock markets and limited liability provided "liquidity" for the investor (Lazonick 2015, 5–7).

There was a perceived reversal of living and dead labor (Marx 1947, Vol. I, Ch. 7, Section 2, 195), with capital as agent and the worker as object. An increase in wages merely extends "the length and weight of the golden chain the wage worker has already forged for himself" (Vol. I, Ch. 25, Section 1, 618).

Once the worker no longer owns the product of labor (Marx 1967, Vol. I, Ch. 24, 587), the state defines and enforces "paradoxical" divisions, such as the public/private divide. That is, the whole of the economic system must be divided into factory and household, or work and nonwork. This division enables the owner to maintain control of production by specific rules, and the individual household to maintain the "independence" vis-à-vis reliance on the state and the employer, according to the self-ownership of labor model (Davis 2017). Further, the family constitutes the "public" in terms of citizenship, labor force, and population, while also shouldering the responsibility of the individual "private" household in terms of provision of necessities, education, and socialization. This externalization of the costs of the reproduction of the labor force helps differentiate and define the limits of the financial circuit, such as children, and circumscribe the costs that can be attributed to the firm, such as day care (with health care and pensions subject to variable contributions by firms). A similar "externalization" of environmental costs of disposal protects the firm from potential claims or deductions from its profit due to ecological disruption.

Money is the financial token that helps to externalize some costs and internalize others, defining the boundary of the financial circuit. Money is a symbol of delegated sovereignty that allows the control of property and aids the state in managing decentralized agents and their division of tasks along the financial circuit. Completion, or "realization," of the financial circuit is necessary for both firms and the state, and they maintain complementary roles. Completing the financial circuit by means of realization, by sales of the "final product" to the household and payment of taxes to the state, is increasingly complex, given the geographic extension and institutional innovation of financial forms and institutions. The definition of money is endogenous, instrumental, and evolutionary, as are theories of what constitutes money (Mehrling 1997, 2011; Minsky 1986, 223–229; Streeck 2015).

Financial institutions vary historically and comparatively (Hall and Soskice 2001), with a variety of arrangements of banks, stock markets, and state-owned enterprises, as well as provision of public goods. The state must regulate credit to maintain its "credibility," whereas financial agents will seek to escape that regulation in order to expand credit and their associated interest payments and fees. The result is an ongoing regulatory arbitrage (Minsky 1986, 250–251). Like property, the state both creates money and allows for the relative autonomy of financial institutions, which is in turn protected from and enforced by the state.

That is, the state divides the economy according to the mandates of individual private property, adjudicated by courts and legislatures, and provides for its reintegration by means of the financial circuit. Although considered "private," this financial circuit is ultimately "public," subject to state control and regulation. The hierarchy of money is based on proximity to the state, with the associated institutional arrangements to assure that "money always trades at par on demand" (Pozsar 2014, 7–23).

Public finance can provide a means of financing public goods as well as defense. Marx viewed public finance as a means of extracting wealth from the people.

National debts, i.e., the alienation of the state – whether despotic, constitutional or republican —marked with its stamp the capitalistic era. The only part of the so-called national wealth that actually enters into collective possessions of modern peoples is – their national debt ... Public credit becomes the *credo* of capital. And with the rise of national debt-making, want of faith in the national debt takes the place of the blasphemy against the Holy Ghost, which may not be forgiven. (Marx 1967, Vol. I, Ch. 31, 754–755)

For example, the formation of the Bank of England in 1694 as a joint stock company enabled it to raise its own capital to lend to the government and to coin money to distribute to the public. It became the "receptacle of the metallic hoard of the country and the centre of gravity of all commercial credit" (Marx 1967, Vol. I, Ch. 31, 755; see also Vol. III, Ch. 33). As Marx noted, "the nation with its total wealth backs up the Bank of England" (Marx 1967, Vol. III, Ch. 33, 540).

The role of a central bank also varies historically. The central bank can become more like a securities dealer, in Shaw's balance sheet framework (Garbade 2012; Mehrling 1997, 187–190). In this case, financial deepening is a substitute for price adjustment by means of specialized assets and institutions, or "financial intermediation over financial markets" (Mehrling 1997, 209–211). The central bank can become the "dealer of last resort" to maintain stable asset values and avoid bubbles (Mehrling 2011, 2012).

VI.   Keynes: Money and Liquidity

For Keynes, a central aspect of money is its liquidity, compared with other assets (Keynes 1964, 194–209). With the development of money as a means of payment, there is a tendency to "accumulate money against the dates fixed for the payment of the sums owing" (Marx 1967, Vol. I, Ch. 3, Section 3b, 142). When the accumulation of money becomes the "end and aim" of the production of commodities, money becomes a store of value, and along with it there arises a "gold fetish" (Marx 1967, Vol. I, Ch. 3, Section 3a, 130, 133). This is similar to Keynes' notion of the precautionary demand for money (Keynes 1964, Ch. 13, 166–172; Ch. 15, 194–199). The ability to convert assets into means of payment quickly with no loss in value is often defined as "liquidity." At times in the trade cycle, demand for liquidity can be absolute (Keynes 1964, 207, 239–242, 316). Yet Keynes was aware that holding money as an asset can deter investment (Keynes 1964, 212–213, 222–225, 234–235) and so reduce economic growth.

A.   The Source of Value

For Marx, the measure of value is "socially necessary abstract labor" (Postone 1993, 190–200). That is, labor that counts as value producing must achieve the level of productivity of the economy as a whole. Simply taking more time for production won't increase "value." In this sense, socially necessary labor time is already disciplined by competition in the workplace and among commodity producers. There is an implicit standard, reflecting the social dimension of labor even for the individual worker.

Productivity is commonly and frequently measured by economists and business owners at all levels of production. Productivity is simply expressed as Q/L, where Q is output and L is labor time. Yet quantity cannot be measured for the economy or industry as a whole simply by adding up diverse physical units. Implicit in the productivity measure is a market price as a common unit of account. And as productivity increases in a given industry, the market price of the commodity will fall. In this sense, increasing productivity will increase the physical quantity of output, but will not necessarily increase the value of output. As Postone emphasizes (Postone 1993, 288–292), the *value* produced by a given unit time measure of labor expended is constant, even if that value is embodied in increased quantities of physical output. Postone highlights this difference between value and material wealth. Direct living human labor is necessary to embody value in the commodity, even as progress in science and technology reduces the amount of living labor necessary for production (Postone 1993, 196–200, 346–354).

Once there are limits to the working day, increasing surplus value can result from increases in the productivity of wage goods and the subsequent increase in relative surplus value (Postone 1993, 308–314). That is, productivity increases surplus value and profit only indirectly and must take place at an accelerated rate.

B. Keynes' Units of Analysis

Keynes' money wage-unit avoids some of the ambiguity of attempting to measure physical output by using nominal measures to express the capacity for command of labor (Hayes 2013, 34–35; Keynes 1964, Chapter 4, 37–45). That is, Keynes estimates aggregate output by expenditures for the purchase of labor time paid for in units of money wage, in order to incorporate the effect of changes in productivity and technology. In Keynes' terminology:

$$E = N\,W$$

where E is the wages and salaries bill, W is the money wage-unit, and N is the quantity of employment (Keynes 1964, 41). That is, labor is aggregated into a homogeneous unit instead of output (Keynes 1964, 41–45). The real wage is then determined by the marginal productivity of labor in the wage-goods industries (Keynes 1964, 29).

Money is the standard of value as the medium in which wages and debt are fixed (Keynes 1964, 236–239, 302). Keynes mentions legal tender in a footnote on p. 167, along with an arbitrary distinction between money and debt.

The money wage-unit is the means of aggregation for both aggregate demand and supply (Keynes 1964, Ch. 3 and Ch. 20), emphasizing the central role for labor (Keynes 1964, 213–214). "Stickiness" in the money wage-unit was also a condition for stability (Keynes 1964, 239, 251, 253, 304, 309).

The actual quantitative production of value is unknown in advance, although anticipated by production decisions. That is, there is a potential difference between the production and realization of value of aggregate output. The "realization" problem may be due to the lack of effective demand, to be managed if full employment is to be achieved, as well as a coordination problem among multiple individual actors within the economy. The statistical estimates for gross domestic product, for example, are revised several times.

The yield to all capital assets is calculated in its "own rate of return" (Keynes 1964, 222–229). The possible conversion of physical yield (wheat in Keynes' example) into monetary yield allows the convertibility of yields among various assets in money terms. Along with the categorization of types of risk (Keynes 1964, 144), this analysis helps to standardize financial assets and so increase liquidity by facilitating exchange among them.

Keynes defined the marginal efficiency of capital as present discounted value of the expected yield, affected by changes in technology and business confidence (Keynes 1964, 135–137, 141–143, 148–149, 204, 308, 316–320, 325). It is possible to have a declining marginal efficiency of capital (MEC) over time, as technology improves and prices decline. This sets up the challenge for the monetary authority to lower the rate of interest to allow for continuing rates of investment (Keynes 1964, 216–218, 221, 308–309, 316).

Keynes made note of the circularity of the definition of capital. That is, the interest rate is necessary to measure the quantity of capital, and the quantity of capital also determines the interest rate (Keynes 1964, 137, 140; Minsky 1986, 213–218). Quantitative measures of capital are also affected by taxes and accounting conventions (Shaikh 2016, 243–256), as well as depreciation (Kliman 2012, 138–148).

C. Money and Other Assets

Unlike Marx and his distinction between property in capital and labor, Keynes aggregates across all types of property, or "assets." Keynes assumes that all assets have yield and can be compared based on rate of return, time to maturity, and risk (Keynes 1964, 222–230). Money has a liquidity premium because it is a standard of value (Keynes 1964, 230, 236–239). Money is also unique in its conditions of production and substitution (Keynes 1964, 230–234).

Keynes' approach leads to a standardization of financial assets and a perspective that leads to the calculation of the relative desirability of each. Unlike Marx, Keynes' analysis is primarily in nominal terms. The demand for money or alternative assets is separate from real investment, measured by the MEC (Keynes 1964, 141–143, 145–146, 308, 316–320, 325). The MEC is in nominal terms, but is affected by changes in productivity and prices.

The supply of money is controlled by the monetary authority and is not connected with the production of total social value. Money has a scarcity value, similar to the Quantity Theory of Money (Keynes 1964, 208–209, 304–306). As a result, liquidity becomes a purely monetary phenomenon unlinked to the production of total value. Yet monetary policy becomes a method of controlling the rate of investment (Keynes 1964, 326–327).

For Keynes, like the Classical economists, a distinction between money and real is possible. For Marx, the financial circuit involves both money and real in a continual, contingent transformation.

VII.   The Paradox of Liquidity

Both Marx and Keynes make note of the need for liquidity.

A.   The Pursuit of Liquidity

Capital markets emerged to provide an exit strategy for investors in fixed capital with long-term commitments. So-called "liquid" stock markets developed once limited liability and perpetual corporations enabled investors to exchange holdings of corporate securities (see Chapter 5).

From the point of view of money as capital, there is a contradiction between money as a qualitative representation of the totality of social power and the open-ended potential of production and innovation, as compared with the actual quantity of production of surplus in a given period.

> Marx elaborates a logical contradiction between the boundlessness of money, when considered qualitatively as the universal representation of wealth that is directly convertible into any other commodity, and the quantitative limitation of every actual sum of money. (Postone 1993, 267)

Both Marx and Keynes were critical of the Quantity Theory of Money (Marx 1967, Vol. I, Ch. 3, 123–124; Vol. III, Ch. 34, 554; Vol. III, Ch. 35, 573–574; Moseley 2005, 143–174). There is a need to limit credit to maintain competition, but also to relax restrictions to enable entrepreneurship and to prevent collapse of expectations.

Keynes notes the paradox of liquidity but sees it in purely psychological terms related to the demand for money (Keynes 1964, 166–172, 202, 246–247, 315–316).

> Speculators may do no harm as bubbles on a steady stream of enterprise. But the position is serious when enterprise becomes the bubble on a whirlpool of speculation. When the capital development of a country becomes a by-product of the activities of a casino, the job is likely to be ill-done … These tendencies are a scarcely avoidable outcome of our having successfully organized "liquid" investment markets. (Keynes 1964, 159)

With the separation between ownership and management which prevails to-day and with the development of organized investment markets, a new factor of great importance has entered in, which sometimes facilitates investment but sometimes adds greatly to the instability of the system … It is as though a farmer, having tapped his barometer after breakfast, could decide to remove his capital from the farming business between 10 and 11 in the morning and reconsider whether he should return to it later in the week … Investments which are "fixed" for the community are thus made "liquid" for the individual. (Keynes 1964, 150–151, 153)

Of all the maxims of orthodox finance none, surely, is more anti-social than the fetish of liquidity, the doctrine that it is a positive virtue on the part of investment institutions to concentrate their resources upon the holding of "liquid" securities. It forgets that there is no such thing as liquidity of investment for the community as a whole. (Keynes 1964, 155)

… the liquidity of investment markets often facilitates, though it sometimes impedes, the course of new investment. For the fact that each individual investor flatters himself that his commitment is "liquid" (though this cannot be true for all investors collectively) calms his nerves and makes him much more willing to run a risk. (Keynes 1964, 160)

To address these problems, Keynes proposes the "Euthanasia of the rentier" (pp. 221, 376) and "comprehensive socialization of investment" (p. 378). Further, "the duty of ordering the current volume of investment cannot safely be left in private hands." (Keynes 1964, 320; 325, 378)

Keynes' policy solution is to expand the role of the state, as if the state were a neutral arbiter capable of long-run stabilization. There are misgivings regarding the role of the state, nonetheless, such as from James Galbraith ("predator state" in Wray 2009) or Shleifer and Vishny (1998) (the "grabbing hand" of the state), or the corporate liberal state (Davis 2015) or exploitative state (Marx 1967). That is, Keynes does not match his analysis of money with the political economy of the state or an analysis of historically specific financial institutions.

B. Managing Liquidity

It is possible that attempts to stabilize the economy have set the conditions for future instability. That is, stabilization and prevention of depressions may weaken the "shake-out" function of financial crises and preserve excess capacity, which in turn may slow recovery from financial crises and undermine long-run growth (Brenner 2009; El-Erian 2016; Roubini and Mihm 2010). The "lender of last resort" function may have stabilized liquidity in the 1970s, but led to inflation as a consequence (Minsky 1986, 254–287). The shift to lower interest rate policies in the 1980s and 1990s may have led to asset bubbles rather than a recovery of investment (Brenner 2009; El-Erian 2016).

Evidence exists to support these hypotheses. There has been a long-term shift toward short-term assets (Tirole 2011), consistent with Keynes' "liquidity fetish" and Too Big To Fail (TBTF) moral hazard. The role of the central bank as a "dealer of last resort" in the 2008 Great Recession to stabilize the asset bubbles (Mehrling 2011) may have inadvertently placed a floor under collateral values and hence removed the limits to credit expansion. This in turn would lead to overinvestment and a decline in the MEC and the negative interest rates, as we now observe in the global economy. This may be an expression of the limits of monetary policy (as well as the political taboo on fiscal policy). Discussion of secular stagnation has reemerged (DeLong and Summers 2012). There may be political fallout as well from slow growth (Bremmer 2010).

Minsky, as well as Marx, differentiates between two types of assets and cash flows: investment in commodity production, or $M - C - M'$, and financial assets, $M - M'$ (Minsky 1986, 69, 174–175, 179). For Minsky, the important distinction is the type of financing, whether hedge, speculative, or Ponzi (Minsky 1986, 70, 206), and the impact of the relative proportion among them on financial instability. For Minsky, the financial system facilitates the extraction of surplus for investment (Minsky 1986, 141–143, 169–170, 224). For Marx, money is also necessary for extraction of surplus, specifically based on extraction of surplus from labor. The analysis of both can be understood with a set of equations with a markup on labor costs (Minsky 1986, 144–157).

Crises are inevitable as long as value is expressed in a form external to the commodity (Marx 1967, Vol. I, Ch. 3, Section 3b, 138; Vol. III, Ch. 32, 516–517; Ch. 35, 573–574).

> As long as the *social* character of labour appears as the *money-existence* of commodities, and thus as a *thing* external to actual production, money crises – independent of or as an intensification of actual crises—are inevitable. (Marx 1967, Vol. III, Ch. 32, 516–517; italics in original)

VIII.   Financialization in the Global Context

There is now widespread discussion of "financialization" in the global economy. In spite of Marx's clear prescription that living labor is the only source of surplus (Christophers 2013, 40–51), financial transactions appear to be increasingly prevalent.

A.   *Definition of Financialization*

One of many possible definitions of financialization is "a pattern of accumulation in which profits accrue primarily through financial channels rather than through trade and commodity production ... [which tends to occur] during periods of hegemonic transition" (Arrighi 1994, 92–96; Davis 2009; Foster and McChesney 2012, 49–63; Kotz 2015, 32–37; Krippner 2005, 174; Lapavitsas 2013, 138–168; Palley 2013: Tymoigne and Wray 2014, 78–83). Arrighi describes several "cycles of accumulation" in which the wealth generated in one hegemonic power is subsequently invested in the next, once profitable opportunities are limited in the context of the first (Arrighi 1994, 109–174, 228–238).

Once "capital has become a commodity," available for loan in financial markets, it can be invested in either commodity production for profit or in financial assets. In either sphere, money loaned will receive a "pro-rata" rate of return relative to its magnitude (Marx 1967, Vol. III, Ch. 21, 338–339). In spite of this appearance of equal return, surplus production only takes place by the employment of living labor.

> Capital exists as capital in actual movement, not in the process of circulation, but only in the process of production, in the process by which labour-power is exploited. (Marx 1967, Vol. III, Ch. 21, 343)

The expansion of capital involves the process of production and circulation as a whole (Marx 1967, Vol. III, Ch. 21, 343–345), with many overlapping circuits on an expanding scale. Financial capital may contribute to surplus in a number of channels: with tighter credit standards, it can lead to the intensification of competition for both labor and capital; it can increase exploitation of workers in other countries by globalization of capital, foreign direct investment (FDI), and supply chains (Ali 2015; Milberg and Winkler 2013); it can increase in centralization due to expansion of hegemonic currency and increase in access to information about profitable investment opportunities; it can increase in velocity and reduction of turnover time, and so increasing profit per time period; it can facilitate the management of war debt to increase hegemonic power relative to other capitalist countries (Eichengreen and Hausmann 2005; Garbade 2012), along with the associated power to determine the international rules of finance (Rodrik 2015a; Stiglitz 2016). In the recent period, there is a tendency toward "predatory" finance, which is a zero-sum game (Akerlof and Shiller 2015; Harvey 2010, 244–245).

There are in fact historical precedents to the international significance of financial institutions. The forms in which money markets have existed can be identified historically, such as "usurer's capital" and "merchant's capital" (Marx 1967, Vol. III, Ch. 20, Ch. 36, 591–600). The "rentier" is a well-known figure in Keynes' writing as well (Adams 2005; Keynes 1964). Long-distance trade and gold payments to merchants and mercenaries in the early modern period in Genoa, Venice, and Florence were noted by Marx as "pre-capitalist relations" (Marx 1967, Vol. III, Ch. 36). The influence of private bankers, or *haute finance,* in alliance with hereditary dynasties, was noted by several historians (such as the Medici, Fugger, Warburg, Rothschild, and Morgan family bankers) (Arrighi 1994, 54–56, 96–109; Polanyi 1944, 9–27). With the rise of the fiscal/military state, new financial forms developed, as did a new form of citizenship based on taxes and public expenditures (Arrighi 1994, 36–47; Celik 2016; Davis 2015). In certain circumstances, the leading hegemonic power is able to organize global financial relations with the hegemonic currency, such as Britain's gold standard, a core aspect of the "liberal creed" (Polanyi 1944, 3, 135–142).

B. Hegemonic Currency

Marx was also clear that gold was the universal commodity in international relations. Although some theorists interpret Marx as a commodity theorist (Shaikh 2016), there is an informative discussion in Vol. I, Ch. 3, Section 2c (124–129) regarding the possibilities of symbols of money, including paper. Historically gold was established as an "ideal measure of value," as "hard cash" (Marx 1967, Vol. I, Ch. 3, Section 1, 103). With commodity production, the function of money emerges as a means of expressing the value of commodities as an "independent reality" (Marx 1967, Vol. I, Ch. 3, Section 2b, 116). Coining and other designations of the money commodity is a function of the state (Marx 1967, Vol. I, Ch. 3, Section 2c, 125–129).

> The independent existence of the exchange-value of a commodity is [in circulation] a transient apparition ... Hence, in this process ... the mere symbolical existence of money suffices ... Being a transient and objective reflex of the prices of commodities, it serves only as a symbol of itself, and is therefore capable of being replaced by a token ... This token must have an objective social validity of its own, and this the paper symbol acquires by its forced currency ... this compulsory action of the State. (Marx 1967, Vol. I., Ch. 3, Section 2c, 129)

Both Polanyi and Marx view such a national fiat currency as unable to circulate beyond the territory of the state, and so a gold standard is necessary for international trade (Marx 1967, Vol. I, Ch. 3, Section 3c, 142–145; Polanyi 1944, 192–193). Similar views were expressed by modern monetary theorists after the end of the Bretton Woods dollar/gold standard in 1973. World trade has expanded since that period, nonetheless, with a new international financial institutional architecture, although with increasingly frequent financial crises.

The potential contributions to surplus from a hegemonic fiat currency are important to consider. The dimensions of hegemonic power include determination of the means of payment and the "rules of the game." The hegemonic currency is also a store of value for global central banks, and the hegemonic country can issue debt in its own currency to finance public goods such as the military and economic innovation. As a reserve asset, the hegemonic currency would then be more stable and have favorable terms of trade for outward FDI. During the Bretton Woods period (1944–1973), the U.S.-led International Monetary Fund (IMF) provided a buffer for domestic economic policy, and global capital flows and currency conversions were restricted.

C. International Financial Institutions

During the Bretton Woods system, from 1944–1973, the U.S. dollar became the key currency of global capitalism because of its convertibility to gold and to the supremacy of the U.S. economy and military. Even after the Bretton Woods period, the U.S. dollar and U.S. Treasury bonds became the safe asset for foreign central banks, a legacy role from the Bretton Woods period. Once a currency has a status of "safety," it is likely to maintain that status from the use of the asset as reserve currency in central banks. This enables that country to issue its own debt more easily and so also finance military spending to maintain its status. Countries that are not able to issue debt in their own currency are subject to "original sin" and must earn "hard" currencies on the global financial markets by exports, subject to shifting terms of trade (D'Arista 2007; Eichengreen and Hausmann 2005). There is a self-reinforcing dimension to the status of key currency (He, Krishnamurthy and Milbradt 2016).

Beginning in the United States in the 1960s, financial innovation developed new forms of money, such as the government securities market, certificates of deposit, the federal funds market, and repurchase agreements (Minsky 1986, 72–77). Since the end of the Bretton Woods era in 1973, there was both an opportunity and a necessity for new financial institutions to ensure against exchange rate risk (Friedman 1960, 2011). The emergence of the unregulated Eurodollar market provided the opportunity (Wachtel 1986). In this context there was rapid innovation in currency futures contracts and new forms of unregulated credit default swaps (Carruthers 2013). There has been an increasing reliance on "private" capital markets (Tymoigne and Wray 2014, 93). The so-called "Washington Consensus" at the IMF after 1980 increased currency conversions and capital flows, as well as privatization. There was an increase in third world debt and tighter conditions regarding its availability, leading to a new form of debt discipline. There has been a decrease in aid and an increase in borrowing by emerging countries (D'Arista 2007) and expanded global circuits of capital (Vasudevan 2013), along with an increasing frequency and scale of international financial crises.

The institutional structure of international finance since the early 1970s can be variously interpreted to reveal the risks of a noncommodity money, as well as the feasibility of a long-term international fiat currency. In spite of currency competition during this period, a hierarchy of national currencies has remained, with the U.S. dollar remaining the hegemonic currency (Cohen 2015; Goldberg 2013; Prasad 2014). It is possible that the legacy of the Bretton Woods period, as well as the continuing dominance of the U.S. economy and military power, has enabled this "exorbitant privilege" to continue (Eichengreen 2011). The legacy role of the U.S. dollar also helped sustain the leading role of the United States in institutions such as the IMF and to change their orientation after the 1980s toward the "Washington Consensus," which then further reinforced that leading role. Arguably this was a period of increasing "financialization" and financial innovation, an aggressive attempt to provide "safe assets" to the world economy to help maintain the role of the dollar as a key currency. Without this hegemonic role of the U.S. dollar, the global feasibility and pervasive influence of "financialization" would not have been possible, in my view.

D.   *Financialization: Tools, Techniques, and Conditions of Possibility*

Conceptual and financial institutional innovations often occur together. For example, risk can only be "priced" as a separate conceptual category once stable financial institutions are in place to support regular financial circuits. That is, there is an "institutional complex," consisting of specific institutions, categories, and knowledge (Davis 2015). According to Minsky, "what is money is determined by the workings of the economy" (Minsky 1986, 228), and these financial institutions are in flux historically.

For example, the insurance industry emerged in a particular historical circumstance: maritime insurance emerged with the increasing regularity of foreign trade in Venice in the thirteenth century (Baskin and Miranti 1997). There was an emergence of a culture of life insurance in eighteenth-century England, partly based on recent financial innovations and Enlightenment attitudes regarding progress (Clark 1999). Further, "modern" financial systems require the presence of six related institutions: stable public finances and debt management, stable money, an effective central bank, a functioning banking system, an active securities market, and a growing number of business corporations, both financial and nonfinancial (Sylla, Wright, and Cowen 2009, 62). It is these institutional components, along with the symbol of money and credit, that make a resilient financial system.

The conceptualization and quantification of risk (Goeztmann 2016, 276–288, 504–518; Mehrling 2005) have institutional prerequisites, such as existing and stable financial circuits, which can be measured and assessed. Further there is an assumption of efficient financial markets, with a stable central value. Consequently risk is seen as measured by volatility of financial assets, which are expected to return to their long-term value. Because return is proportional to risk, there is a drive for return by means of increasing leverage (risk) to increase yield (Rajan 2005). With large financial institutions, this leads to risk for the system as a whole.

The institutional complex for the emergence of financial innovation can be viewed as follows:

1   Stable modern financial institutions
2   Information technology
3   Theoretical advances based on assumptions of perfect financial markets; pricing of risk (Mehrling 2005, 2011)

4 Key currency, even after Bretton Woods, and the associated international financial institutions to support the dollar
5 Incentives regarding risk (Rajan 2005)
6 Political support (Roe 2006)

As suggested by Cooper (2015), there is a linkage across contexts, from finance, corporations, and government. That is, financial institutions do not exist separately from the political economic situation, as illustrated in Table 6.1.

There is an evident evolution of what are considered "safe assets" historically, along with associated political and legal institutions, as illustrated in Table 6.2.

For example, the Bank Act of 1844 delegated the management of the nation's gold reserve to the Bank of England (BOE), a form of monetizing the gold stock (Marx 1967, Vol. III, 572–574). The BOE notes were also backed by government securities, as well as gold reserve (Andreades 1966, 84–85, 290), like the U.S. dollar subsequently (Mehrling 2011, 37). Once "naturalized," any safe asset seems obviously secure, like gold. There was an institutional evolution, nonetheless, which led to the installation of each type/genre, along with political and legal backstops, without which the asset would not have been considered "safe." That is, an institutional process occurred to define and identify the physical characteristics of each entity and to secure its meaning.

There is a need for a "safe asset" to secure the rewards of capital accumulation. Yet further growth, technological innovation, and competition, as well as the business cycle, may undermine the safety of any asset. The legal/institutional backstop requires the support of the state, even for financial assets that are presumably "private." Regulatory arbitrage occurs to seek profitable niches, even while the regulation is necessary for stability. This dynamic of private innovation beyond the public backstop then results in rescue and re-regulation and a possible ever-widening public responsibility for financial stability. There is a long-run institutional plasticity that is best submerged in the consciousness of investors in the present, in the interests of confidence in the stability of the financial system. That is, reification is functional.

Table 6.1 Institutional Linkages

Role of Government	Corporate Form	Financial Institutions	Period
Public insurance	Fordist capital/labor accord	Regulated banks	1930–1980
Neoliberal privatization and Washington Consensus	New Economy Business Model with contingent labor; supply chains	Private capital market with public collateral as "safe asset"	1980–2015

Table 6.2 History of Safe Assets

Safe Asset	Financial/ Political Institution	Legal Institution	Period
British consols	Exchange Alley	Bank of England charter revisions	1720
Bank notes	Bank of England 1694 Federal Reserve 1913	Bank Act of 1844 Federal Reserve Act of 1913	1844 1913
Corporate stock	Private business corporations; stock markets	Dartmouth General incorporation statutes; protection of outside investors	1819 1880s
U.S. dollars	Banks	National Currency Act of 1863; Gold Standard Act of 1879	1863
U.S. Treasury bonds	Dealers	Federal Reserve Act of 1913, 1916	1916
Derivatives	Brokers	Commodity Exchange Act of 1936 Commodity Futures Modernization Act of 2000	1980s 2000s

IX.   Periodization: The Rise of Neoliberalism

Distinct financial institutions can be observed in particular periods (Kotz 2015; Tabb 2012). The 1970s were a transitional period that helped pave the way for a new regime.

The end of the Bretton Woods system was partly due to the loss of international competitiveness by the United States, its persistent balance of payments deficits, and the loss of the gold reserve (Brenner 2009; Harvey 2010). There was both an opportunity and a need to develop financial instruments to counteract the instability of currency exchange rates (Friedman 1960, 2011). Several authors note a change in regime, such as the "Wall Street-Treasury Complex" (Bhagwati 2004, 199–207); the "state-finance nexus" (Harvey 2010, 204–209); "asset price Keynesianism" (Brenner 2009, 3); Washington Consensus (Stiglitz 2002); and "privatized Keynesianism" (Celik 2016).

With near-full employment in the 1960s, there were rising labor costs (Tymoigne and Wray 2014, 68), along with an increasing price of oil from the formation of the Organization of the Petroleum Exporting Countries (OPEC), and intensification of religious conflict in the Middle East. The turn to U.S. "exorbitant privilege" of the key currency can be understood in this context, parlaying the remaining strength on international capital markets, even with a fiat currency. The U.S. dollar became the "safe haven" of last resort, a reified asset in financial markets. For the leading hegemonic country, this financial power still enabled the financing of the military in an increasingly unpredictable global political economy.

With the reassertion of prerogatives of capital in the Reagan/Thatcher period, there was deregulation, tax cuts, and privatization, as well as an increasing divergence of wages and productivity growth (Shaikh 2016, 60, 731) and increasing inequality.

Neoliberal "financialization" developed in the context of OPEC and the recycling of petrodollars (Wachtel 1986) through U.S. banks and the third world debt crisis. Deregulation of finance with the Eurodollar market and competition among global financial centers (with London's "big bang" in 1986) increased regulatory competition. Volcker's Monetarism Experiment in 1979–1981 raised interest rates and attracted global investment into dollars until the Plaza Accord (and crash of 1987), which led to the bursting of Japan's property bubble in the 1990s. The Washington Consensus at the IMF and the opening of third world markets to FDI at the same time facilitated the outsourcing of U.S. multinational corporations (MNCs), beginning with electronics. The decline of unions and the reassertion of shareholders' control over corporations reinforced inequality, with the growing power of institutional investors leading to more assets under management and the rise of shadow banking (Pozsar 2011, 2015). The low interest rates of the 2001 period were intended to release equity in residential real estate via securitization, and Greenspan's preferences for self-regulation of financial markets were intended to avoid deflation like Japan.

With China's entrance into the world market with membership in the World Trade Organization (WTO) in 2000, there developed a new international division of labor: "Chimerica" (Ferguson and Schularick 2007). This new relationship was based on manufacturing in China organized by MNC supply chains and exporting to the U.S. market. This interdependency may have limits, nonetheless, with U.S. consumers still in debt and with China increasingly able to produce at the leading edge of technology, learned from inward FDI from MNCs. Even after 2008, China's continual growth maintained an export market for commodity, supplying emerging market countries. The recovery since 2008 has also relied upon extraordinary measures by central banks, with the series of Quantitative Easing experiments and, more recently, negative interest rates. Recently China has reduced its accumulation of U.S. Treasury reserves, with its increasing outward FDI directed toward resource acquisition in Africa, as well as mergers and acquisition of leading technology companies in the West. China has recently founded an international development bank and is launching a "New Silk Road" with infrastructure investment in Central Asia. China's recent efforts to open its financial sector have been compromised by high indebtedness, as well as instability in its stock market and currency. If the U.S. Federal Reserve does raise interest rates, there is a risk of another global debt crisis centered in emerging countries (IMF FSR 2016).

In spite of some success to maintain its hegemonic currency role, there may be a decline in U.S. prestige and influence after 2008 (Kirshner 2014), along with increasing neomercantilism in China regarding the role of the renminbi (Prasad 2016). A focus on financial investment alone may succeed in increasing the rate of profit, at least in the case of the hegemonic currency, where the hegemon can write the rules of international finance. Debt is also useful as a discipline, for countries as well as households and CEOs, at least until global excess capacity, lack of effective demand, and distribution of advanced production techniques due to MNC FDI and local investments in learning exacerbate the "race to the bottom" (Brenner 2009; Rodrik 2015b; Yu Zhou, Lazonick, Sun 2016). There is evidence of an emerging "mercantilist" response in the present to compete with U.S. financial power. The potential increase in financial return with the hegemonic currency may then provide a higher threshold for real investment, delaying the embodiment of new techniques of production in a new capacity. Reliance on the reified dollar may work to undermine economic performance and confidence in the long term and lead to increasing international competition for the next hegemon.

X. Finance as Fetters

With "financialization," there was a change in the financial institutions. There was a period of a secure banking system from 1933–1980, with public insurance and regulation (Cooper 2015; Tymoigne and Wray 2014). The subsequent growth in the "shadow banking" sector was based on repurchase agreements of U.S. Treasury bonds as the safe asset to backstop increasing inventories of derivatives.

The definition of "shadow banking" includes extension of credit beyond the reach of financial regulation and insurance (Adrian and Ashcraft 2012; Gorton and Metrick 2010; Krugman 2009, 158–162;; Pozsar 2015; Pozsar, Adrian, Ashcraft, and Boesky 2013; Tabb 2012, 93–131).

There was a shift to a "private market" insurance provision with rising assets under management, such as credit default swaps. With the deregulation after 1980, new financial institutions developed, such as brokerage firms. With the end of Bretton Woods, there was more exchange rate risk and more need to insure against it. There was a large accumulation of cash pools in excess of the Federal Deposit Insurance Corporation (FDIC) insurance cap due to increasing income inequality, rising corporate profits, foreign exchange holdings, and an aging population (Pozsar 2015). There was an expansion in institutional investors such as pension funds, money market funds, hedge funds, and private equity.

Evidence of financialization includes the rising ratio of financial assets to GDP (Adrian 2014; Tabb 2012, 100; Tymoigne and Wray 2014, 100–101), increasing shares of short-term/long-term assets (Tirole 2011), cash hoards in U.S. information technology corporations (Gruber and Kamin 2015), negative interest rates (Palley 2016), declining rates of investment (IMF 2015; Eggertsson, Mehrotra, and Summers 2016; Tabb 2012, 219–224, 237–241), increase in cash under management with rising inequality (Pozsar 2011), and an increase in the search for yield (Pozsar and Singh 2011).

The irony is that so-called "private" insurance depends on the existence of public debt. That is, the global "safe financial asset" is U.S. Treasury bond, or "repo," used as collateral for a "private" capital market, the rapid growth of which potentially destabilizes the entire system. There is a "Triffin Dilemma" of sorts, with an excess demand for the safe asset that may lead to a potential increase in public debt (Cabellero, Farhi, and Gourinchas 2016; Pozsar 2011). There is a "shortage of safe assets" because of the limits on public debt due to neoliberal austerity, whereas the new purpose of this public debt is to stabilize the value of "private" financial assets.

Negative interest rates may also represent a charge for the provision of liquidity, much as Mehrling (2011) would support. That is, the provision of safe assets for the large global accumulation of financial wealth incurs a considerable cost in the maintenance of an inventory of financial assets and the provision of the role of "dealer of last resort." The safe asset is the U.S. Treasury bond, which depends on the public credit and projection of long-term growth. If, however, there is global stagnation instead, then the public credit will no longer be safe, with no increment to surplus with the decline of investment. Having witnessed the Great Depression, Keynes foresaw the possibility an MEC is equal to zero and a low or negative interest rate (Keynes 1964, 215–221, 315–324). His solution was not financial, but was for a larger role for the government investment and for income redistribution. The longer that the government assumes the role of financial manager instead of public investor, the greater the possibility of economic collapse.

That is, the ultimate purpose of the public sphere in the tax/credit state is to support private wealth. Such protection of the value of existing financial assets may ultimately prevent the adjustment of obsolete capital values to new vintages of more productive capital and so delay new investment. Thus, too much support for existing financial assets may delay Schumpeter's "creative destruction," a periodic aspect of capital accumulation.

There are two different approaches to managing liquidity and risk in the current context.

Recommendation 1: Extend the role of the Fed to dealer of last resort, to stabilize asset values in the now-global private capital markets (Gabor and Vestergaard 2016; Mehrling 2011).

Recommendation 2: Increase taxes and government investment to reduce cash pools and to stimulate consumption, private investment and GDP (Keynes 1964, 320–326; Summers 2014).

The first extends the recent role of the Federal Reserve to provide a backstop in a global financial crisis. The Fed would take upon its balance sheet the private "safe assets" and maintain liquidity for them. The second would return to a Keynesian view of the government, to make public investments based on a system-wide perspective of needs and opportunities, replacing the casino-like capital markets.

Financialization increases claims to surplus, but without producing surplus. The rush to "hard cash" in the crisis appears to be a shortage of means of payment, but is actually a shortage of total surplus production with which to meet those claims. That is, there is a distinction between "currency and capital" (Marx Vol. III, Ch. 28, 442). The availability of "liquidity" is pro-cyclical, a function of expansion of credit (Minsky 1986) and "fictitious capital" (Marx 1967, Vol. III, Ch. 25, 27, 29, 30, 33).

There is an irony of financial power: the focus solely on M – M' leads to lower total social surplus and so less success in expansion of value through money. The social power of money is misleading; hoarding and the increasing velocity of money and the focus on liquidity lead to a decline in the global economy.

Money is the only expression of the totality of capital. Central banks are the "only game in town" (El-Erian 2016) while a decreasing share of financial assets are regulated and insured by central banks. Credit continues to expand for profit, making the task of rescue like the one facing the Red Queen in *Alice in Wonderland*.

XI. Fetishism and Knowledge

A. *Meanings of Money*

In a historical institutional context, money can be conceptualized as a crucial link between firms, households, government, and its central bank once production and households have been separated. Money is not just a crystalized relation between credit and debt, but a historically specific kind of credit and debt. That is, in a capitalist economy, workers provide credit to the firm by working first and receiving payment afterwards. Then firms provide credit to the worker by allowing a time lag between the purchase of consumer goods and the payment. The time lag between work and pay and between purchase and sales receipt can provide a means of accumulation to financial intermediaries. These financial intermediaries can provide credit for improved or expanded production technology, increase in scale and scope, and extension of time to maturity. These financial intermediaries are supported by the state, for assistance in the management of public finances, the issue of debt, and the collection of taxes. Such a stable circular flow of finances was put in place, along with a new form of the state, from 1688–1694 in England, followed by other modern industrial powers (United States in 1776, France in 1789, Germany and Italy in the 1880s after unification), replacing the hereditary monarchy allied with the church (Adams; Arrighi 1994; Davis 2015). That is, money is not an "object" but a "relation," an aid to state power in a system of competing states.

Marx clearly differentiated between types of property, capital, and labor. Only living labor contributed to surplus, although the substitution for labor in production is a central dynamic of capitalist production for both Smith and Marx. Marx differentiated between flows that incorporated living labor in commodity production, M – C – M', and financial flows, M – M', which did not. For Postone this dynamic represents a contradiction between use value and value, the increase in wealth which capitalism is capable of producing, compared with its decreasing foundation in living labor (Postone 1993, 348, 358–359).

Unlike Marx, other theorists of money did not clearly differentiate between types of property. Keynes merged all types of property into a generalized concept of "assets," with yields that could be transformed into money. Keynes also noted the central importance of wages as a source of income and aggregate demand. Minsky focused on cash flow and types of cash flow. He analyzed financial institutions and banking as a for-profit activity, with a possible impact on macroeconomic outcomes such as the rate of investment and financial fragility. Minsky also noted the importance of financial flows to validate capital asset values and to carry the surplus. Keynes and Minsky did not examine the two types of capital flows differentiated by Marx: the commodity production and the financial flows. Without this differentiation, there is no clear explanation for the macro indicators such as declining investment, declining profit rates, declining capacity utilization, and slow growth, which are now widely noted as characteristic of the global economy.

The increasingly widespread acceptance of the term "financialization" after the financial crisis of 2008 provides an opening to a critique of the concept of money as valuable in itself. This step has not yet been taken in most analyses today.

B. Paradigms

Essentially the concept of "fetishism" is a critique of a way of thinking—what might be called a paradigm. Money is taken as valuable in itself, instead of a means of facilitating the relationship among key institutions, in the pursuit of the accumulation of capital. Money is understood as unrelated to labor, as a convenience, rather than as the abstract expression of socially necessary labor time as value.

> Marx's notion of the fetish is centrally related to his theory of alienation as social constitution ... It is integral to Marx's theory of social constitution, which relates forms of thought, worldviews, and beliefs to the forms of social relations and the ways in which they appear to immediate experience. (Postone 1993, 224)

Keynes was consciously mediating between the Classical tradition and Marx (Keynes 1964, 3, 32, 353–358, 371, 379). Keynes was a reformist, but was nonetheless aware of the weaknesses of capitalism, including the circularity of the definition of capital (Keynes 1964, 137, 140) and the potential for technological unemployment (Keynes 1963). In fact, the ambiguity of capital valuation may lead to the instability of the MEC and vulnerability to shifting expectations.

Keynes assumed that all assets have a yield, or their "own rate of return." For Keynes, the demand for financial assets was a function of psychological phenomena. In contrast, Marx's analysis was structural. For him, the return to money lending constituted a claim to a share of the surplus. If the surplus wasn't forthcoming in the process of production, there was no surplus to be shared. Marx's analysis of crises consisted of at least three aspects: the instability of credit, the decline in surplus due to increasing automation, and the lack of effective demand due to limits on labor income. In the recent crisis of 2007–2008, all three factors may have contributed to the long-delayed recovery.

Forms of knowledge, such as contemporary social science, can be influenced by certain paradigms. That is, it is possible to analyze modern social sciences as subject to the pervasive logic of a paradigm of maximizing the financial circuit, M – M'. In general there is an emphasis on abstraction and auto-mation, control and optimization, as well as objectification. In economics and business, such methods as increasing productivity, economizing on fixed assets, and reducing the turnover time of currency and credit would all con-tribute to the expansion of M – M'. The structure of modern social sciences, including management and economics, may also contribute to this outcome.

There is a rough parallel between theories of institutions and the operation of those institutions. Arguably the form of knowledge helps to legitimize and reinforce the specific operation of the institutions (Davis 2015). For example:

- Theories of the firm have evolved Maximization of Shareholder Value (MSV), as well as the specific institutional forms of the corporation (Chandler and Mazlish 2005; Davis 2009, 53–58; Fligstein 1990; Lazonick 2009; Stout 2012).
- Theories of money have evolved (CAPM, EMH), as well as specific finan-cial institutions (Garbade 2006; Mehrling 1997, 2005, 2011, and 2013; Rajan 2005).
- Theories of the state have evolved, as well as specific forms of the state (Celik 2016; Davis 2015).
- Theories of information have evolved, as well as information technology for storage, retrieval, and processing (Gleick 2011; Edwards 1996).
- Theories of labor organization have evolved, as well as specific types of employment relations, from the commodification of labor, the separa-tion of mental from manual, mechanization, and automation, as well as abstraction of knowledge and information processing with the develop-ment of Information, Communication, and Technology industries (ICT) industries (Fisk 2009; Ford 2015; Lazonick 2009; Marx 1967).
- Theories of the economy have evolved, along with the specific organization of economic institutions (MacKenzie 2006; Mirowski and Plehwe 2009; Nelson 2016; Postone 1993; Zelizer 2008).
- Cultural incentives have evolved from the "motive of gain" (Polanyi 1944, 30) to a motive for safe assets in the "portfolio society" (Davis 2009).

That is, fetishism as a form of knowledge leads to a distorted analysis of eco-nomics and to inadequate policies. For example, in the contemporary period, financial innovation tends to increase the number of financial assets, without understanding their relation to the production of total value by the employ-ment of living labor. By multiplying the number of claims on an ever-limited surplus, there is a tendency to create asset bubbles and then collapse. Keynes' "fetish of liquidity" is still the reigning strategy, with an increasing share of assets in short-term rather than long-term securities (Tirole 2011).

During the financial crisis of 2008, the role of the state was to increase liquidity and to save large financial institutions. But an increase in the supply of money does not necessarily induce investment, or employment, or production of surplus. Quantitative measures do not address the qualitative structure of financial institutions. Such efforts can then lead to a loss of confidence in the state, with political ramifications.

A critique of the fetishism of money has yet to take place.

Bibiliography

Acharya, Viral V., Thomas F. Cooley, Matthew Richardson, and Ingo Walter (eds.). *Regulating Wall Street: The Dodd-Frank Act and the New Architecture of Global Finance*. New York: John Wiley & Sons, Inc., 2011.

Acharya, Viral V., Matthew Richardson, Stijn Van Nieuwerburgh, and Lawrence J. White. *Guarantee to Fail: Fannie Mae, Freddie Mac and the Debacle of Mortgage Finance*. Princeton, NJ: Princeton University Press, 2011.

Adams, Julia. *The Familial State: Ruling Families and Merchant Capitalism in Early Modern Europe*. Ithaca: Cornell University Press, 2005.

Adrian, Tobias. "Financial Stability Politics for Shadow Banking," *Federal Reserve Bank of New York Staff Report No. 664*, February 2014.

———. "Discussion of 'Systemic Risk and the Solvency-Liquidity Nexus of Banks'" *Federal Reserve Bank of New York Staff Report No. 722*, April 2015.

Adrian, Tobias and Adam B. Ashcraft. "Shadow Banking: A Review of the Literature," *Federal Reserve Bank of New York Staff Report No. 580*, October 2012.

Adrian, Tobias and Hyun Song Shin. "Liquidity and Leverage," *Federal Reserve Bank of New York Staff Report No. 328*, December 2010.

Aizenman, Joshua, Yothin Jinjarak, and Huanhuan Zheng, "Chinese Outwards Mercantilism—The Art and Practice of Bundling," *NBER Working Paper No. 21089*, June 2015.

Akerlof, George and Robert J. Shiller. *Phishing for Phools: The Economics of Manipulation and Deception*. Princeton, NJ: Princeton University Press, 2015.

Ali, Mona. "Dark Matter, Black Holes and Old-Fashioned Exploitation: Transnational Corporations and the US Economy," *Cambridge Journal of Economics*, Vol. 40, No. 4, 2015 , 997–1018.

Allen, Franklin and Jun "QJ" Qian. "Comparing Legal and Alternative Institutions in Finance and Commerce," in James J. Heckman, Robert L Nelson, and Lee Cabatingan (eds.), *Global Perspectives on the Rule of Law*. New York: Routledge, 2010, 118–144.

Andreades, Andreas Michael. *History of the Bank of England 1640 to 1903*. New York: Augustus M. Kelley, 1966.

Arrighi, Giovanni. *The Long Twentieth Century: Money, Power, and the Origins of Our Times*. London: Verso, 1994.

Atack, Jeremy and Larry Neal (eds.). *The Origin and Development of Financial Markets and Institutions: From the Seventeenth Century to the Present*. New York: Cambridge University Press, 2009.

Baker, Dean, Gerald Epstein, and Robert Pollin (eds.). *Globalization and Progressive Economic Policy*. New York: Cambridge University Press, 1998.

Baskin, Jonathan Barron and Paul J. Miranti, Jr. *A History of Corporate Finance*. New York: Cambridge University Press, 1997.

Bhagwati, Jagdish. *In Defense of Globalization*. New York: Oxford University Press, 2004.

Bremmer, Ian. *The End of the Free Market: Who Wins the War Between States and Corporations?* New York: Penguin, 2010.

Brenner, Robert. "The Capitalist Economy, 1945–2000: A Reply to Konings and to Panitch and Gindin," in David Coates (ed.), *Varieties of Capitalism, Varieties of Approaches*. New York: Palgrave MacMillan, 2005, 211–241.

_____. "What Is Good for Goldman Sachs Is Good for America: The Origins of the Current Crisis," introduction to *Economics of Global Turbulence*. Spanish translation. London: Verso, 2009.

Brunhoff, Suzanne de and Duncan K. Foley. "Karl Marx's Theory of Money and Credit," in Philip Arestis and Malcolm Sawyer (eds.), *A Handbook of Alternative Monetary Economics*. Cheltenham, UK: Edward Elgar, 2006, 188–204.

Brunnermeier, Markus K, Luis Garicano, Philip R. Lane, et al. "The Sovereign-Bank Diabolic Loop and ESBies," *American Economic Review*, 2016, Vol. 106, No. 5, 2016, 508–512.

Caballero, Ricardo J., Emmanuel Farhi, and Pierre-Olivier Gourinchas. "Safe Asset Scarcity and Aggregate Demand," *American Economic Review*, Vol. 106, No. 5, 2016, 513–518.

Carruthers, Bruce G. "Diverging Derivatives: Law, Governance and Modern Financial Markets," *Journal of Comparative Economics*, Vol. 41, 2013, 386–400.

Celik, Tim Holst. "Fiscal State-Citizen Alignment: Tracing the Sociohistorical Conditions of the Financial Crisis," *Critical Historical Studies*, Spring 2016, 105–141.

Chandler, Alfred D. Jr. and Bruce Mazlish (eds.). *Leviathans: Multinational Corporations and the New Global History*. New York: Cambridge University Press, 2005.

Christophers, Brett. *Banking Across Boundaries: Placing Finance in Capitalism*. Oxford, UK: Wiley-Blackwell, 2013.

Clark, Geoffrey. *Betting on Lives: The Culture of Life Insurance in England, 1695-1775*. Manchester, UK: Manchester University Press, 1999.

Cohen, Benjamin J. *Currency Power: Understanding Monetary Rivalry*. Princeton, NJ: Princeton University Press, 2015.

Cooper, Melinda. "Shadow Money and the Shadow Workforce: Rethinking Labor and Liquidity," *South Atlantic Quarterly*, Vol. 114, No. 2, 2015.

D'Arista, Jane. "U.S. Debt and Global Imbalances," *PERI Working Paper No. 136*, May 2007.

_____. "The Evolving International Monetary System," *Cambridge Journal of Economics*, Vol. 33, 2009, 633–652.

Daily, Gretchen. *Nature's Services: Societal Dependence on Natural Ecosystems*. Washington, D.C.: Island Press, 1997.

Davis, Ann E. "Marx and the Mixed Economy: Money, Accumulation, and the Role of the State," *Science & Society*, Vol. 74, No. 3, July 2010, 409–428.

_____. "The New 'Voodoo Economics': Fetishism and the Public-Private Divide," *Review of Radical Political Economics*, Vol. 45, No. 1, 2013, 42–58.

_____. *The Evolution of the Property Relation: Understanding Paradigms, Debates, Prospects*. New York: Palgrave MacMillan, 2015.

_____. "Paradoxical Positions: The Methodological Contributions of Feminist Scholarship," *Cambridge Journal of Economics*, 2017. Vol. 41, No. 1, 181–201.

Davis, Gerald F. *Managed by the Markets: How Finance Reshaped America*. New York: Oxford University Press, 2009.

DeLong, J. Bradford and Lawrence H. Summers. "Fiscal Policy in a Depressed Economy," *Brookings Papers on Economic Activity*, Spring 2012, 233–297.

De Vries, Jan. *The Industrious Revolution: Consumer Behavior and the Household Economy, 1650 to the Present*. New York: Cambridge University Press, 2008.

Edwards, Paul N. *The Closed World: Computers and the Politics of Discourse in Cold War America*. Cambridge, MA: MIT Press, 1996.

Eggertsson, Gauti B., Neil R. Mehrotra, and Lawrence H. Summers. "Secular Stagnation in the Open Economy," *American Economic Review*, Vol. 106, No. 5, 2016, 503–507.

Eichengreen, Barry. *Exorbitant Privilege: The Rise and Fall of the Dollar and the Future of the International Monetary System*. New York: Oxford University Press, 2011.

Eichengreen, Barry and Ricardo Hausmann (eds.). *Other People's Money: Debt Denomination and Financial Instability in Emerging Market Economies*. Chicago: University of Chicago Press, 2005.

El-Erian, Mohamed A. *The Only Game in Town: Central Banks, Instability, and Avoiding the Next Collapse.* New York: Random House, 2016.

Epstein, Gerald (ed.). *Financialization and the World Economy.* Cheltenham, UK: Edward Elgar, 2005.

Farhi, Emmanuel and Jean Tirole. "Deadly Embrace: Sovereign and Financial Balance Sheets Doom Loops," *NBER Working Paper 21843*, January 2016.

Ferguson, Niall and Moritz Schularick. "'Chimerica' and the Global Asset Market Boom," *International Finance*, Vol. 10, No. 3, 2007, 215–239.

Fisk, Catherine L. *Working Knowledge: Employee Innovation and the Rise of Corporate Intellectual Property, 1800-1930.* Chapel Hill, NC: University of North Carolina Press, 2009.

Fligstein, Neil. *The Transformation of Corporate Control.* Cambridge, MA: Harvard University Press, 1990.

Ford, Martin. *Rise of the Robots: Technology and the Threat of a Jobless Future.* New York: Basic, 2015.

Foster, John Bellamy and Robert W. McChesney. *The Endless Crisis: How Monopoly-Finance Capital Produces Stagnation and Upheaval from the USA to China.* New York: Monthly Review Press, 2012.

Frank, Robert H. *Luxury Fever: Weighing the Cost of Excess.* Princeton, NJ: Princeton University Press, 2010.

Friedman, Milton. "In Defense of Destabilizing Speculation," in Ralph W. Pfouts (ed.), *Essays in Economics and Econometrics.* Chapel Hill, NC: University of North Carolina Press, 1960, 133–141.

_____. "The Need for Futures Markets in Currencies," *Cato Journal*, Vol. 31, No. 3, 2011, 635–641.

Gabor, Daniela and Jakob Vertergaard. "Towards a Theory of Shadow Money," *INET Working Paper*, 2016.

Garbade, Kenneth D. "The Evolution of Repo Contracting Conventions in the 1980s," *FRBNY Economic Policy Review*, Vol. 12, No. 1, 2006, 27–42.

_____. *Birth of a Market: The U.S. Treasury Securities Market from the Great War to the Great Depression.* Cambridge, MA: MIT Press, 2012.

Gleick, James. *The Information: A History, a Theory, a Flood.* New York: Pantheon, 2011.

Goetzmann, William N. *Money Changes Everything: How Finance Made Civilization Possible.* Princeton, NJ: Princeton University Press, 2016.

Goldberg, Linda S. "The International Role of the Dollar: Does It Matter If It Changes?," in Yin-Wong Cheung and Frank Westermann (eds.), *Global Interdependence, Decoupling, and Recoupling.* Cambridge, MA: MIT Press, 2013, 243–262.

Gordon, Peter E. "Secularization, Dialectics, Critique," in *The Weight of All Flesh: On the Subject-Matter of Political Economy*, edited by Kevis Goodman. New York: Oxford University Press, 2016, 183–203.

Gorton, Gary. *Slapped by the Invisible Hand: The Panic of 2007.* New York: Oxford University Press, 2010.

Gorton, Gary and Andrew Metrick. "Regulating the Shadow Banking System," *Brookings Papers on Economic Activity*, 2010, 261–297.

Gruber, Joseph W. and Steven B. Kamin. "The Corporate Saving Glut in the Aftermath of the Global Financial Crisis," Board of Governors of the Federal Reserve System, June 2015, Washington, DC.

Hall, P. A. and D. Soskice (eds.). *Varieties of Capitalism: The Institutional Foundations of Comparative Advantage.* New York: Oxford University Press, 2001.

Harris, Ron. "Law, Finance, and the First Corporations," in James J. Heckman, Robert L Nelson, and Lee Cabatingan (eds.), *Global Perspectives on the Rule of Law.* New York: Routledge, 2010, 145–171.

Harvey, David. *The Enigma of Capital and the Crisis of Capitalism.* Oxford, UK: Oxford University Press, 2010.

Hayes, M. G. "Ingham and Keynes on the Nature of Money," in Jocelyn Pixley and G. C. Harcourt (eds.), *Financial Crises and the Nature of Capitalist Money: Mutual Developments from the Work of Geoffrey Ingham*. New York: Palgrave MacMillan, 2013, 31–45.

He, Zhiguo, Arvind Krishnamurthy, and Konstantin Milbradt. "What Makes US Government Bonds Safe Assets?," *American Economic Review*, Vol. 106, No. 5, 2016, 519–523.

International Monetary Fund (IMF). *Global Financial Stability Report*, Ch. 4, "Private Investment: What's the Holdup?" April 2015, 111–143.

_____. *Financial Stability Report: Fostering Stability in a Low-Growth, Low-Rate Era*. October 2016.

Keynes, John Maynard. "Economic Possibilities for Our Grandchildren," *Essays in Persuasion*, New York: W.W. Norton & Co., 1963, 358–373.

_____. *The General Theory of Employment, Interest, and Money*. New York: Harcourt, Brace & World, 1964.

Kirshner, Jonathan. *American Power after the Financial Crisis*. Ithaca, NY: Cornell University Press, 2014.

Kliman, Andrew. *The Failure of Capitalist Production: Underlying Causes of the Great Recession*. London: Pluto Press, 2012.

Konings, Martijn (ed.). *The Great Credit Crash*. New York: Verso, 2010.

_____. *The Emotional Logic of Capitalism: What Progressives Have Missed*. Stanford, CA: Stanford University Press, 2015.

Kotz, David M. *The Rise and Fall of Neoliberal Capitalism*. Cambridge, MA: Harvard University Press, 2015.

Krippner, Greta R. "The Financialization of the American Economy," *Socio-Economic Review*, Vol. 3, 2005, 173–208.

_____. *Capitalizing on Crisis: The Political Origins of the Rise of Finance*. Cambridge, MA: Harvard University Press, 2011.

Krugman, Paul R. *The Return of Depression Economics and the Crisis of 2008*. New York: W.W. Norton, 2009.

Lapavitsas, Costas. *Profiting Without Producing: How Finance Exploits Us All*. London: Verso, 2013.

Lazonick, William. *Sustainable Prosperity in the New Economy? Business Organization and High-Tech Employment in the United States*. W.E. Upjohn Institute for Employment Research. Kalamazoo, Michigan, 2009.

_____. "Stock Buybacks: From Retain-and-Reinvest to Downsize-and-Distribute." Center for Effective Public Management, Washington, D.C.: Brookings Institution, 2015, 1–22.

MacKenzie, Donald A. *An Engine Not a Camera: How Financial Models Shape Markets*. Cambridge, MA: MIT Press, 2006.

Marx, Karl. *Capital*. Vol. I–III. New York: International Publishers, 1967.

McKinnon, Ronald I. *The Unloved Dollar Standard: From Bretton Woods to the Rise of China*. New York: Oxford, 2013.

Milberg, William and Deborah Winkler. *Outsourcing Economics: Global Value Chains in Capitalist Development*. New York: Cambridge University Press, 2013.

Mehrling, Perry. *Fischer Black and the Revolutionary Idea of Finance*. Hoboken, NJ: John Wiley and Sons, 2005.

_____. *The Money Interest and the Public Interest: American Monetary Thought, 1920–1970*. Cambridge, MA: Harvard University Press, 1997.

_____. *The New Lombard Street: How the Fed Became the Dealer of Last Resort*. Princeton, NJ: Princeton University Press, 2011.

_____. "Essential Hybridity: A Money View of FX," *Journal of Comparative Economics*, Vol. 41, 2013, 355–363.

Mehrling, Perry, Zoltan Pozsar, James Sweeney, and Dan Neilson. "Bagehot Was A Shadow Banker: Shadow Banking, Central Banking and the Future of Global Finance," *INET*, November 5, 2013.

Meister, Robert. *Political Identity: Thinking Through Marx*. Oxford, UK: Basil Blackwell, 1990.

Minsky, Hyman P. *Stabilizing and Unstable Economy*. New Haven, CT: Yale University Press, 1986.

Mirowski, Philip and Dieter Plehwe (eds.). *The Road from Mont Pelerin: The Making of the Neoliberal Thought Collective*. Cambridge, MA: Harvard University Press, 2009.

Monson, Andrew and Walter Scheidel (eds.). *Fiscal Regimes and the Political Economy of Premodern States*. New York: Cambridge University Press, 2015.

Moseley, Fred (ed.). *Marx's Theory of Money: Modern Appraisals*. New York: Palgrave MacMillan, 2005.

Nelson, Julie. *Economics for Humans*. Chicago: University of Chicago Press, 2016.

Nersisyan, Yeva and L. Randall Wray. "The Global Financial Crisis and the Shift to Shadow Banking," *Levy Institute Working Paper No. 587*, February 2010.

Orren, Karen. *Belated Feudalism: Labor, the Law, and Liberal Development in the United States*. New York: Cambridge University Press, 1991.

Pak, Susie J. *Gentlemen Bankers: The World of J.P. Morgan*. Cambridge, MA: Harvard University Press, 2013.

Palley, Thomas I. *Financialization: The Economics of Finance Capital Domination*. New York: Palgrave MacMillan, 2013.

_____. "Why Negative Interest Rate Policy (NIRP) is Ineffective and Dangerous," Private Debt Project, June 24, 2016.

Phillips-Fein, Kimberly (ed.). *What's Good for Business: Business and American Politics Since World War II*. Oxford, UK: Oxford University Press, 2012.

Polanyi, Karl. *The Great Transformation: The Political and Economic Origins of Our Time*. Boston: Beacon Press, 1944.

Poovey, Mary. *A History of the Modern Fact: Problems of Knowledge in the Sciences of Wealth and Society*. Chicago: University of Chicago Press, 1998.

Postone, Moishe. *Time, Labor, and Social Domination: A Reinterpretation of Marx's Critical Theory*. New York: Cambridge University Press, 1993.

Pozsar, Zoltan. "Institutional Cash Pools and the Triffin Dilemma of the U.S. Banking System," *IMF Working Paper WP/11/190*, August 2011.

_____. "Shadow Banking and the Global Financial Ecosystem," VOX CEPR's Policy Portal, November 7, 2013.

_____. "Shadow Banking: The Money View," *Office of Financial Research Working Paper 14-04*, U.S. Treasury, Washington, DC, July 2, 2014.

_____. "A Macro View of Shadow Banking: Levered Betas and Wholesale Funding in the Context of Secular Stagnation," SSRN #2558945. Shadow Banking Colloquium (Institute for New Economic Thinking). January 2015.

Pozsar, Zoltan, Tobias Adrian, Adam Ashcraft, and Hayley Boesky. "Shadow Banking," *FRBNY Economic Policy Review*, December 2013, 1–16.

Pozsar, Zoltan and Manmohan Singh. "The Nonbank-Bank Nexus and the Shadow Banking System," *IMF Working Paper WP/11/28*. Washington, DC., International Monetary Fund, December 2011.

Prasad, Eswar S. *The Dollar Trap: How the U.S. Dollar Tightened Its Grip on Global Finance*. Princeton, NJ: Princeton University Press, 2014.

_____. "China's Efforts to Expand the International Use of the Renminbi," A Report Prepared for the U.S.-China Economic and Security Review Committee. Washington, DC: Brookings Institution. 2016.

Rajan, Raghuram G. *Has Financial Development Made the World Riskier?* NBER Working Paper 11728, 2005.

Rodrik, Dani. *Economics Rules: The Rights and Wrongs of the Dismal Science*. New York: W.W. Norton, Inc., 2015a.

_____. "Premature Deindustrialization," Institute for Advanced Study, Princeton University, 2015b.

Roe, Mark. "Legal Origins, Politics, and Modern Stock Markets," *Harvard Law Review*, Vol. 120, No. 2, December, 2006, 460–527.

Roubini, Nouriel and Stephen Mihm. *Crisis Economics: A Crash Course in the Future of Finance*. New York: Penguin, 2010.

Rousseau, Peter L. "The Politics of Financial Development: A Review of Calomiris' and Haber's *Fragile by Design*," *Journal of Economic Literature*, Vol. 54, No. 1, 2016, 208–223.

Searle, John R. *Making the Social World: The Structure of Human Civilization*. New York: Oxford University Press, 2010.

Shaikh, Anwar. *Capitalism: Conflict, Competition, Crises*. New York: Oxford University Press, 2016.

Shleifer, Andrei and Robert W. Vishny. *The Grabbing Hand: Government Pathologies and Their Cures*. Cambridge, MA: Harvard University Press, 1998.

Singh, Manmohan and James Aitken, "The (Sizable) Role of Rehypothecation in the Shadow Banking System," *IMF Working Paper WP/10/172*, 2010.

Smith, Adam. *An Inquiry into the Nature and Causes of the Wealth of Nations*. New York: Modern Library, 1994.

Stiglitz, Joseph E. *Globalization and Its Discontents*. New York: W.W. Norton & Co., 2002.

_____. *Rewriting the Rules of the American Economy: An Agenda for Growth and Shared Prosperity*. New York: W.W. Norton & Co., 2016.

Stout, Lynn A. "Derivatives and the Legal Origin of the 2008 Credit Crisis," *Harvard Business Law Review*, Vol. 1, 2011, 1–38.

_____. *The Shareholder Value Myth: How Putting Shareholders First Harms Investors, Corporations, and the Public*. San Francisco: Berrett-Koehler Publishers, Inc., 2012.

Streeck, Wolfgang. "Why the Euro Divides Europe," *New Left Review*, Vol. 95, September/October 2015, 5–26.

Summers, Lawrence H. "U.S. Economic Prospects: Secular Stagnation, Hysteresis, and the Zero Lower Bound," *Business Economics*, Vol. 49, 2014, 65–73.

Sylla, Richard, Robert E. Wright, and David J. Cowen. "Alexander Hamilton, Central Banker: Crisis Management During the U.S. Financial Panic of 1792," *Business History Review*, Vol. 83, 2009, 61–86.

Tabb, William K. *The Restructuring of Capitalism in Our Time*. New York: Columbia University Press, 2012.

Tirole, Jean. "Illiquidity and All Its Friends," *Journal of Economic Literature*, Vol. 49, No. 2, 2011, 287–325.

Tymoigne, Eric and L. Randall Wray. *The Rise and Fall of Money Manager Capitalism: Minsky's Half Century from World War Two to the Great Recession*. New York: Routledge, 2014.

Vasudevan, Ramaa. *Things Fall Apart: From the Crash of 2008 to the Great Slump*. London: Sage Press, 2013.

Wachtel, Howard M. *The Money Mandarins: The Making of a Supranational Economic Order*. New York: Pantheon, 1986.

Wolfson, Martin H. and Gerald A. Epstein. *Handbook of Political Economy of Financial Crises*. New York: Oxford University Press, 2013.

Wray, L. Randall. "The Rise and Fall of Money Manager Capitalism: A Minskyian Approach," *Cambridge Journal of Economics*, Vol. 33, 2009, 807–828.

Yu Zhou, William Lazonick, and Yifei Sun (eds.). *China as an Innovation Nation*. New York: Oxford University Press, 2016.

Zelizer, Julian E. (ed.). *Rightward Bound: Making America Conservative in the 1970s*. Cambridge, MA: Harvard University Press, 2008.

7 Money and Abstraction

I. Methodology: Money as Concept, Institution, and Knowledge

The methodology of historical institutionalism analyzes the changing meanings of a key term and the associated institutions and related knowledge (Davis 2015). In this context, the key term is money—as a symbol, a means of communication, and a type of writing (Poovey 1998). In the case of money in particular, the importance is in the "flow," the use of money to make transactions and to serve as a store of value over time. Money does not serve its function unless it is in motion, and such motion is necessary to preserve its value by constant demonstration of its convertibility to another asset or material object. The movement of money is tracked by information, such as double-entry bookkeeping, which maintains records of financial transactions. Such movement of information requires agents and institutions that understand its meaning and transmit it in a consistent way, according to discrete rules. These institutions must also actively maintain this meaning, within standard definitions, reinforced with discipline on the institutional actors. Entire institutional complexes are involved and evolve historically.

II. The Corporation as Stabilizer of Financial Flows

The corporate form was used to stabilize financial flows and was in turn continually transformed by them.

The long history of the corporation begins with communes and city-states that were able to issue their own debt based on a collective promise to repay. Their robust political process enabled the issue of securities that these territorial entities could repay based on future tax revenues. The finance was often used for military self-defense against other warring city-states. Gold coin was necessary for long-distance trade and payment of mercenaries.

Early shipping ventures from city-states were conducted with partnerships and an advance of finance to purchase ships and crew, called the "corpo." These partnerships were time limited, lasting only the duration of the voyage, and proceeds were shared upon the return.

The importance of commerce for national power provided a "reason of state," a logic of mercantile calculation to expand trade. The subsequent use of the corporate form was the monopoly merchant corporation, such as the Dutch East India Corporation and the English East India Corporation. This entity commissioned by the state was used to explore, subdue territories, and establish trade routes. These corporations were often able to use force and to claim territories on behalf of the nation-state.

The function of defense was internalized with the liberal state, or tax/credit state, based on regular taxation and representative political institutions. The United Kingdom after the Reform Act of 1832 (Marazzi 2011, 116–119) and the United States at its founding were the exemplars of this form of the liberal state. In early nineteenth-century United States the corporate form expanded as a private business entity distinct from the state and protected by it (Davis 2016, 7).

After the Civil War, public/private partnership produced the transcontinental railroads, whereas other private rail corporations received support from local municipalities along their routes. The multidivisional corporation emerged from these large complex entities (Chandler 1977). Economies of scale in production, along with transportation and communication technologies, facilitated the growth of large-scale enterprises. Trusts were replaced by corporations after the antitrust laws of 1890 and 1914. Bankers such as J. P. Morgan formed the first large corporations, such as U.S. Steel and General Electric, by merging a new entity among existing competing firms and replacing the founding entrepreneurs, such as Carnegie, Edison, and later Ford (Davis 2016, 19, 24–25).

The multinational firm emerged in the early twentieth century (Chandler and Mazlish 2005) and spread with the growth of mass production and marketing. The holding company form in the 1920s led to abuse and regulation in the 1930s. The separation of ownership and control with the rise of the stock market and dispersal of ownership led to the large, stable managerial enterprise, especially after World War II (Cheffins 2015).

International competition in the 1970s, as well as inflation and deregulation, led to the growth of conglomerates in the 1980s (Davis, Diekmann, and Tinsley 1994). The subsequent leveraged buyout movement by management and private equity firms made use of the stock market to gain control and to reorganize companies that had grown too large and complex (Appelbaum and Batt 2014). As providing consumer credit became more important to the sales effort, manufacturing corporations become less distinguishable from financial corporations (Krippner 2011). The return to "core competencies" and to allowing large investors to manage and diversity their portfolios, rather than view the corporation with its own internal capital market, facilitated the emphasis on the stock price and the new ideas regarding "maximizing shareholder value" (Fligstein and Shin 2007).

Gains in information technology and global capital markets, especially after the end of Bretton Woods and the fall of the USSR, enabled Western companies to develop global supply chains (Antras 2016; Baldwin 2016; Brown and Linden 2009; Prechel 2000, 226–229), which "disintegrated" production (Feenstra 2010; Urry 2014). The information technology industry itself was the first to separate design from execution geographically, with "fabless" and "fab," or foundry firms, respectively (Angel 1994). Computer chips are design intensive with capital-intensive production methods and are high-value and low-weight commodities, ideal for trade in components. The location of foundries in low-wage Asian countries reduced capital costs of the U.S.-based design firms and helped offset the high research and development expense. The information technology industry also provided the capacity to track the dispersed units across global locations, with ongoing improvements in hardware and software. The corporate logo became the symbol of an integrated yet geographically dispersed system of production, marketing, and distribution, increasingly a "hollow" corporation that no longer generated stable domestic employment, replaced by subsidiaries and contractors throughout Asia.

In the twenty-first century, corporations manage global capital flows within their own treasuries, as well as their own production and distribution systems. Their flexible form and geographic reach, nonetheless, enables evasion of taxes and regulation and exacerbates wage competition on a global scale. High CEO salaries and bonuses combined with low wages exacerbate inequality and reduce effective demand.

III.   Abstraction of the Production Process

As discussed in Chapter 3, abstraction is a social and institutional as well as a conceptual process. To constantly improve the methods of production, analysis of the process was necessary from an objective point of view, which is another form of abstraction from its concrete material features. For the business firm to abstract from the production process, to discipline labor and organize greater efficiencies, there was an early application of science to the production process. In response to the monopoly of the guilds, which was criticized by Adam Smith and others, which had been the dominant institution of training and organizing craft workers, and protecting their knowledge, there was a long term effort at abstracting knowledge from the workers.

For example, Pascal and Leibniz had designed and constructed calculating machines in the mid-seventeenth century (Jones 2012). Pascal had been granted a "privilege" in 1649 by the French Academy of Sciences. The privilege protected the idea and enabled protection of the production of the machine, an early form of intellectual property granted by a new type of organization, a science society authorized by the state. Rather than simply protecting the artisanal skill of making the machine, this privilege protected the idea, for the public welfare, with no specific timetable or requirement for actual production (Jones 2012, 127–132). Leibniz made reference to this earlier invention in his request in 1675, which included a business model (Jones 2012, 134–141). In spite of relying heavily on a skilled artisan for production, he claimed the idea as his own, supporting a new romantic model of the individual inventor with rights to his invention. This notion of invention as an abstract process separate from production helped solidify later divisions of labor which separated conception from execution, later extended by Charles Babbage in 1832. The invention and production of a calculating machine, itself a form of information technology, or "smart machine," helped to stimulate a new division of labor.

> The difficulties in producing calculating machines served as an emblem for needed reforms of work and a major spur for the development of new machining techniques and organization of labor. The ability to create a regime of standardized manufacture of form helped to legitimate a conception of invention as a mentalistic "form" independent of a process of the actual production. Manufacture so reduced grounded a severing of form and matter. (Jones 2012, 141)

Tacit knowledge, which is only imperfectly captured in the machine algorithms, would hamper efforts to maintain efficient production while deskilling the workers (Marglin 2008, 128–168).

Babbage continued the dream of "mechanization of intelligence" (Schaffer 1994, 207). There was a complementarity between Smith's division of labor and the "Babbage principle," which involved analysis of production into its simplest components and reorganized these components with the aid of machinery. That is, the use of intelligent machines also involved the reorganization and discipline of labor. Experimentation with developing entire systems of production was important for improvements in military production, such as the Royal Navy between 1795 and 1807, where an automatic machine tool system was first implemented (Schaffer 1994, 211). The factory system was a "vast automaton," a marvel for tourists (Schaffer 1994, 222), emblematically locating intelligence in the machine and the "mental capital of the mill owners," rather than the workers (Schaffer 1994, 224).

> The apotheosis of the intelligent machine was an integral part of Babbage's ambitious programme … These techniques helped make a new social order and a new form of knowledge. (Schaffer 1994, 226)

Marx, writing *Capital* in 1867, noted the role of science in the aid of industry (Marx 1967, Vol. I, Ch. 15, 386, 436–437, 461, 486). Quoting Ure about the automatic factory, he notes that there are two descriptions:

> These two descriptions are far from being identical. In one, the collective labourer, or social body of labour, appears as the dominating subject, and the mechanical automaton as the object; in the other, the automaton itself

is the subject, and the workmen are merely conscious organs, co-ordinate with the unconscious organs of the automaton, and together with them, subordinated to the central moving–power ... The second is characteristic of its use by capital, and therefore the modern factory system. (Marx 1967, Vol. I, Ch. 15, Section IV, 419)

So-called "Fordist" methods of mass production made commodity production a "continuous flow" operation by means of machine pacing of the production process, along with detailed division of labor. The transition to more flexible "post-Fordist" methods required more integral use of information technology to produce customized products and to adjust the rate of production to consumer demand to minimize accumulation of unsold inventories (Marazzi 2011, 17–35).

IV.   The Corporation as Producer and Mediator of Financial Flows

The role of the corporation straddling financial and real flows can mediate many of the contradictions of money discussed in Chapter 2:

*   Abstract and concrete
*   Real and financial
*   National and international
*   Interface with financial markets
*   Interface with labor markets
*   Interface with product markets (consumer and investment goods)
*   Interface with the state via taxes and subsidies
*   Interface with the state in terms of form of property and associated regulation
*   Interface with the state as a citizen with rights (Ciepley 2013)

That is, the financial circuit, $M - C - M'$, is a combination of both abstract and concrete flows over time, which are mediated by the corporation. First, the concrete labor process is managed by engineers and managers in factories, $C - C'$. Second, the financial flows are captured with information regarding both costs and revenues, $M - M'$. Third, the information regarding the production process, including design, marketing, distribution, and realization, is captured at each stage of the circuit and at each site. The information flows are increasingly captured within the machine complex of information technology and used to further automate the production and realization process. This capture of information enables further conceptualization and rationalization of the entire process and an increase in the speed of production and realization, further affecting the continual reorganization of the entire process. According to the logic of the division of labor and the "Babbage principle," the entire process is divided into components and reassembled in new forms to facilitate automation and to increase the speed of turnover, affecting the organization of work and the corporate form.

The corporation was originally territorial in the commune and city-state before becoming a vehicle of world trade, with the monopoly merchant corporation. After the Industrial Revolution and the separation of home from factory, the private business corporation was a mediator of spaces as well. The wholly owned factory organized the labor process with machines and mobile energy sources, drawing labor from the household. The final product was in turn sold to the household. The integration of these specialized spaces occurred by means of financial flows, including the corporation, the household, and the nation-state. The currency was issued by the territorial nation-state as its own liability, based on expected tax returns by means of that same currency as a means of payment and as an asset. Yet the national currency also circulated globally, first the gold standard under the British hegemon, and later the U.S. dollar under the succeeding hegemon. The nation-based corporation was able to use these domestic currencies to expand globally, with the favorable terms of trade in investment and purchase of raw materials, extending the power of the nation-state geographically.

V.   The Corporation as an Agent of Abstraction

The corporation is an abstract entity itself (Barkan 2013; Davis 2015; Searle 2010), defined by linguistic statements with collective recognition of the appropriate behavior that is associated with these statements. The corporate form is impersonal, organized by rules regarding decision-making authority for the collective entity as a whole. In this way it can become perpetual, existing beyond the life of any particular member. There was a long historical evolution of the corporate form from the early modern to the modern period, from guilds and communes and city-states, as well as merchant monopoly corporations. The use of the corporate form in the United States was resisted based on the experience of colonial governance and the fear of centralized power. Once recognized by law and freed from specific charters from the state legislature, the use of the form of the business corporation expanded (Prechel 2000, 25–39; Wright 2014).

Scientific management developed by Frederick Taylor provided a framework for standardizing the labor process in terms of optimizing the use of labor time. Taylor provided the tools for establishing standard rates for associating labor time with material flow in production, as well as the information systems to manage the progressive separation of conception from execution (Prechel 2000, 99–100, 177–178, 203). This separation was facilitated by the organizational hierarchy in which mental workers, or professionals, had more status and higher pay than manual workers. The financial accounting innovations by Donaldson Brown provided financial controls to link management decisions with returns for corporate investors. Brown's concept of ROI (return on investment) captured the rate at which revenue was returned from a given initial outlay relative to the size of the original outlay. It was a measure of speed of financial "turnover," or the time lag between outlay and cash receipts (Prechel 2000, 99–110, 204–205, 251–252).

The focus on financial accounting helped to abstract from the concrete labor process of production. That is, the particular skill of the workers and the shape of the mechanical equipment will vary by industry and technology. These physical characteristics will be important to engineers and, ultimately, to consumers. Yet the accounting system of the corporation can track these same processes in a parallel abstract fashion, by the financial outlay for the workers and for the equipment, in financial terms. What matters for financial accounting is the size of the initial outlay for the equipment, the regular pattern of wage payments, which vary with volume of output, and the rate at which the products can be sold and the value realized in financial proceeds. There is considerable uncertainty in the financial return due to the rate at which the equipment is utilized, the potential obsolescence of any given embedded technology, the flow of inventory and sales, and the expected future value of output of the particular type of product. These specific features of a given corporation in a given industry can be translated into financial flows per unit of time, providing abstract information to corporate investors on a timely basis. Using these organizational and accounting techniques, a centralization of financial control with a delegation of managerial responsibility could be achieved (Prechel 2000, 100, 107).

VI. The Corporation as a Producer and User of Information

The organization of the managerial hierarchy, as well as the relationship among discrete corporate entities, was the subject of considerable experimentation. The holding company permitted one company to hold stock in another and so allowed the pyramiding of capital by the investors in the top of the corporate hierarchy (Prechel 2000, 30–39, 44–57, 62–78). With complex mergers, the multidivisional form became more useful, with separate divisions for each product line, followed by the multilayered subsidiary form (Boies and Prechel 2002; Prechel 2000, 79–87, 105–113, 207–216, 251–265). The conglomerate movement followed by the leveraged buyout model helped to establish a "market for corporate control" (Appelbaum and Batt 2014). The changing corporate form was motivated by profitability crises, which mobilized corporate leaders to engage in political strategies to allow for legal changes in the corporate form. The resulting process facilitated consolidation of market control and extension across product lines as well as geographic reach.

In financial accounting systems, economies in labor time of production, or "throughput," are indistinguishable from increases in the speed of turnover for financial assets; both increase the rate of profit, at least in the short term. That is, efficiencies in the flow of funds and the choice of financial vehicles can affect the calculated rate of profit independently of production and sales of the product. The shift from cost to financial accounting can produce misleading information and inefficiencies, which mask those differences as to the source of profits, whether production or finance, and so potentially distort investment decision in the firm's own "internal capital market" (Coffee and Palia 2015; Prechel 2000, 108–113).

With improvements in information technology, management information systems, and openness to global capital flows, the corporation was able to operate a supply chain composed of subsidiaries and subcontractors located in geographically dispersed locations to serve both foreign and domestic markets. The brand was the unifying concept behind the geographically and organizationally dispersed functions of design, marketing, engineering, component production, and distribution.

The organization of production with information technology is possible to the extent that automation is feasible with advanced manufacturing techniques and the modularity of production processes and software (Brown and Linden 2009; Prechel 2000, 197–202). With cloud computing and software, the corporation can evolve into an Internet platform for the aggregation of both consumers and suppliers and for the conduct of trade and financial investment (Davis 2016; Evans, Hagiu, and Schmalensee 2006).

VII.   Theories of the Corporation

There are many theories of the corporation: from law, from economics, and from political science and history.

Within economics, the focus has been on the choice of markets or hierarchies, or the "make or buy" decisions. The firm, which represents the "make" position, can instruct labor as needed when the ability to specify the content of the assignment before hiring is not possible. This is considered an information problem, which prevents efficient contracting (Lamoreaux, Raff, and Temin 2003). When the cost of contracting in the market diminishes with information technology, there will be more "buy" decisions, as access to the market is more feasible. A recent contribution stresses the efficiency of the corporation form when the entrepreneur makes the transition from founding to external finance, when differences in product attributes must be abstracted to facilitate comparisons of rates of return for investors (Rajan 2012). An alternative tradition within economics emphasizes the hierarchical nature of the firm, the control of labor, and its focus on profits (Edwards 1979; Marglin 2008).

There are also varieties of legal theories of the firm, from "entity" (Hansmann, Kraakman, and Squire 2006) to "nexus of contracts" (Jensen and Meckling 1976). That is, rather than a single entity that represents the stockholders, the firm is simply an aggregation of separate voluntary contracts by autonomous individuals, with no recognition of the collective operating as a whole. There is also a political view of the corporation, which stresses its access to the public power of the state, as well as a "legal origins" view, which analyzes the legal institutional history of each country and its impact on corporate forms (Ciepley 2013; Roe 2006).

Smith and Marx both referred to the corporation as an entity that makes use of "other people's money" (Smith 1994, Part III, Article I, 799–801, 815–818; Marx 1967, Vol. III, Ch. 27, 436–441), and so does not effectively represent the owner. The attempt to discipline management after the separation of ownership and control at the turn of the twentieth century, along with the ascendance of free-market views, led to the development of the renewed focus of the corporation on "maximizing shareholder value." This focus on shareholder returns and profit enabled the vertical disintegration and global distribution of components of the supply chain, facilitated by information technology to reintegrate the discrete pieces into a conceptual whole.

The position here is that the corporation is a legal entity with a long history and shifting forms and functions, as discussed in more depth elsewhere (Davis 2015; 2016). A similar approach (Hockett and Omarova 2016a and 2016b) emphasizes the public nature of the corporation. This is particularly true of financial firms, which manage the "faith and credit of the United States," monetized by the financial system in coordination with the central bank. Access to this public resource occurs by delegation of the government according to a "franchise" model, which renders regulation of this resource as a legitimate protection of the public interest. This "franchise" approach differs from the view of money as a scarce private resource accumulated from saving and from returns to investment, and so beyond the appropriate reach of government regulation.

The relevance of the corporation to the topic of money is based on the role of financial corporations in the management of money. The early resistance to the founding of the Bank of the United States by President Jackson is well known, as is the relatively late foundation of the central bank in 1913. The separation of commercial and investment banks in the Glass-Steagall Act of 1933 and the restriction on branch banking maintained a large number and moderate size of most financial firms. In the twentieth and twenty-first centuries, the organizational form of the finance industry has continued to evolve, from partnerships and syndicates to public corporations (Akerlof and Shiller 2015; Pak 2013). Deregulation beginning in the 1980s facilitated further division of labor among types of financial firms, comprising a linked chain of financial intermediation across different organizational entities. These new entities were designed to evade regulation and so became a "shadow banking" system (Gorton and Metrick 2010). After the financial crisis of 2008, the bank holding company (BHC) has become the predominant form after the repeal of Glass-Steagall in 1999 and its replacement with the Gramm-Leach-Bliley Act, and the rescue of "too big to fail" banks by merging weaker ones into larger stronger units.

The oligopoly structure, size, and integration of the BHCs remain issues, nonetheless, with the potential of systemic risk, now identified and regulated according to the provisions of the Dodd-Frank Act of 2010.

VIII.   The Corporation and Reification

With the scaffolding of the institutions of the perpetual state and the perpetual corporation, one territorial and one mobile, there can exist a global financial market across space and infinite time. Financial assets can command living labor in any location in the present.

A.   The Importance of "Representation"

Searle stresses the importance of representation for the durability and recognition of institutions. A "status function declaration" must be capable of being represented in documents or symbols. But there are important double meanings of the term "representation." On the one hand, representation can refer to political and legal processes by which governance institutions can articulate the needs and interests of their constituents. On the other hand, representation is a linguistic term, referring to the correspondence between "words and things." Metaphors such as the "body" and "land" provide a semblance of materiality for such mental concepts as corporation and property (Santner 2016; Underkuffler 2003, 16–17). According to Poovey, there can be a "problematic of representation," nonetheless, by which the assumed correspondence can be challenged and questioned (Poovey 2008, 5, 7, 15, 62, 72–73, 221–223, 229).

This double entendre of the term "representation" has special resonance in the history of money and credit, institutional forms that were first developed by communes and city-states. The legitimate political processes by which early modern states were capable of decision-making provided the credibility by which such institutions were able to issue debt (Stasavage 2015). That is, political representation in parliaments facilitated the issue of debt, a symbolic form of representing the solemn commitment of the entire community, a "bond."

The corporation itself is characterized by dualities and divisions; it is at once public and private, financial and real, personal and impersonal, as well as abstract and concrete. These diverse aspects are relatively invisible due to its specific representation in each context. On the other hand, the unity of the corporation as a single body facilitates the integration of each aspect, primarily in the context of the financial circuit. The corporation can integrate across space and time as a single privileged agent.

B.   Functions of Reification

In such situations, the process of "reification" can be important (Honneth 2008). If the word is taken *as* the thing itself, such as the term "property" standing for the object, such as land, then the questioning of this representation is less likely. As the word *becomes* the thing, in normal parlance, its meaning becomes etched in an enhanced institutional *reality* that exists in everyone's mind as shared "background" (Searle 2010). No one questions the existence of money with a U.S. dollar bill in hand, with its authoritative text, symbols, and signatures, as well as its purchasing power. Yet money, even U.S. dollars, is like a modern metaphysical being with preternatural powers, which is presumed to exist and so guides daily behavior in the moment. All contingency based on human institutions becomes irrelevant to the reality of the financial "instrument." A currency with global recognition, favorable terms of trade, strict enforcement, and demonstrable purchasing power becomes a "hard" currency, as if it were actually made of precious metal. There is a hierarchy of currencies, reflecting the degree of confidence in the nation that is represented, as well as its economic, political, and military power. The nation with a credible currency can then issue debt in its own currency and achieve access to credit more easily (Eichengreen 2011; Terzi 2006), and hence can finance increased military power.

Reification of money is also important in its role as a medium of exchange—Smith's "great wheel of circulation" (Smith 1994, 314–317). Property must circulate to maintain and *expand* its value, but the process of circulation itself involves changes in ownership and location minimally, as well as possibly transformation in production, which pose *challenges* to value. While the value of commodities is in constant flux with the continuing increases in productivity (Postone 1993), the firm is able to maintain a fixed price of the product and facilitate completion of the financial circuit by sales of the product. The belief that the value of money is stable facilitates the maintenance of a fixed sales price, even while real purchasing power of money may ultimately change with the changing costs of production and new product competition. In modern economies, this management of the value of the currency is the role of the central bank and financial innovations such as credit default swaps. That is, reification is important when both the value of money and the price of the product can vary over time, potentially jeopardizing the completion of the financial circuit, as well as credit and debt contracts.

C. Perpetuity

With the existence of perpetual institutions, like the corporation and the state, an infinite money market can be constructed on that institutional scaffolding. The money market, or "finance," stretches into the future with no limit—its existence a daily reality. Governments can issue "perpetual" bonds and so raise money in the present. Corporations with perpetual lives can issue stock and become a vehicle for entrepreneurship, investment, and accumulation. Money is a symbol of the infinite state and the perpetual corporation. The corporation and the state cooperate in the management of the financial circuit, which maintains flows of real goods and labor, production and consumption. The central bank manages the value of the purchasing power of money in the present and the future. "Interest is a premium on present over future purchasing power … regarded as a means of control over production goods" (Schumpeter 1983, 157, 184), which embodies innovation permitting increasing productivity of labor.

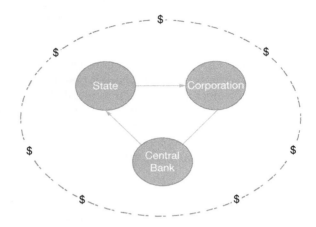

Figure 7.1 Modern Corporations

This tripartite system, as illustrated in Figure 7.1, consisting of private business corporations, central banks, and the state, originates and manages financial assets and allocates investment by means of the financial markets. The direction of the economy is the outcome of the competition for surplus between corporations and the state, while they also collaborate in maintaining the stability and integrity of the financial system. The state, a corporate form defined by territory, becomes mobile by means of its private business corporations, which organize investment and reap surplus on a global scale. Together these interlocking corporate forms manage space and time.

This representation of money enables the *trading in time*, such as saving now for the future, and taking future returns and calculating "present discounted value" in the moment. With the deregulation of finance in the United States beginning in the 1980s, after the end of Bretton Woods, the trading of financial assets expanded to arbitrage the differences in present value, with the financial assets taken as valuable in themselves (Poovey 2008, 16, 26). The function of intertemporal intermediation, whereby banks acquire short-term liabilities and manage long-term assets, resolves increasingly to rely on short-term arbitrage and the rise of the counterparty to manage risk in the present. Further, high-frequency trading developed with advancing information technology, which allowed trading in the instant on differences in expected present discounted value among alternative financial assets (MacKenzie 2015). Finally, the reification of money cements its claim to the first share of the surplus in the settlement of debt contracts and bankruptcies.

D.   *Modernity*

In this context, the definition of modernity is the foundation based on this tripartite system of power: the corporation, the state, and the central bank. This interlocking complex of institutions issues currencies and debt and uses and manages the financial markets in a complementary fashion. This modern institutional complex contrasts with the medieval constellation of town, guild, and church, as illustrated in Figure 7.2.

This medieval complex is evident in the European architecture of every urban center, such as the Guildhall in the City of London. In the medieval context, the foundation was land and its management, along with the production and distribution of the surplus. In the modern complex, the foundation is finance, a fluid, "fictional" entity, "liquid," subject to "flows," which are more contingent and more challenging to manage. The corporate form of the guild was repurposed to operate in a new commercial context with the emergence of long-distance trade and provided a transitional institutional mechanism or "homology" (Padgett and Powell 2012). In this context, reification of money and property served the purpose of promoting the image of "permanence" in spite of the ubiquity of an intangible medium of money and credit based on public confidence and "belief." In this context, orthodoxies become important (Poovey 2008, 17–19) and such mantras as "there is no alternative."

The modern "individual" is abstract, as illustrated in Figure 7.3 (Davis 2011), along with "property." The individual's right to his own property, emphasized by Locke and Smith, becomes compromised with the separation of the individual from his property with the introduction of money and the division of labor. Property and its increase remain the rationale of the system, the "wealth of nations," over abstract space and continuous time.

The status and character of the individual are nonetheless reflected in his "own" property, a mirroring relationship. That is, if property is no longer *owned* by the individual worker, property is at least *displayed* by the individual consumer. This reflection of oneself is especially important with the separation of ownership of the worker and his product, a form of reintegration in the private sphere, for the purposes of display in the public sphere via an equalizing "conspicuous consumption" (Sewell 2014).

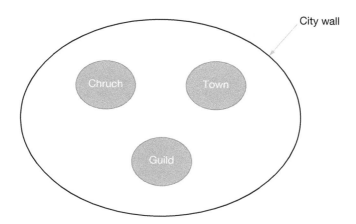

Figure 7.2 Medieval Corporations

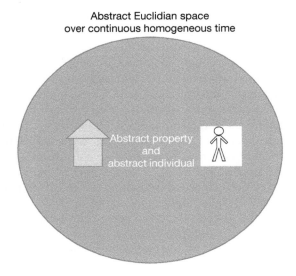

Figure 7.3 Modernity

Corporate sovereignty can undermine the state, but financial flows can strengthen the state. Competing corporations on behalf of competing nation-states can increase their "competiveness" reflected in balance of payments surpluses, thereby strengthening their currency. In some ways, the hierarchy of nations and their currencies depends on the relative success of competing corporations. The "competitiveness" of nations was still a topic of national pride (Berger 2005; Dertouzas, Lester, and Solow 1989; Porter 1980, 1990; Porter, Rivkin, and Desai 2016) after World War II and in the context of competition with the USSR, ending in 1989 with the apparent victory of the Western liberal model.

IX.   Information Technology and Dynamic Abstraction in the Pursuit of Profit

Financial firms were early adopters of information technology in order to speed up the financial circuit and to reduce turnover time. The Morse code, transatlantic cables, the ticker tape, and the computer were adapted quickly to financial functions (Knorr-Cetina and Preda 2007) and in turn helped to stimulate further innovation in information technology.

Flows of financial information, along with flows of production information, were combined to produce entire systems of finance. The double-entry bookkeeping form was used in both corporate and government accounting to facilitate the "flow of funds" reporting for the macroeconomy as a whole, reflected in statistics regularly available from the Federal Reserve Board.

The representation of the corporation by the stock price and the nation by the sovereign bond enables rapid processing of information regarding each.

The trading of both symbols on global capital markets provides greater liquidity and stability. Yet in the process of representing the social institution by means of a symbol, there is a potential irrational element involving projections of human emotions such as image and status, security and desire (De Goede 2005), onto the symbol itself.

This integrated system is reflexive (Soros 2013), providing information to participants, yet also reactive, responding to the actions of those participants. The greater the speed of reaction and the more comprehensive the system, the greater the potential of large movements within the system. Movements of the dynamic system itself can create "manias" and euphorias, noted with the early emergence of the financial markets (Kindleberger 1989; Pocock 1975).

The overnight repurchase agreements of U.S. Treasury bonds, the "repo," are a key source of liquidity, at the same time that it is a symbol of a sovereign nation. Repos are the "safe asset" at the base of a shadow financial system, with no regulation and infinite possible expansion of credit (Gorton 2010, 43–51; Hockett and Omarova 2016b, 28–34). At times these interactions can generate instability (Shin 2010) and sovereign debt loops (Farhi and Tirole 2016). The flexibility of exchange rates after the end of the Bretton Woods system provided more opportunities for trading and hedging (Krippner 2011, 88–92), while also making the system vulnerable to currency crises and self-fulfilling bubbles and bursts.

There are several examples of destabilizing feedback loops in the financial system. One example is "socially necessary labor time," which provides the basis for productivity comparisons and market price (Postone 1993). The "first mover" to improve productivity can charge the same price while having lower costs. This increase in profits will generate imitative behavior by other firms, who then are pressured to improve productivity as well. As average productivity increases, the average price will decline, decreasing profits for the follower firms. This general dynamic tends to reduce labor input and employment throughout the economy, undermining effective demand. Another example is how easy credit can increase the price of collateral, such as homes and real estate. This increase in the value of collateral then provides the basis for further expansion of credit, like the housing bubble in the early 2000s (Soros 2013, 323–324). A third example is the repo market, where U.S. Treasury bonds and other securitized assets are accepted as collateral for overnight loans. The decline in home prices starting in 2006 suddenly raised the question of the safety of the mortgage-backed security (MBS), whose composition was obscure. This switch in perception reduced the liquidity of these assets, and trades were unable to be executed, creating a "run on repo" (Gorton and Metrick 2010) as investors raced for cash when the safety of the MBS was in doubt. The decline in price of the MBS then spread the panic to other types of financial assets. Ultimately the shadow banking system collapsed and "toxic assets" were taken onto the balance sheet of the Federal Reserve (Ricks 2012). Finally, rescued large financial holding companies were allowed to remain in derivatives and commodity trading, driving a commodity price cycle in 2011 and 2012 (Omarova 2013).

X. Knowledge and Episteme

The question has been raised as to whether finance is a separate type of knowledge or episteme (Knorr-Cetina and Preda 2007). The aspect of human systems as reflexive based on changes in understanding has been stressed by Soros, who had extensive experience in the financial sector along with academic training. According to his "reflexive system," human perceptions influence intentions, which then have an effect on social reality. In turn, that social reality can change perceptions based on experience and observations (Soros 2013, 314). One modification of his "reflexive system" may include the linguistic structure of institutions, based on "status function declarations" (Searle 2010). That is, there is a social context for human beliefs, where common terms such as property and money are defined by expert systems, such as law and corporate governance. These terms and common understandings influence behavior, or social reality, as well as perceptions of reality, like the proverbial "rose-colored glasses." Because of the complex division of function among a set of institutions, including corporations, courts, and legislatures, along with legitimate social norms, these common understandings change slowly, but evolve over time (Davis 2015, 28–54). However, at historic junctures, these common understandings can change dramatically, constituting a "crisis" of understanding and coordination, and likely to lead to changes in knowledge paradigms. New paradigms can emerge at such crisis periods. Such a revised "reflexive system" is illustrated in Figure 7.4.

Rather than understand finance as a different type of epistemology, the view here is that existing frameworks can apply to finance, with the only difference being that much more of the activity is conducted in symbolic form

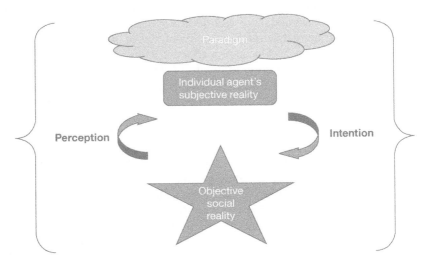

Figure 7.4 Reflexive System with Paradigm

at very high speeds, with implications for national and international economic systems. Such meaning systems, or paradigms, can persist for decades, such as in the case of the New Deal financial regulatory system, or they can evolve rapidly, such as the trend toward deregulation that began in the 1980s along with "neoliberalism." For example, the regulatory framework was undermined quickly once the noncorporate "special-purpose vehicles" were able to issue money-like securities, which were off the balance sheets of regulated insured commercial banks (Gorton and Metrick 2010).

Changes in paradigms can influence public discourse as well as the function of important institutions. For example, the importance of the transformation to a "portfolio society" has been noted by Gerald F. Davis (2009). That is, the primary function of the financial system has become the preservation of the value of financial assets, rather than the channeling of investment into profitable and productive ends for growth and employment. This transformation has been noted by Gary Gorton as well in terms of the increasing share of privately produced "safe assets" rather than public safe assets like insured bank deposits and Treasury bonds. Although these privately produced safe assets fill a demand, they are still less stable and likely to experience crises of confidence, or "runs." As the financial system has changed to accommodate these large pools of investment funds, he does not see a return to the previous system, with implications for macro stability (Gorton 2016).

XI. The Corporation Brings Money to Life

The corporation enlivens financial flows, like living labor brings value to the dead labor of the machine (Marazzi 2011 80–81). Yet the corporation is a legal fiction, a corporate "personality," recognized by law and by the coordinated behavior of its members.

The corporation itself is symbolized by a logo, an icon, which communicates for consumers a certain status and lifestyle to other consumers. Yet the corporation and its operations can increasingly be summarized by a code and the automatic operations of intelligent software systems. Similarly the currency is a symbol of the nation, and its stability and exchange rate are a reflection of its commercial and military power.

Currencies and sovereign debt are freely traded on global financial markets, along with corporate stocks and bonds. These symbols of the collective provide liquidity for investors, with options for balancing portfolios, and providing leverage over the entity itself, whether corporation or nation. They are also merely symbols, whose reference to the original party becomes weakened with the growing length of the intermediation chain. In financial crises, money reverts to its public nature. Ultimately each nation is responsible for providing a backstop for wagers beyond its control and beyond its borders, potentially reducing confidence in the nation as well as the global financial system.

References

Akerlof, George and Robert J. Shiller. *Phishing for Phools: The Economics of Manipulation and Deception*. Princeton, NJ: Princeton University Press, 2015.

Angel, David P. *Restructuring for Innovation: The Remaking of the U.S. Semiconductor Industry*. New York: Guilford Press, 1994.

Antras, Pol. *Global Production: Firms, Contracts, and Trade Structure*. Princeton, NJ: Princeton University Press, 2016.

Appelbaum, Eileen and Rosemary Batt. *Private Equity at Work: When Wall Street Manages Main Street*. New York: Russell Sage, 2014.

Baldwin, Richard. *The Great Convergence: Information Technology and the New Globalization*. Cambridge, MA: Harvard University Press, 2016.

Barkan, Joshua. *Corporate Sovereignty: Law and Government Under Capitalism*. Minneapolis: University of Minnesota Press, 2013.

Berger, Suzanne. *How We Compete: What Companies Around the World Are Doing to Make It in Today's Global Economy*. New York: Doubleday, 2005.

Boies, John and Harland Prechel. "Capital Dependence, Business Political Behavior, and Change to the Multilayered Subsidiary Form," *Social Problems*, Vol. 49, No. 3, 2002, 301–326.

Brown, Claire and Greg Linden. *Chips and Change: How Crisis Reshaped the Semiconductor Industry*. Cambridge, MA: MIT Press, 2009.

Chandler, Alfred D. Jr. *The Visible Hand: The Managerial Revolution in American Business*. Cambridge, MA: Belknap Press, 1977.

Chandler, Alfred D. Jr. and Bruce Mazlish (eds.). *Leviathans: Multinational Corporations and the New Global History*. New York: Cambridge University Press, 2005.

Cheffins, Brian R. "Corporate Governance Since the Managerial Capitalism Era," *Business History Review*, Vol. 89, 2015, 717–744.

Ciepley, David. "Beyond Public and Private: Toward a Political Theory of the Corporation," *American Political Science Review*, Vol. 107, No. 1, 2013, 139–158.

Coffee, John C. and Darius Palia. "The Wolf at the Door: The Impact of Hedge Fund Activism on Corporate Governance," *Columbia Law School Working Paper No. 521*, September 4, 2015.

Davis, Ann E. *The Evolution of the Property Relation: Paradigms, Debates, Prospects*. New York: Palgrave MacMillan, 2015.

_____. "Contested Continuity: Competing Explanations of the Evolution of the Corporate Form," *Journal of Economic Issues*, Vol. 50, No. 2, 2016, 611–619.

Davis, Gerald F. *Management by the Markets: How Finance Reshaped America*. New York: Oxford University Press, 2009.

_____. *The Vanishing American Corporation: Navigating the Hazards of a New Economy*. Oakland, CA: Berrett-Koehler Publishers, Inc., 2016.

Davis, Gerald F., Kristina A. Diekmann, and Catherine H. Tinsley. "The Decline and Fall of the Conglomerate Firm in the 1980s: The Deinstitutionalization of an Organization Form," *American Sociological Review*, Vol. 59, No. 4, 1994, 547–570.

Davis, John B. *Individuals and Identity in Economics*. New York: Cambridge University Press, 2011.

De Goede, Marieke. *Virtue, Fortune, and Faith: A Genealogy of Finance*. Minneapolis, MN: University of Minnesota Press, 2005.

Dertouzas, Michael L., Richard K. Lester and Robert M.Solow. *Made in America: Regaining the Productive Edge*. New York: HarperCollins, 1989.

Edwards, Richard. *Contested Terrain: Transformation of the Workplace in the Twentieth Century*. New York: Basic Books, 1979.

Eichengreen, Barry. *Exorbitant Privilege: The Rise and Fall of the Dollar and the Future of the International Monetary System*. New York: Oxford University Press, 2011.

Evans, David S., Andrei Hagiu, and Richard Schmalensee. *Invisible Engines: How Software Platforms Drive Innovation and Transform Industries*. Cambridge, MA: MIT Press, 2006.

Farhi, Emmanuel and Jean Tirole. "Deadly Embrace: Sovereign and Financial Balance Sheets Doom Loops," *NBER Working Paper 21843*, January 2016.

Feenstra, Robert C. *Offshoring in the Global Economy: Microeconomic Structure and Macroeconomic Implications*. Cambridge, MA: MIT Press, 2010.

Fligstein, Neil and Taekjin Shin. "Shareholder Value and the Transformation of the U.S. Economy, 1984-2000," *Sociological Forum*, Vol. 22, No. 4, 2007, 399–424.

Gorton, Gary. "The History and Economics of Safe Assets," *NBER Working Paper*, August 31, 2016.

Gorton, Gary and Andrew Metrick. "Regulating the Shadow Banking System," *Brookings Papers on Economic Activity*, Fall 2010, 261–297.

Hansmann, Henry, Reinier Kraakman, and Richard Squire. "Law and the Rise of the Firm," *Harvard Law Review*, Vol. 119, No. 5, March 2006, 1333–1403.

Hockett, Robert C. and Saule T. Omarova. "'Special,' Vestigial, or Visionary? What Bank Regulation Tells Us About the Corporation – and Vice Versa," *Seattle University Law Review*, Vol. 39, 2016a, 453.

––––––. "The Finance Franchise," *Cornell Law School Research Paper* No. 16–29, 2016b.

Honneth, Axel. *Reification: A New Look at an Old Idea*. New York: Oxford University Press, 2008.

Jensen, Michael C. and William H. Meckling. "Theory of the Firm: Managerial Behavior, Agency Costs and Ownership Structure," *Journal of Financial Economics*, Vol. 3, No. 4, October 1976, 305–360.

Jones, Matthew L. "Improvement for Profit: Calculating Machines and the Prehistory of Intellectual Property," in Mario Biagioli and Jessica Riskin (eds.), *Nature Engaged: Science in Practice from the Renaissance to the Present*. New York: Palgrave MacMillan, 2012, 125–146.

Kindleberger, Charles P. *Manias, Panics, and Crashes: A History of Financial Crises*. New York: Basic Books, 1989.

Knorr-Cetina, Karin and Alex Preda. "The Temporalization of Financial Markets: From Network to Flow," *Theory, Culture, and Society*, Vol. 24, No. 7–8, 2007, 116–138.

Krippner, Greta R. *Capitalizing on Crisis: The Political Origins of the Rise of Finance*. Cambridge, MA: Harvard University Press, 2011.

Lamoreax, Naomi R., Daniel M. G. Raff, and Peter Temin. "Beyond Markets and Hierarchies: Toward a New Synthesis of American Business History," *American Historical Review*, Vol. 108, No. 2, 2003, 404–433.

MacKenzie, Donald A. "Mechanizing the Merc: The Chicago Mercantile Exchange and the Rise of High-Frequency Trading," *Technology and Culture*, Vol. 56, No. 3, 2015, 646–675.

Marazzi, Christian. *Capital and Affects: The Politics of the Language Economy*. Los Angeles: Semiotexte, 2011.

Marglin, Stephen A. *The Dismal Science: How Thinking Like an Economist Undermines Community*. Cambridge, MA: Harvard University Press, 2008.

Marx, Karl. *Capital*, Vol. I–III. New York: International Publishers, 1967.

Omarova, Saule T. "The Merchants of Wall Street: Banking, Commerce, and Commodities," *Minnesota Law Review*, Vol. 98, 2013, 265–355.

Padgett, John F. and Walter W. Powell. "The Problem of Emergence," in *The Emergence of Organizations and Markets*. Princeton, NJ: Princeton University Press, 2012, 1–29.

Pak, Susie J. *Gentleman Bankers: The World of J. P. Morgan*. Cambridge, MA: Harvard University Press, 2013.

Pocock, John G. A. *The Machiavellian Moment: Florentine Political Thought and the Atlantic Republican Tradition*. Princeton, NJ: Princeton University Press, 1975.

Poovey, Mary. *A History of the Modern Fact: Problems of Knowledge in the Sciences of Wealth and Society.* Chicago: University of Chicago Press, 1998.
_____. *Genres of the Credit Economy: Mediating Value in the Eighteenth-and Nineteenth-Century Britain.* Chicago: University Press, 2008.
Porter, Michael E. *Competitive Strategy: Techniques for Analyzing Industries and Competitors.* New York: The Free Press, 1980.
_____. *The Competitive Advantage of Nations.* New York: The Free Press, 1990.
Porter, Michael E., Jan W. Rivkin, and Mihir A. Desai with Manjari Raman. "Problems Unsolved and a Nation Divided: The State of U.S. Competitiveness 2016." Cambridge, MA: Harvard Business School.
Postone, Moishe. *Time, Labor, and Social Domination: A Reinterpretation of Marx's Critical Theory.* New York: Cambridge University Press, 1993.
Prechel, Harland. *Big Business and the State: Historical Transitions and Corporate Transformation, 1880s-1990s.* Albany, NY: State University of New York, 2000.
Rajan, Raghuram G. "The Corporation in Finance," *The Journal of Finance,* Vol. 67, No. 4, 2012, 1172–1217.
Ricks, Morgan. "The Case for Regulating the Shadow Banking System," in *Too Big to Fail? Resolving Large Troubled Financial Institutions in the Future.* Washington, DC: Brookings Institutions, 2012.
Roe, Mark J. "Legal Origins, Politics, and Modern Stock Markets," *Harvard Law Review,* Vol. 120, No. 2, 2006, 460–527.
Santner, Eric L. *The Weight of All Flesh: The Subject-Matter of Political Economy.* New York: Oxford University Press, 2016.
Schaffer, Simon. "Babbage's Intelligence: Calculating Engines and the Factory System," *Critical Inquiry,* Vol. 21, No. 1, 1994, 203–227.
Schumpeter, Joseph A. *The Theory of Economic Development: An Inquiry into Profits, Capital, Credit, interest, and the Business Cycle.* London: Transaction Books, [1934] 1983.
Searle, John R. *Making the Social World: The Structure of Human Civilization.* New York: Oxford University Press, 2010.
Sewell, William H. Jr. "Connecting Capitalism to the French Revolution: The Parisian Promenade and the Origins of Civic Equality in Eighteenth-Century France," *Critical Historical Studies,* Vol. I, No. 1, 2014, 5–46.
Shin, Hyun Song. *Risk and Liquidity.* New York: Oxford University Press, 2010.
Smith, Adam. *An Inquiry into the Nature and Causes of the Wealth of Nations.* New York: Modern Library Edition, 1994.
Soros, George. "Fallibility, Reflexivity, and the Human Uncertainty Principle," *Journal of Economic Methodology,* Vol. 20, No. 4, 2013, 309–329.
Stasavage, David. "Why Did Public Debt Originate in Europe?," in Andrew Monson and Walter Scheidel (eds.), *Fiscal Regimes and the Political Economy of Premodern States,* New York: Cambridge University Press, 2015, 523–533.
Terzi, Andrea. "International Financial Instability in a World of Currencies Hierarchy," in Louis-Philippe Rochon and Sergio Rossi (eds.), *Monetary and Exchange Rate Systems.* Cheltenham, UK: Edward Elgar, 2006, 3–21.
Underkuffler, Laura S. *The Idea of Property: Its Meaning and Power.* New York: Oxford University Press, 2003.
Urry, John. *Offshoring.* Cambridge, UK: Polity, 2014.
Wright, Robert E. *Corporation Nation.* Philadelphia: University of Pennsylvania Press, 2014.

8 Conclusion

I. Review of Money's Three Aspects: Symbol, Discipline, and Sovereignty

At the outset we identified three aspects of money. These aspects—symbol, discipline, and sovereignty—are interpreted in conventional financial theory as real, voluntary, and individual. That is, the operation of money in modern financial institutions is interpreted as the opposite by orthodox financial expertise, as real value, as free choice, and as individual private property. The concept of the whole is understood only as the "invisible hand" guiding individuals, a somewhat ephemeral force, the "specter of capital" (Rothschild 2001, 116–156; Santner 2016, 80, 100, 104; Vogl 2015, 24–27), maintained by the monopoly of the state on the issue of the currency. That is, the academic disciplines of economics and finance are part of the "misrecognition" of money (LiPuma and Lee 2012, 298).

Money is a symbol that serves as a communication vehicle in a self-referential meaning system and that also delineates its boundaries. A national currency is used by domestic citizens as well as international tourists and investors. That is, the boundary is at once fixed and permeable, like a network or club. Prices are produced and observed as indicators of the state of the system, which then inform further actions of the system. Because not everyone can participate in the coded exchange operations of money, and not every object is traded, there is a distinction between monetary and nonmonetary spheres. A set of meanings is understood by those who participate, which can establish separate spaces and times for monetary transactions, like shopping malls, stock markets, and casinos. Although justified as a convenience, trading money for money can become an end itself. The stock market is essential to the "market imaginary," with elements of both reality and fantasy (Staheli 2013, 23, 66–72, 82–93).

Money is an abstract "fiction" with real effects (Marx 1967; Polanyi 1944; Poovey 2002; Searle 2010). Money is only "real" when traded for other commodities, including material objects as well as financial assets. Because participants accept money as "real," it is accepted in exchange for products, making it real. In this sense, money has performative dimensions (Lee 2016). It is only an effective medium of payment because it is believed to be such, based on confidence. Consequently, money is subject to the "problematic of representation." Because money is widely accepted, it supports a broader culture of fictionality and performativity, including and beyond the sphere of circulation (LiPuma and Lee 2004). Value can be based on expectations, including the value of a financial asset in the future, as well as the status effect of consumer durables and the appropriate fashion, or "symbolic capital" (Wacquant 2013). The importance of appearances facilitates personal mobility, as well as questions of authenticity and loss of stable personal identity (Pocock 1975). Money serves as an incentive system, which is effective only to the extent that it is widely believed to represent "value."

The social whole is less visible than the divisions, with private freedom counterposed with public coercion, according to the neoliberal politics of property (Davis 2015). The public/private divide organizes the whole, the public, to support private production for the purposes of expansion of wealth as a principle of the system. As Smith enumerates, the labor force and the capital stock of the entire nation are the resources to produce its wealth (Smith 1994, Book II, Introduction and Ch. 1, 299–309). As Marx notes, the wealth of the entire nation backs the Bank of England to provide public credit (Marx 1967, Vol. III, Ch. 33, 524, 540). For Smith, the "stability of the Bank of England [was] equal to that of the British government … It [was] a great engine of state" (Smith 1994, Book II, Ch. 2, 348). That is, the entire set of public resources and productive capacity backs the credit of the nation for use in the provision of private credit for production and circulation (Davis 2010, 2013). In a sense the entire national productive capacity is double-counted, once as public credit and once as private credit, once as liability and once as asset, each backstopping and reinforcing the other (Davis 2015 129–133). Money is the "great wheel of circulation" for Smith (Smith 1994, Book II Ch 2, 314–317, 322), for the purposes of expanding that wealth, according to both Smith and Marx. The "formal rationality" of calculability and expansion does not guarantee the "substantive rationality" of provision of basic needs, however, according to Weber (Weber 1978, Vol. 1, Part 1, Ch. II, Section 9, 85–86; Section 11, 94; Section 13, 108).

Money is both abstract and concrete, expressing the general capacity to exchange products, as well as having a tangible, recognizable form, if only in computer code. The use of money enables purchasing of products and investment for the future, as well as measuring the contributions of one's own life. Money is also used as a measurement of labor productivity and the capacity of firms to maintain a positive balance on their balance sheets and income flows—Minsky's "survival constraint." Money is necessary for the liberal state to balance expenditures with tax revenues, a measure of the state capacity.

The term money has been observed across millennia, yet also relates to changing institutional forms. In turn, institutional forms are affected by the use of money. The type of knowledge in a given era is related to money (Kaye 1998; Postone 1993; Simmel 1978). The importance of calculation

(Weber 1978) and empirical "facts" described with numbers (Poovey 1998) help substantiate the concept of the economic system.

The study of financial institutions in a given period provides great insight into their structure.

II. Money as a Representation of Collective Governance

The basic premise of this book is that money is a symbol that represents a given collective, constituted by rules of governance and meaning systems. The currency of a nation-state or the stock of a business corporation both represent the relevant institution and provide a means for specific actions on its behalf. With the rise of trade, city-states developed techniques for perfecting coin made of precious metal to compensate mercenaries and long-distance merchants. As trade became more widely established, these coins and their symbolic representations were useful in organizing production, first in the putting-out system and subsequently in factories owned by merchants. The separation of households from the factory then made effective use of wage payments as a means of providing access to necessities, as well as a motivation for labor.

The now-permanent states and corporations were able to trade their respective corporate symbols on perpetual financial markets, made more liquid by the issue of their respective promises to pay. With the development of technology for large-scale production, the corporate form was repurposed to access finance and organize product distribution, as well as income distribution to factor inputs. That is, the corporate form was central to the coordination of flows of material, product, and income and assets. As it developed in the nineteenth-century United States as a protected private business corporation, the state recognized it as a separate entity, although complementary with the goal of economic growth and development.

With the expansion of global trade and finance, especially in the mid-twentieth century, the trading of financial assets like corporate stock and sovereign currencies became more rapid and more concentrated in global multinational financial corporations (Block 2014). These symbols of the collective became considered valuable in themselves. With changes in laws and regulations, these symbols were used to reorganize other corporations and national production systems, in turn fragmenting the previous collective forms. The increasingly frequent financial crises since the late twentieth century represent a questioning of the value of the symbol, long assumed to be a "safe asset" backed by the collective entity. The continual reorganization of production on a global scale by means of these assets in fact undermined their stability and security.

Transformations in the economy may affect worldviews, and vice versa (Biagioli 2006; Maifreda 2012). From a mercantile perspective, the entire world may be a potential commodity—the more exotic, the more valuable. From the perspective of the modern "portfolio society" (Davis 2009), the orientation is toward protected spaces, for luxury consumption, protection, and preservation of value as collateral.

Arguably money was historically always about the symbolic linkage of flows of objects and labor across spaces on behalf of corporate bodies whose organization was reshaped by those flows. This interaction is evident in the history of the forms of the state, the corporation, and money, as well as their mutual interconnections. Money became the measure of profit and the expansion of wealth, which was the fundamental purpose of the state. Money disciplines human behavior at all levels—the household, the firm, and the nation, as well as international commerce. As such it becomes valuable in itself, a measure of the ultimate value.

Representations of the whole remain ambiguous in the current period. On the one hand, money is the symbol of the whole, represented by the bankers, according to Marx. The ultimate goal is freedom in the private sphere for individuals and owners of individual private property. On the other hand, from the Civic Republican Tradition, the state is the whole, represented by the sovereign currency. This tradition makes an appeal to the inherently political nature of humans, drawing from Aristotle and Arendt.

There is some potential conflict between these two representations. On the one hand, there is a potential conflict over distribution of the surplus, between "capital" and the state. On the other hand, the production and expansion of surplus is a complementary effort between the state and capital. Growth rates and income distribution become the metrics for judging the performance of the whole (Milanovic 2016; Piketty 2014) in quantitative terms. The period of intensified class conflict in the later nineteenth century was resolved by Progressivism and the turn to impartial expertise. If the state during the 1930s New Deal era favored income distribution to labor and the lower classes, then the neoliberal period after the 1980s favored income distribution to the elite. Since the Full Employment Act of 1946, the metric of performance of the state is the number of "jobs." Still the Progressive era institution, the Federal Reserve represents the whole in the twenty-first century, even if its role is under new debate and challenge.

III.   Innovations in Institutions for Human Development

In spite of its centrality to the Western tradition and his own stress on "collective intentionality," Searle expresses skepticism regarding democracy. The most important decisions are better left to other methods than the popular vote, in his view (Searle 2010, 171–173). By contrast, the position here is that the meaning of "modernity" is the capacity for human societies to imagine and to organize their own institutions and to commit to their own constitutions. That is, instead of reliance on traditional authority or religion, the design of institutions is newly recognized as possible and desirable in the modern era. Yet the models for human communities are widely in flux. Drawing upon a tradition of "reciprocal awareness" (Wolff 1968) and reflexivity (Postone 1993; Soros 2008), the social can be conceived as community-based interpersonal "recognition" (Fraser 2013, 2016; Honneth 2008, 2012) within privileged and stable institutions, like the household, the workplace, schools, and voluntary associations. There is need for a "third term" mediating between the relevant interpersonal dyads, but this object of the relationship can be flexible and "transparent," like parenting and stewardship, rather than an objectified and mystified mediation like money (Simmel 1978). From Habermas and Searle, that transparent third term can be language and communication to facilitate recognition and human development. From ecology, the human community can be "grounded" in place, with a full awareness of its connection to and effect on the global ecosystem.

In Western tradition there is a long list of potential bases for social relationships from a wide range of thinkers, including work (Marx 1967), parenthood (Rich 1976; Chodorow 1978; Winnicott 1986), and sexuality (De Beauvoir 2010; Freud 1955; Foucault 1986), as well as language (Austin 1962; Searle 2010; Wittgenstein 2001), the market (Hayek 1941), patriarchy (Filmer 1991), property (Hegel 1991; Locke 1988; Smith 1994), the gift (Appadurai 1986; Mauss 1967), conspicuous consumption (Veblen 1934), land (Pocock 1975), and rationality (Habermas 1984; Israel 2011). Instead of money as the generalized medium of exchange, one could conceive of community as a generalized, mutual, deliberative, respectful relationship, which could potentially encompass any or all of the items just mentioned. An ecologically based regional community that cherishes the source of food and habitat for all living things is a potential model (Davis 2017b forthcoming). Like the shift from Ptolemy to Copernicus, a new paradigm of human awareness could emerge from the knowledge of humankind as the dominant species in a complex evolving ecology on earth, apparently the only living planet in the universe.

IV. Money as the Organizing Institution

A summary view of the sociology of Max Weber, celebrant of rational calculation, can help conceptualize the irrational basis of the financial system in capitalism. As a sociologist he emphasizes the human dimension, the relevant group involved, and the probability of a given rate of exchange. That is, money is a material object offered as a "medium of exchange," assuming that recipients can exchange it for goods or money at an acceptable rate "within the relevant time horizon" and "within the membership of a group of persons or within a territorial area" (Weber 1978, 75–76). Such an "indirect exchange" relationship by means of money "results in a tremendous extension of the area of possible exchange relationships ... With this goes the orientation of acquisitive activities to all the opportunities which are made available ... [and] the most important fact of all, the possibility of monetary *calculation*" (Weber 1978, 80–81; italics in original).

The habits of calculation seem to derive from money itself in Weber's treatment. In the analysis earlier, by contrast, the emergence of calculation was in pursuit of collective organizational goals, such as credit of a commune, or payment for war by a fiscal-military state. The emphasis here is the interrelationship of the organizational form and the use of money to support that organization. In turn, the emergence of money as a tool makes other types of relationships possible.

Weber does acknowledge the role of "power" in economic organization (Weber 1978, 67–68, 95, 97, 108, 137–138, 161–164). He also distinguished between formal and substantive rationality (Weber 1978, 85–86, 108–109), with the former concerned with calculation in general, versus the pursuit of particular social criteria such as equality or provision. Weber himself displays his exceptional skills at formal rationality with his comparison of slave labor to wage labor (Weber 1978, 162–163):

> When workers are employed for wages, the following advantages to industrial profitability and efficiency are conspicuous: (a) Capital risk and the necessary capital investment are smaller; (b) the costs of reproduction and of bringing up children fall entirely on the workers. His wife and children must seek employment on their own account; (c) largely for this reason, the risk of dismissal is an important incentive to the maximization of production; (d) it is possible to select the labor force according to ability and willingness to work. (Weber 1978, 163)

It appears as though money itself has succeeded in ordering and organizing modern life. Every person throughout every day encounters and makes use of money: for necessities, for future plans, for entertainment, to reveal status, to reward effort and innovation. Major sectors of the economy are coordinated by means of the cash nexus and "bottom line."

Money is a "steering mechanism," creating channels for credit and distribution (Palley 2013; Quint and Shubik 2014). In these circumstances, the financial sector itself may accumulate power and influence (Krippner 2011). The role of the financial sector as mediator for financial flows of the modern liberal state provides information and political perspective, as well as personal contacts and deliberative power regarding the appropriate social investments.

To the extent that money is a tool to maximize individual pleasure by rational calculation, the market system can be rendered absurd. This awkward combination of rationality and emotion is possible only in widely disparate contexts and settings, such as the institutional separation of work and consumption. To the extent that Weber understood the role of advertising in creating desires, the system was admittedly self-contained and self-referential, even circular.

> It goes without saying that in terms of *economic* theory the direction in which goods can be profitably produced by profit-making enterprises is determined by the marginal utilities for the last consumers in conjunction with the latter's incomes. But from a *sociological* point of view it should not be forgotten that, to a large extent, in a capitalistic

economy (a) new wants are created and others allowed to disappear and (b) capitalistic enterprises, through their aggressive advertising policies, exercise an important influence on the demand functions of consumers. Indeed, these are essential traits of a capitalist economy. It is true that this applies primarily to wants which are not of the highest degree of necessity, but even types of food provision and housing are importantly determined by the producers in a capitalistic economy. (Weber 1978, Vol. I, Ch. II, Section 11, 99–100; italics in original)

Important elements of the system are based on fantasy, including confidence in money as "real" (Davis 2015, 124–125). The system consists of investors borrowing money for the production of goods and services, which may appeal to the fashion sensibility of consumers, itself in rapid flux influenced by fads. Similarly, "investment" in financial assets depends on the ultimate ability to exchange for other financial assets in the future, the value of which is influenced by "expectations."

As a self-contained system, there is the possibility of the production of ignorance, or "agnatology," of anything that is outside the system. For example, the abstraction from natural resources by the concept of homogeneous "inputs" in the neoclassical economic production function has facilitated the application of assumptions and models with characteristics that are separate and unrelated to natural biogeochemical systems (Bonneuil and Fressoz 2015, 198–221; Locher and Fressoz 2012, 595) and is possibly misleading. Further, the history of alternative points of view is often forgotten.

V. Money and the Liberal State

By internalizing its own money and finance rather than relying on private bankers or tax farmers, the liberal state can establish new principles of operation. The state protects individual private property in return for the authority to tax it and the obligation to provide opportunities for public participation in governance. The shared resources then provide for defense of the state and its territory and public and private finance for its growth. Within the financial circuit, *de jure* equal individuals can produce and trade their own property on a voluntary basis while nonetheless subject to the discipline of productivity and competition. Money is reified as valuable in itself, which stabilizes the contingent financial circuits. Such a financial republic (or citizen/tax state) is a new paradigm, in contrast to the long history of empires (Darwin 2008), providing a conditional, if fragile, personal autonomy. The experience of personal freedom is circumscribed by the operation of an autonomous economy conceived as an automatic system, beyond the individual citizen's control, even if actually driven by each person's life choices. The republican form of government is historically vulnerable (Pocock 1975), even without the presumed separation of economy and state, along with its actual interpenetration (Habermas 1989; Vogl 2012).

The *de jure* rules of the financial system recognize equal rights for all property owners. The presence of *de facto* discrimination, by class, race, and ethnicity, along with pervasive inequality, undercuts the legitimacy of the system (Searle 2010, 165–166). The presumed equality of nations in an international marketplace is obviated by the role of the hegemon and the currency hierarchy, making access to credit dependent on the conditions of the leading state. The presence of populism as a dissenting social movement challenges the equality of the abstract individual and reasserts the superiority of racial, national, and ethnic groups. This rhetorical appeal to historic group allegiance and claims for the constitution of the real "people" sets a new collective unity in the face of disciplinary individualism and global capital flows.

VI.   Management of Time

Money is an instrument for managing time. "In essence, financial technology is a time machine we have built ourselves" (Goetzmann 2016, 2). Financial markets are social constructions, nonetheless, with money based on a series of interlocking "status function declarations," or statements and rules for what symbols can indicate what operations in what contexts (Searle 2010), like the rules of the game.

Capitalism is an institution of labor exchange (see Chapter 3), built upon the segmentation and exchange of units of time. That is, the worker is compensated per unit of time and uses that money to purchase and consume products, produced by the time of other workers. What appears to be an exchange of money is an exchange of time—work time for leisure time among the collective labor force. Similarly, savings is money offered this period for a greater return next period, traveling along a time dimension by the exchange of money. Further, "capital" is borrowed now for an increase in returns later—also a movement along the time dimension. Parents work now to provide for children, retirement, and the next generation. Knowledge and equipment appear as "dead labor," occurring in the past to facilitate labor in the present. Permanent corporations and the perpetual state are institutions that manage the movement along the time dimension by means of money. The exchange of money along the time dimension, nonetheless, would not be possible without the perpetual institutions that recognize that contract and the equivalence of payments through time. Divisions among institutions and their representations enable money and capital to appear to be the source of the movement and growth through time, rather than the society's own collective decisions, capacities, and human reproduction.

With population as a resource for the production of wealth, the development of "political arithmetic" enabled the state to calculate the optimum management of that resource by means of "biopolitics" (Foucault 1978, 126–127, 139–145). With the emergence of labor time at a factory as a resource, the norms of "calculation" became widespread, both for the public as a whole and for the occupation of management in particular

(Weber 1978, 85–100, 165–166). Calculating labor productivity became a standard practice—output per unit of labor time—along with "transactions costs" (Coase 1998) and "turnover time" (Marx 1967), with an ever-increasing scale of reference in space and time. The notion of "opportunity costs" encourages comparison of *any* choice in life with the next best foregone alternative, as part of the economics way of thinking introduced in economics courses in high school and college.

With the standardization of labor time, the treatment of the economy as a machine, and the reification of money, the awareness of the time dimension of the capitalist economy tends to disappear. Money becomes the vehicle for time and serves to standardize its passage. The technical problem of managing money and providing a stable standard for long-term contracts assumes the priority, rather than managing human provision and the development of human capacities. The habits and norms of calculation enable the rationalization of the production process and facilitate further abstraction.

VII.   The Development of Knowledge and Information

The role of knowledge and information has become increasingly important with the development of capitalism. The "eternal present" of living labor is the standard of value (Postone 1993, 295–296, 299–301, 303, 346–347), in spite of infinite financial markets that manage time. According to Postone's analysis of "historical time," the productivity of living labor is increasingly influenced by science and technology (Postone 1993, 296):

> The productivity of labor … is a function of scientific, technical, and organizational knowledge and experience … This process entails the development in alienated form of socially general forms of knowledge and experience which are not a function of, and cannot be reduced to, the skills and knowledge of the immediate producers. (Postone 1993, 296)

Postone's notion that our sense of time is affected by improvements in productivity at the workplace is reinforced by the phrase "living on Internet time," used by Andrew Grove, CEO of Intel (Gleick 2016, 303), who personally was an integral part of that phenomenon.

The extraction of knowledge from the craft worker has been a motivation in common for both military and commercial production for purposes of control and optimization. Major improvements in technology have been associated with the fiscal/military state in examples such as the employment of Galileo in the Venetian Arsenal (Biagioli 2006), interchangeable parts in the production of Civil War rifles (Smith 1977), and the development of computers during World War II (Edwards 1996; Marazzi 2011, 86–96). This separation of knowledge from the worker was aided by the development of information technology in the postwar period, culminating in the development of the Internet and artificial intelligence (AI). The widespread diffusion of personal computers, and later mobile phones, enabled the collection of comprehensive data for consumers, producers, and distributors. The meaning of these data and information would not be consistent without standards for socially necessary labor time and the ongoing discipline of competition among workers and firms. This comprehensive data collection, in turn, has facilitated the development of machine learning (Varian 2014). This capacity is useful in advertising, production, and finance. The comparison of expected rates of return for various financial assets in the present has provided opportunities for profit from arbitrage, as well as increasing the speed of turnover (Lee and LiPuma 2004, 37–38, 124, 127–129; Vogl 2015, 53–57, 122–127).

VIII.   Money and Information

The circulation of money provides information regarding prices and the state of the system by means of metrics such as growth rate and profitability. Money mediates between the individual and social by providing a tool for surveillance of the individual, by means of the abstract social medium of money to represent the whole. The social nature of the collective enterprise becomes hidden by the evident role of money treated as individual private property. That is, money appears to be one's own, enabling purchases of a unique basket of commodities according to one's own taste. The money is acquired through distinct channels, such as conditional bank loans or payment for labor under conditions specified by the employer. These channels for distribution of money are supervised and regulated by the state, at least to some degree.

Money and credit are based on "credibility" of the promise to repay. The probability of repayment is based on size, diversification, trust, creditworthiness, innovation, state of the business cycle, type of financial circuit, and income distribution. The corporation and the state are complementary in pooling risk, and also competitive in the distribution of surplus.

As a self-referential communication system, money is the unit of account for all relevant flows. These flows are recorded in consistent balance sheets at a point in time—for the income-pooling household, for the corporation, and for the nation-state. Composed of offsetting assets and liabilities, the balance sheets for the financial system as a whole cancel, leaving real relations with the nonfinancial world to comprise net worth (Shin 2010, 12). All growth is represented by the expansion of the size of the balance sheet through the monetary system (Hockett and Omarova 2016) through endogenous money creation. Yet the entire real world is capable of being represented, once it is considered a legal commodity and a claim can be established. Once incorporated into the financial circuits, the material inputs into the process of commodity production and realization tend to produce symbolic wealth, "only by sapping the original sources of all wealth—the soil and the labourer" (Marx 1967, Vol. I, Ch. 15, Section 10, 507).

The role of money and the quality of "safe assets" has been related to information. That is, the liquidity of a given asset is related to its ability to exchange at par with "no questions asked" and with no need to incur information costs (Gorton 2015, 5; 2016). This economy of information reduces transaction costs. For example, such relevant information regarding coin could be its purity and weight, as well as the validity of the stamp of the sovereign. The credibility of the bill of exchange is the reliability of its signatories. The liquidity of a mortgage-backed security (MBS) could be based on the value of the real estate collateral. In the latter case, the need for further information was reduced by the reputation of the rating agency. According to Gorton, public-sector assets are generally more credible than private sector, which are always subject to question. The financial crisis of 2008 was related to a sudden switch in the view of these privately produced MBS assets as being unreliable based on new information.

Market signals can also be misleading. For example, the accumulation of large cash pools among institutional investors in the early 2000s led to an increase in the demand for safe assets. The private production of those assets increased the vulnerability to questioning, which led to runs on the shadow banking system. That is, the quality and accuracy of the price signals can be influenced by the overall state of the system, and in turn destabilize that system.

IX. Objectification as a Social Contract

Searle suggests that the use of money is a form of social contract, like all forms of promising (Searle 2010). That is, each person agrees to abide by certain rules regarding types of property in return for the social operation of the totality. The consumer benefits by increased purchasing power, the worker by more employment options and workplace instruments, the investor by greater range of financial assets from which to choose. The efficiency of the whole makes everyone better off, according to mainstream economic theory.

But is the type of self-objectification with regard to money one that undermines individual expression and autonomy? For example, does the promise of obedience at the workplace undermine agency and self-respect and contribute to alienation?

According to Foucault, the "truthful confession" has been "inscribed at the heart of the procedures of individualization by power" since the Middle Ages (Foucault 1978, 58–59). The process of self-objectification occurs in the process of converting labor to labor power, according to Marx's theory of the fetish (Lee 2016, 129–130). There is an associated "objectification of subjectivity," whereby one observes oneself, speaks through novels and diaries of one's own efforts at betterment, and tries to shape one's own attractiveness to potential employers. There is a similar notion, like Smith's "impartial spectator" or investing in one's own "human capital" (Cooper 2014, 40–43; Kuiper 2003; Lee 2016, 131–139;). The importance of "identity" may increase in this context, even abstract expressions of belonging such as similar consumer styles. According to Wu, all desire above basic necessities is "mimetic," intensifying the phenomena of fashion fads (Wu 2016, 315).

It is possible that the operation of the market system itself may have an effect on personal and cultural values (Bowles 2016; Sandel 2012). That is, the offer of and orientation to financial incentives may undercut the salience of moral incentives.

X.   Dynamic of Abstraction

As discussed in Chapter 7, the corporation is a tool of abstraction. Using the techniques of scientific management and automation, the formation of "homogeneous labor" is an active and ongoing process.

Increasing capacity to represent production with information technology enables further automation and control (Brynjolfsson and McAfee 2014; Vogl 2015, 74–77). The circulation of finance on a global scale "takes on the function of an information-producing apparatus" (Vogl 2015, 77). Operating according to the efficient market hypothesis,

> [t]o the extent that prices on financial markets simultaneously compile information about the future of prices, information about money has become more important in transactions than money itself. The market installs an information-automatism. (Vogl 2015, 77)

Machine learning promises to achieve breakthroughs, making use of the voluminous "Big Data" produced by online commerce, mobile communication, and social media. Advances in genetic engineering (Venter 2013) and software code (Lessig 2006) are new forms of representation, enabling new methods of production. The replacement of labor has reached the stage that the issue of new forms of remuneration are contemplated, rather than individual factor returns based on contribution in production, as well as shrinking value of the contribution of direct living labor (Postone 1993).

Given the commodity labor power, the institutions related to the public/private divide, and the self-ownership of labor (Davis 2017a), there is a built-in coercion that strongly shapes modern life forms. Existing institutions accomplish individualization as part of liberal governmentality. In this context abstraction is powerful, enabling existing institutions to have broader reach and information processing capacity to monitor labor and market to consumers (Head 2003, 2014).

In the "age of the smart machine" (Brynjolfsson and McAfee 2014; Zuboff 1984), innovation produces more abstraction, more surveillance, more marketing, faster consumer fads, as well as less collective agency. The information produced regarding prices, quantities, productivity, and revealed preferences related to personal characteristics can be processed in the abstract, increasingly by automated processes internal to computer information systems (Arthur 2011).

XI.   Agency and Collective Intentionality

The tools of automation and AI have been designed by military and commercial innovation in order to substitute for labor and abstract knowledge into the machine, now increasingly digital. On the other hand, the widespread dissemination of personal computers and participation in social media may have enabled a new type of public sphere in the information age. These two different trajectories have distinct characteristics and may shape the further "path-dependent" evolution of these technologies in two very different directions: one toward more control in the workplace and the other toward greater freedom of expression and sharing in civil society.

Rather than consider information in the abstract, apart from meaning (Gleick 2011, 217–231, 246–248, 416–418), like a new type of "modern fact" (Poovey 1998), the approach here is to link digital information to human users, institutions, and paradigms. The current period is the context for widespread experimentations in new forms of linking information technology with social institutions. We may consider these variations according to two dimensions: first, the relative segmentation or integration of knowledge, and second, the degree of subjectivity or objectification, as illustrated in Table 8.1. That is, to what degree can information technology provide more agency and greater capacity to represent the social world than money?

Habermas' original notion of the "public sphere" (Habermas 1989) was based on rational property-owning bourgeoisie, capable of critical reflection on the performance of the state via access to publicity. He also recognized the "transformation" of the public sphere based on commercial motives and the erosion of the separation of the public and private divide. With consumers increasingly concerned with self-presentation and one's "image" before the public, there emerges a "self-surveillance" (Turkle 2011, 261–264) on the Internet, where one's identity is based on the number of "likes" on Facebook or the number of followers on Twitter. Computers are used less for calculation and more for simulation (Turkle 1995, 18–20), to promote addictive (Turkle 2011, 226–227), immersive experiences in cyberspace and "virtual reality." Although communication on the Internet is less restrictive in participation and in forms of expression (Warner 1992), it has facilitated individual participation in the culture of celebrity (Wu 2016, 306–317).

Table 8.1 Social Implications of Information Technology

Degree of Knowledge Integration	Degree of Agency/Objectification	
	Agency	*Objectification*
Divided by sphere	Makers; Linux; Creative Commons	AI and robots at work; Internet of things at home
Integrated across spheres	Interactive democracy; public education; news; public R&D	Government surveillance, propaganda, and censorship

Once a commons that fostered the amateur eccentric in every area of interest, the web, by 2015, was thoroughly overrun by commercial junk, much of it directed at the very basest human impulses of voyeurism and titillation. (Wu 2016, 322)

The turning point seems rather stark. On the one hand, according to Foucault, "man" disappears (into workplace automaton and AI) or, on the other, may become newly embedded in purposeful ecological communities (Davis forthcoming 2017b). It is possible to develop a new model of democracy that is no longer based on a male household head with dependent household, *oikos*, with hierarchy based on gender and property-owning status (Cooper 2014, 45–52). A new model of collective intentionality can develop new institutions based on a new language and new forms of knowledge, with capacity of the global reach of new communication technologies, or "infotopia" (Fung 2013).

XII.   The New Public Sphere: Internet and Information Technology

One question is whether the Internet and information technology can provide a new form of the public sphere, a new center for public life. Information technology is the outcome of the dynamic of abstraction and automation in the context of World War II and the Cold War (Edwards 1996). Yet knowledge is a pubic good (Block 2011; Hess and Ostrom 2007; Stiglitz and Greenwald 2014). Information technology has been widely adopted in both the public and the private sphere. Will the public have access to ever greater publicity, increasing the responsiveness of the state? Further, the ever-decreasing cost of information technology services may provide for new forms of vigorous market competition. On the other hand, the economies of scale and network externalities in commercial provision of information technology services tend to lead toward oligopoly (Varian 2001), such as in cloud computing services.

At present there is evidence of both orientations, toward greater agency, on the one hand, and toward greater surveillance on the other. The sharing economy has institutional developments such as open source and the Creative Commons (Benkler 2006, 2011; Lerner and Schankerman 2010; Lessig 2008; Weber 2004, 2005). The importance of software code and the privileged position of computer programmers may enable the development of new norms for sharing among the software community.

The Internet could be a platform for deliberative democracy and public education (Fung 2013). Accumulation of Big Data can provide superior social planning (Varian 2010), far beyond the Lange/Hayek socialist planning debate. The Internet can organize production as well as circulation, with examples such as Linux and 3D manufacturing. The Internet could help articulate and disseminate collective intentionality beyond the abstract individual relating to other such individuals through the mediation of money and branded consumer products.

The Internet had seemed to provide a free cyberspace, independent of territorial governments, a libertarian dream. National governments have reasserted control, nonetheless, including censorship in China (Goldsmith and Wu 2006). Within the context of the reigning episteme, the Internet has been used to automate and replace labor and to control the individual (Zuboff 2015), rather than to empower the community with information, deliberation, and real-time consultation. The Internet is used as a vehicle for personalized commercial advertising rather than information for personal development and global sustainability. In information technology industries, with marginal production costs near zero, the product is marketed based on the consumer's willingness to pay (Brynjolfsson and MacAfee 2014; Shapiro and Varian 1999). Without free entry, such IT firms are capable of extracting consumer surplus with perfect price discrimination (Varian 2010, 6), instead of "free" for the benefit of the community.

Platform competition may enable a new form of the firm with economies of scale, network externalities, and zero marginal costs (Shapiro and Varian 1999). It is possible to consider price structure as well as price level and different types of market structure, such as profit-maximizing monopoly, Ramsey planner, as well as not-for-profit firm (Rochet and Tirole 2003). Although these models of platform competition typically study exchanges, it is possible to organize production by means of the Internet, given the example of open-source software.

The structure of employment is in flux (Davis 2016), with decreasing job security and benefits. There is a new "gig" economy, including shorter engagements and more specific "tasks" instead of jobs, such as Mechanical Turk at Amazon or "Task Rabbit" (Kuttner 2013). There is a new class of contingent workers, called the "precariat" (Katz and Krueger 2016; Standing 2011), vulnerable to imposition of costs of providing equipment and insurance, as well as training.

The existing institutions for public participation—the U.S. Congress as well as state and local governments—have been the target of concerted efforts to empower large donors with "special interests" and particular political orientations (Mayer 2016). The "disruption" of the newspaper business, with advertising revenue migrating to the Internet, may serve to undermine the institution of the free, independent press (Greenstein 2015, 378–391).

The alternatives, which are polar opposites from those identified in Table 8.1, have also been discussed by Castells, where he articulates the options of "communication democracy versus political control" (Castells 2006, 20–21). Without a reinvigorated public sphere and new forms of community (Weber 2016, 20–21), there is not much of a vehicle for countervailing power and reassertion of collective control.

XIII.   Experimentation: New Forms of Money

To the extent that money is a form of communication and provides information, it is possible that the information/communication technology (ICT) industry can replace money. One way to briefly consider this topic is to examine the extent to which the functions of ICT and money are similar and complementary. Another approach is to consider whether they are more likely substitutes.

The financial system is like a computer "platform" to organize payments, consisting of the providers of money, the central bank, and the Treasury along with commercial banks, on the one hand, and the users of money, firms, and consumers, on the other. But every role has two sides: the providers of money are also the collectors of money via the tax system. The users of money, the firms and consumers, are also the source of money. In this sense, the financial system is like a two-sided platform, like malls or credit card companies, or retail computer platforms like Amazon (Evans, Hagiu, and Schmalensee 2006). Money facilitates the aggregation of actors on both sides. In that sense, the function could be performed by electronic money, such as Bitcoin.

On the other hand, the associated institutions, such as property definition and enforcement, judicial resolution of conflicts, and allocation and utilization of credit, are actions far beyond the platform function. In this sense, the financial system is like a set of status function declarations that are reflected in documents and could be recorded in code. But the relevant actions are human, requiring "nonlinguistic" actions by the parties, as Searle discusses (Searle 2010, 109–115). That is, Bitcoin and its electronic verification functions can provide the same role as documentation, but the human actions—borrowing money, producing products with greater value, realizing the value of those commodities in sales to households—are greater than the electronic platform of verification of the transaction (Weber 2016). Similarly, the store of value function must be recognized by other perpetual institutional players for it to be meaningful over time. That is, Bitcoin must be expected to have perpetual life, like a government bond, for it to be successful as a "safe asset."

Bitcoin and blockchain and other advances can lower the cost and speed up the verification of trading of financial assets and the processing of payments. The payments themselves need to be incurred by human actors. In this sense, electronic money is a complement to financial institutions, not a substitute. Governments may even make use of electronic currency to facilitate negative interest rates and to reduce tax evasion and money laundering (Rogoff 2016). In fact, other crypto-currencies and related financial institutions have arisen, already challenging the monopoly of Bitcoin as the leading virtual currency (Bohme, Christin, Edelman, and Moore 2015).

Likewise, the euro was a new currency created by the European Union that facilitated trade across the borders of the member countries. The associated institutions, such as common fiscal policy, were assumed to follow.

The financial crisis of 2008 created stresses on the still-separate countries before such a unified fiscal policy was established. The alternative of austerity imposed on debtor countries may have worsened the financial crisis (Stiglitz 2016).

XIV.   Possibility of Noneconomic Cooperation

Societies have existed throughout the millennia with other leading institutions besides money and property. It is possible that the last four or five centuries of the market dominance have been exceptional within that long time frame.

Anthropological studies of the "gift" (Appadurai 2016) or traditional societies (Calhoun 2013), or observers of the commons and other forms of human cooperation (Benkler 2011; Bowles 2016; Ostrom 1990) are reminders that financial incentives are not the only, or always the dominant, human motives.

Similarly, new views of science can overcome the positive/normative split, with holistic methods and embodying ethical values (Tresch 2012). Global agreements such as the Kyoto Protocol and the Paris Accord of 2016 occur, reflecting a new vision of the role of human institutions in an ecological context. A long-term historical perspective can restore the awareness that the dominance of financial institutions in the capitalist system is historically unique (Weber 2016, 32, 36–37).

XV.   Return of Fundamentalism/Populism

Periods of slow growth, such as the 1930s, the 1970s, and 2000s, can lead to social and political unrest. Even before the election of 2016, there was evidence of growing fundamentalist and populist movements in the United States, Europe, and the Middle East. The turmoil in the Middle East from the 1950s to the 1970s, for example, revealed both left and right, religious-based opposition to the dominant U.S./Western European model.

In the twenty-first century, there has been a greater resurgence of right-wing populism in the United States and Europe. According to Judis (2016), there have been populist candidates in the nineteenth and twentieth centuries in the United States, but the election of Donald J. Trump represents the first populist electoral victory. Ironically Trump also represents the apotheosis of the "rich man," where the possession of money itself is a status symbol, the victor of the "winner take all" contests like the U.S. electoral system (Dahl 2001) and CEO pay (Frank and Cook 1995), as well as the ubiquitous casino.

One possibility is that this turn to populism represents a form of "Polanyian double movement" (Block and Somers 2014). In the analysis here, rather than the market and a social backlash, the political reaction may be understood as a resistance to the ubiquitous individualizing discipline of financial circuits. That is, rather than conceive of the existence of a protected social sphere, which is an alternative to the market, the extent of the political reaction in the early twenty-first century is due to the pervasive and systemic influence of financial flows throughout various spheres and life forms.

The global liberal order is based on the competing individual. The group identity with respect to money is fluid and ambiguous in terms of nationality and class. The abstract "liberal individual" can make use of money in a neutral, anonymous fashion based on rational calculus, but the variability of financial flows can undercut stable social relations. The discourse is dominated by the elite experts, as well as the guidance of impersonal financial circuits. The "systematic fallout" (Searle 2010, 22, 116–119, 120–121) of the malfunction of markets falls unevenly, such as the Great Depression and the Great Recession. The tendency was to "save the currency" (Polanyi 1944) in the financial crisis of the 1930s, which was viewed as the essential, objective, and most efficient method of governance. The response in 2008 was similarly to save the banks, perceived as the heart of the economic system.

With the return of populism, the birthplace regains importance, with the so-called "nativism" and nostalgia for the nation's purity prior to the influx of marginal populations, including refugees, immigrants, and the other newly illegitimate beneficiaries of the welfare state (Marazzi 2011, 141–144). With the incarceration of the majority of young minority males in U.S. cities, the "iron fist of the penal state" has reinforced the invisible hand of the neoliberal market (Alexander 2010; Wacquant 2012).

The global financial system has lost legitimacy in the early twenty-first century, but its repair or replacement has not yet emerged. Asserting and reinforcing traditional hierarchies like nation, gender, and class and demonizing and objectifying the "other" appear to be winning strategies in the United States and Europe in the aftermath of the financial crisis of 2008.

XVI. Return to Ecological Time

From Benjamin Franklin's aphorism, "time is money" (quoted in Lee 2016, 84) to the metaphor that money "grows," money absorbs the characteristics of the human life cycle and the natural environment. Or, more accurately, as the medium for acquiring the necessities of life and social status, humans project onto money what are social and natural features. While money increases over time with the financial circuit, $M - M'$, resources for the development of human capacities are reduced and natural environments are disturbed. Money seems to master time and become the instrument of its management, but only by the social construction of perpetual financial markets, which ultimately rely on human institutions and knowledge paradigms.

This infinite, abstract, fictitious financial treadmill of the fiscal/military/industrial/financialized state has replaced ecological time and appears to overcome the limits of human mortality, while it actually disciplines every moment of every day throughout the globe.

Other worlds and worldviews are possible.

Bibliography

Alexander, Michelle. *The New Jim Crow: Mass Incarceration in the Age of Colorblindness.* New York: The Free Press, 2010.

Anderson, Chris. *Makers: The New Industrial Revolution.* New York: Crown Business, 2012.

Appadurai, Arjun (ed.). T*he Social Life of Things: Commodities in Cultural Perspective.* New York: Cambridge University Press, 1986.

_____. *Banking on Words: The Failure of Language in the Age of Derivative Finance.* Chicago: University of Chicago Press, 2016.

Arthur, W. Brian. "The Second Economy." *McKinsey Quarterly*, October 2011.

Auletta, Ken. *Googled: The End of the World as We Know It.* New York: Penguin Press, 2009.

Austin, J.L. *How to Do Things with Words.* Oxford: Clarendon Press, 1962.

Battelle, John. *The Search: How Google and Its Rivals Rewrote the Rules of Business and Transformed Our Culture.* New York: Portfolio, 2005.

Benkler, Yochai. *The Wealth of Networks: How Social Production Transforms Markets and Freedom.* New Haven, CT: Yale University Press, 2006.

_____ "Designing Cooperative Systems for Knowledge Production: An Initial Synthesis from Experimental Economics," in Mario Biagioli, Peter Jaszi, and Martha Woodmansee (eds.), *Making and Unmaking Intellectual Property: Creative Production in Legal and Cultural Perspective.* Chicago: University of Chicago Press, 2011, 149–163.

Biagioli, Mario. *Galileo's Instruments of Credit: Telescopes, Images, Secrecy.* Chicago: University of Chicago Press, 2006.

Biagioli, Mario and Peter Galison (eds.). *Scientific Authorship: Credit and Intellectual Property in Science.* New York: Routledge, 2003.

Block, Fred L. *State of Innovation: The US Government Role in Technological Development.* Boulder, CO: Paradigm Publishers, 2011.

_____. "Democratizing Finance," *Politics and Society*, Vol. 42, No. 1, 2014, 3–28.

Block, Fred L. and Margaret R. Somers. *The Power of Market Fundamentalism.* Cambridge, MA: Harvard University Press, 2014.

Bohm, Rainer, Nicolas Christin, Benjamin Edelman, and Tyler Moore, "Bitcoin: Economics, Technology and Governance," *Journal of Economic Perspectives*, Vol. 29, No. 2, 2015, 213–238.

Bonneuil, Christophe and Jean-Baptiste Fressoz. *The Shock of the Anthropocene: The Earth, History and Us.* New York: Verso, 2015.

Bowles, Samuel. *The Moral Economy: Why Good Incentives Are No Substitute for Good Citizens.* New Haven, CT: Yale University Press, 2016.

Bresnahan, Timothy F, Shane Greenstein, and Rebecca M. Henderson. "Schumpeterian Competition and Diseconomies of Scope: Illustrations from the Histories of Microsoft and IBM," in Joshua Lerner and Scott Stern (eds.), *The Rate and Direction of Inventive Activity Revisited.* Chicago: University of Chicago Press, 2012, 203–276.

Brynjolfsson, Erik and Andrew McAfee. *The Second Machine Age: Work, Progress and Prosperity in the Age of Brilliant Machines.* New York: W.W. Norton, 2014.

Calhoun, Craig (ed.). *Habermas and the Public Sphere.* Cambridge, MA: MIT Press, 1992.

_____. "For the Social History of the Present: Pierre Bourdieu as Historical Sociologist," in Philip S. Gorski (ed.), *Bourdieu and Historical Analysis: Politics, History and Culture.* Durham, NC: Duke University Press, 2013, 36–67.

Castells, Manuel, "The Network Society: From Knowledge to Policy," in Manuel Castells and Gustavo Cardoso (eds.), *The Network Society: From Knowledge to Policy.* Washington, DC: Johns Hopkins University Press, 2006, 3–21.

_____. *Networks of Outrage and Hope: Social Movements in the Internet Age.* Cambridge, UK: Polity Press, 2012.

Chodorow, Nancy. *Reproduction of Mothering: Psychoanalysis and the Sociology of Gender.* Berkeley: University of California Press, 1978.

Coase, Ronald. "The New Institutional Economics," *American Economic Review,* Vol. 88, No. 2, 1998, 72–74.

Cooper, Melinda. "The Law of the Household: Foucault, Neoliberalism, and the Iranian Revolution," in Vanessa Lemm and Miguel Vatter (eds.), *The Government of Life: Foucault, Biopolitics, and Neoliberalism.* New York: Fordham University Press, 2014, 29–58.

Dahl, Robert A. *How Democratic Is the American Constitution?* New Haven, CT: Yale University Press, 2001.

Darwin, John. *After Tamerlane: The Rise and Fall of Global Empires, 1400–2000.* New York: Penguin Books, 2008.

Davis, Ann E. "Marx and the Mixed Economy: Money, Accumulation, and the Role of the State," *Science & Society,* Vol. 74, No. 3, July 2010, 409–428.

_____. "The New 'Voodoo Economics': Fetishism and the Public/Private Divide." *Review of Radical Political Economics,* Vol. 45, No. 1, March 2013, 42–58.

_____. *The Evolution of the Property Relation: Paradigm, Debates, Prospects.* New York: Palgrave MacMillan, 2015.

_____. "Paradoxical Positions: The Methodological Contributions of Feminist Scholarship," *Cambridge Journal of Economics,* 2017a, Vol. 41, No. 1, 181–201.

_____. "Ecological Community: A Practical Utopia," in Richard Westra, Robert Albritton, and Seongjin Jeong (eds.). *Varieties of Alternative Economic Systems: Practical Utopias for an Age of Global Crisis and Austerity.* New York: Routledge, forthcoming 2017b.

Davis, Gerald F. *Management by the Markets: How Finance Reshaped America.* New York: Oxford University Press, 2009.

_____. *The Vanishing American Corporation: Navigating the Hazards of the New Economy.* Oakland, CA: Berrett-Koehler Publishers, 2016.

De Beauvoir, Simone. *The Second Sex.* New York: Alfred A. Knopf, 2010.

Derman, Emanuel. *My Life as a Quant: Reflections on Physics and Finance.* New York: John Wiley & Sons, Inc. 2004.

_____. "Remarks on Financial Models," in Benjamin Lee and Randy Martin (eds.), *Derivatives and the Wealth of Societies.* Chicago: University of Chicago Press, 2016, 199–239.

Domingos, Pedro. *The Master Algorithm: How the Quest for the Ultimate Learning Machine Will Remake Our World.* New York: Basic Books, 2015.

Edwards, Paul N. *The Closed World: Computers and the Politics of Discourse in Cold War America.* Cambridge, MA: MIT Press, 1996.

Evans, David S., Andrei Hagiu, and Richard Schmalensee. *Invisible Engines: How Software Platforms Drive Innovation and Transform Industries.* Cambridge, MA: MIT Press, 2006.

Filmer, Robert. *Patriarcha and Other Writings.* New York: Cambridge University Press, 1991.

Foucault, Michel. *The History of Sexuality: Volume I. An Introduction.* New York: Pantheon Books, 1978.

Foucault, Michel. *The History of Sexuality.* New York: Pantheon, 1986.

Frank, Robert H. and Philip J. Cook. *The Winner-Take-All Society: How More and More Americans Compete for Ever Fewer and Bigger Prizes, Encouraging Economic Waste, Income Inequality, and an Impoverished Cultural Life.* New York: The Free Press, 1995.

Fraser, Nancy. *Fortunes of Feminism: From State-Managed Capitalism to Neoliberal Crisis.* London: Verso, 2013.

_____. "Contradictions of Capital and Care," *New Left Review*, Vol. 100, 2016, 99–117.

Freud, Sigmund. *The Interpretation of Dreams*. New York: Basic, 1955.

Fung, Archon. "Infotopia: Unleashing the Democratic Power of Transparency," *Politics & Society*, Vol. 41, No. 2, 2013, 183–212.

Garnham, Nicholas, "The Media and the Public Sphere," in Craig Calhoun (ed.). *Habermas and the Public Sphere*. Cambridge, MA: MIT Press, 1992, 359–376.

Gleick, James. *The Information. A History, A Theory, A Flood*. New York: Pantheon, 2011.

_____. *Time Travel: A History*. New York: Pantheon, 2016.

Goetzmann, William N. *Money Changes Everything: How Finance Made Civilization Possible*. Princeton, NJ: Princeton University Press, 2016.

Goldsmith, Jack and Tim Wu. *Who Controls the Internet? Illusions of a Borderless World*. New York: Oxford University Press, 2006.

Gorton, Gary B. *The Maze of Banking: History, Theory, Crisis*. New York: Oxford University Press, 2015.

_____. "The History and Economics of Safe Assets," *NBER Working Paper #22210*, 2016.

Greenstein, Shane. *How the Internet Became Commercial: Innovation, Privatization, and the Birth of a New Network*. Princeton, NJ: Princeton University Press, 2015.

Habermas, Jurgen. *The Theory of Communicative Action*. Boston: Beacon Press, 1984.

_____. *The Structural Transformation of the Public Sphere: An Inquiry into a Category of Bourgeois Society*. Cambridge, MA: MIT Press, 1989.

Hayek, Friedrich A. Von. *The Pure Theory of Capital*. London: MacMillan, 1941.

Head, Simon. *The New Ruthless Economy: Work and Power in the Digital Age*. New York: Oxford, 2003.

_____. *Mindless: Why Smarter Machines Are Making Dumber Humans*. New York: Basic Books, 2014.

Hess, Charlotte and Elinor Ostrom (eds.). *Understanding Knowledge as a Commons: From Theory to Practice*. Cambridge, MA: MIT Press, 2007.

Hegel, Georg Wilhelm Friedrich. *Elements of the Philosophy of Right*. New York: Cambridge University Press, 1991.

Hirschkop, Ken, "Justice and Drama: On Bakhtin as a Complement to Habermas," in Nick Crossley and John Michael Roberts (eds.), *After Habermas: New Perspectives on the Public Sphere*. Oxford, UK: Blackwell, 2004, 49–66.

Hockett, Robert C. and Saule T. Omarova. "The Finance Franchise," Ithaca, NY: Cornell Law School Research Paper No. 16-29, 2016.

Honneth, Axel. *Reification: A New Look at an Old Idea*. New York: Oxford University Press, 2008.

_____. *The I in We: Studies in the Theory of Recognition*. Cambridge, UK: Polity Press, 2012.

Israel, Jonathan I. *Democratic Enlightenment: Philosophy, Revolution, and Human Rights, 1750–1790*. New York: Oxford University Press, 2011.

Judis, John B. *The Populist Explosion: How the Great Recession Transformed American and European Policies*. New York: Columbia Global Reports, 2016.

Katz, Lawrence F. and Alan B. Krueger. "The Rise and Nature of Alternative Work Arrangements in the United States, 1995–2015," Cambridge, MA: *NBER Working Paper 22667*, September 2016.

Kaye, Joel. *Economy and Nature in the Fourteenth Century: Money, Market Exchange, and the Emergence of Scientific Thought*. New York: Cambridge University Press, 1998.

_____. *A History of Balance, 1250–1375: The Emergence of a New Model of Equilibrium and its Impact on Thought*. New York: Cambridge University Press, 2014.

Krippner, Greta R. *Capitalizing on Crisis: The Political Origins of the Rise of Finance.* Cambridge, MA: Harvard University Press, 2011.

Kuiper, Edith. "The Construction of Masculine Identity in Adam Smith's *Theory of Moral Sentiments*," in Drucilla K. Barker and Edith Kuiper (eds.), *Toward a Feminist Philosophy of Economics.* New York: Routledge, 2003, 145–160.

Kuttner, Robert. "The Task Rabbit Economy," *American Prospect*, Vol. 24, No. 5, September/October, 46–55.

Lee, Benjamin. "From Primitives to Derivatives," in Benjamin Lee and Randy Martin (eds.), *Derivatives and the Wealth of Societies.* Chicago: University of Chicago Press, 2016, 82–142.

Lerner, Joshua and Mark Schankerman. *The Comingled Code: Open Source and Economic Development.* Cambridge, MA: MIT Press, 2010.

Lerner, Joshua and Scott Stern (eds.). *The Rate and Direction of Inventive Activity Revisited.* Chicago: University of Chicago Press, 2012.

Lerner, Joshua and Peter Tufano. "The Consequences of Financial Innovation: A Counterfactual Research Agenda," in Joshua Lerner and Scott Stern (eds.), *The Rate and Direction of Inventive Activity Revisited.* Chicago: University of Chicago Press, 2012, 523–575.

Lessig, Lawrence. *Code.* New York: Basic Books, 2006.

_____. *Remix: Making Art and Commerce Thrive in the Hybrid Economy.* New York: Penguin, 2008.

LiPuma, Edward and Benjamin Lee. *Financial Derivatives and the Globalization of Risk.* Durham, NC: Duke University Press, 2004.

_____. "A Social Approach to the Financial Derivatives Markets," *South Atlantic Quarterly*, Vol. 111, No. 2, 2012, 289–316.

Locher, Fabien and Jean-Baptiste Fressoz. "Modernity's Frail Climate: A Climate History of Environmental Reflexivity." *Critical Inquiry*, Vol. 38, No. 3 (Spring 2012) 579–598.

Locke, John. *Two Treatises of Government.* New York: Cambridge University Press, 1988.

Maifreda, Germano. *From Oikonomia to Political Economy: Constructing Economic Knowledge from the Renaissance to the Scientific Revolution.* Burlington, VT: Ashgate, 2012.

Marazzi, Christian. *Capital and Affects: The Politics of the Language Economy.* Los Angeles: Semiotexte, 2011.

Marx, Karl. *Capital.* Vol. I–III. New York: International Publishers, 1967.

Mauss, Marcel. *The Gift: Forms and Functions of Exchange in Archaic Society.* New York: Norton, 1967.

Mayer, Jane. *Dark Money: The Hidden History of the Billionaires Behind the Rise of the Radical Right.* New York: Doubleday, 2016.

Milanovic, Branko. *Global Inequality: A New Approach for the Age of Globalization.* Cambridge, MA: Harvard University Press, 2016.

O'Mahoney, Siobhan. "Developing Community Software in a Commodity World," in Melissa S. Fisher and Greg Downey (eds.), *Frontiers of Capital: Ethnographic Reflections on the New Economy.* Durham, NC: Duke University Press, 2006, 237–266.

Ostrom, Elinor. *Governing the Commons: The Evolution of Institutions for Collective Action.* New York: Cambridge University Press, 1990.

Palley, Thomas I. *Financialization: The Economics of Finance Capital Domination.* New York: Palgrave MacMillan, 2013.

Piketty, Thomas. *Capital in the Twenty-First Century.* Cambridge, MA: Harvard University Press, 2014.

Pocock, J.G.A. *The Machiavellian Moment: Florentine Political Thought and the Atlantic Republican Tradition.* Princeton, NJ: Princeton University Press, 1975.

Polanyi, Karl. *The Great Transformation.* Boston: Beacon Press, 1944.

Poovey, Mary. *A History of the Modern Fact: Problems of Knowledge in the Sciences of Wealth and Society*. Chicago: University of Chicago Press, 1998.

_____. "The Liberal Civil Subject and the Social in Eighteenth-Century British Moral Philosophy," *Public Culture*. Vol. 14, No. 1, 2002, 125–145.

_____. *Genres of the Credit Economy: Mediating Value in Eighteenth-and Nineteenth-Century Britain*. Chicago: University of Chicago Press, 2008.

Postone, Moishe. *Time, Labor, and Social Domination: A Reinterpretation of Marx's Critical Theory*. New York: Cambridge University Press, 1993.

_____. "Thinking the Global Crisis," *South Atlantic Quarterly*, Vol. 111, No. 2, 2012, 227–249.

Prechel, Harland. *Big Business and the State*. Albany, NY: SUNY Press, 2000.

Quint, Thomas and Martin Shubik. *Barley, Gold, or Fiat: Toward a Pure Theory of Money*. New Haven, CT: Yale University Press, 2014.

Rich, Adrienne. *Of Woman Born: Motherhood as Experience and Institution*. New York: Norton, 1976.

Rochet, Jean-Charles and Jean Tirole. "Platform Competition in Two-Sided Markets," *Journal of European Eco nomic Association*, Vol. 1, No. 4, 2003, 990–1029.

Rogoff, Kenneth S. *The Curse of Cash*. Princeton, NJ: Princeton University Press, 2016.

Rothschild, Emma. *Economic Sentiments: Adam Smith, Condorcet, and the Enlightenment*. Cambridge, MA: Harvard University Press, 2001.

Russell, Andrew L. *Open Standards and the Digital Age: History, Ideology, and Networks*. New York: Cambridge University Press, 2014.

Sandel, Michael. *The Moral Limits of Markets: What Money Can't Buy*. New York: Farrar, Straus, and Giroux, 2012.

Santner, Eric L. *The Weight of All Flesh: On the Subject-Matter of Political Economy*. Oxford University Press, 2016.

Searle, John R. "Language and Social Ontology," *Theory and Society*, Vol. 37, No. 5, 2008, 443–459.

_____. *Making the Social World: The Structure of Civilization*. New York: Oxford University Press, 2010.

Shapiro, Carl and Hal R. Varian. *Information Rules: A Strategic Guide to the Network Economy*. Boston, MA: Harvard Business School Press, 1999.

Shin, Hyun Song. *Risk and Liquidity*. New York: Oxford University Press, 2010.

Simmel, Georg. *The Philosophy of Money*. London: Routledge & Kegan Paul, 1978.

Smith, Adam. *An Inquiry into the Nature and Causes of the Wealth of Nations*. New York: The Modern Library, 1994.

Smith, Merritt Roe. *Harpers Ferry Armory and the New Technology: The Challenge of Change*. Ithaca, NY: Cornell University Press, 1977.

Soros, George. *New Paradigm for Financial Markets: The Credit Crisis of 2008 and What It Means*. New York: Public Affairs, 2008.

Staheli, Urs. *Spectacular Speculation: Thrills, the Economy and Popular Discourse*. Stanford: Stanford University Press, 2013.

Standing, Guy. *The Precariat: The New Dangerous Class*. London: Bloomsbury Academic, 2011.

Stiglitz, Joseph E. *The Euro: How a Common Currency Threatens the Future of Europe*. New York: W.W. Norton, 2016.

Stiglitz, Joseph E. and Bruce Greenwald. *Creating a Learning Society: A New Approach to Growth, Development, and Social Progress*. New York: Columbia University Press, 2014.

Sundararajan, Arun. *The Sharing Economy: The End of Employment and the Rise of Crowd-Based Capitalism*. Cambridge, MA: MIT Press, 2016.

Tresch, John. *The Romantic Machine: Utopian Science and Technology after Napoleon*. Chicago: University of Chicago Press, 2012.

Turkle, Sherry. *The Second Self: Computers and the Human Spirit*. New York: Simon & Schuster, Inc., 1984.

_____. *Life on the Screen: identity in the Age of the Internet*. New York: Simon & Schuster, Inc., 1995.

_____. *Alone Together: Why We Expect More Technology and Less from Each Other*. New York: Basic, 2011.

Varian, Hal R. "High-Technology Industries and Market Structure," Federal Reserve Bank of St. Louis, Jackson Hole Symposium, August 2001.

_____. "Computer Mediated Transactions," *The American Economic Review*, Vol. 100, No. 2, 2010, 1–10.

_____. "Big Data: New Tricks for Econometrics," *Journal of Economic Perspectives*, Vol. 28, No. 2, 2014, 3–28.

Varian, Hal R., Joseph Farrell and Carl Shapiro. *The Economics of Information Technology: An Introduction*. New York: Cambridge University Press, 2004.

Veblen, Thorstein. *The Theory of the Leisure Class: An Economic Study of Institutions*. New York: Modern Library, 1934.

Venter, J. Craig. *Life at the Speed of Light: From the Double Helix to the Dawn of Digital Life*. New York: Viking, 2013.

Vogl, Joseph. "Sovereignty Effects," INET Conference, Berlin, April 12, 2012.

_____. *The Specter of Capital*. Stanford, CA: Stanford University Press, 2015.

Wacquant, Loic. "Three Steps to a Historical Anthropology of Actually Existing Neoliberalism," *Social Anthropology*, Vol. 20, 2012, 66–79.

_____. "Symbolic Power and Group-Making: On Pierre Bourdieu's Reframing of Class," *Journal of Classical Sociology*, Vol. 13, No. 2, 2013, 274–291.

Warner, Michael. "The Mass Public and the Mass Subject," in Craig Calhoun (ed.), *Habermas and the Public Sphere*. Cambridge, MA: MIT Press, 1992, 377–401.

Weatherall, James Owen. *The Physics of Wall Street: A Brief History of Predicting the Unpredictable*. New York: Houghton Mifflin Harcourt, 2013.

Weber, Beat. "Bitcoin and the Legitimacy Crisis of Money," *Cambridge Journal of Economics*. Vol. 40, 2016, 17–41.

Weber, Max. *Economy and Society: An Outline of Interpretive Sociology*. Edited by Guenther Roth and Claus Wittich. Berkeley, CA: University of California Press, 1978. Vol. I.

Weber, Steven. *The Success of Open Source*. Cambridge, MA: Harvard University Press, 2004.

_____. "The Political Economy of Open Source Software and Why It Matters," in Robert Latham and Saskia Sassen (eds.), *Digital Formations: IT and New Architectures in the Global Realm*. Princeton, NJ: Princeton University Press, 2005, 178–211.

Weyl, Glen. "A Price Theory of Multi-Sided Platforms," *The American Economic Review*, Vol. 100, No. 4, 2010, 1642–1672.

Winnicott, D.W. *Home is Where We Start From: Essays by a Psychoanalyst*. New York: Norton, 1986.

Wittgenstein, Ludwig. *Tractatus Logico-Philosophicus*. London: Routledge, 2001.

Wolff, Robert Paul. *The Poverty of Liberalism*. Boston: Beacon Press, 1968.

Wu, Tim. *The Attention Merchants: The Epic Scramble to Get Inside Our Heads*. New York: Alfred A. Knopf, 2016.

Zuboff, Shoshana. *In the Age of the Smart Machine: The Future of Work and Power*. New York: Basic Books, 1984.

_____. "'Big Other' Surveillance Capitalism and the Prospects of an Information Civilization," *Journal of Information Technology*, Vol. 30, 2015, 75–89.

Index

For Product Safety Concerns and Information please contact our EU
representative GPSR@taylorandfrancis.com
Taylor & Francis Verlag GmbH, Kaufingerstraße 24, 80331 München, Germany